CISTERCIAN FATHERS SERIES: N(

GUERRIC OF IGNY

LITURGICAL SERMONS

CISTERCIAN FATHERS SERIES: NUMBER THIRTY-TWO

GUERRIC OF IGNY

Liturgical Sermons

Volume Two

Translated by
Monks of Mount Saint Bernard Abbey

CISTERCIAN PUBLICATIONS
Kalamazoo, Michigan—Spencer, Massachusetts

© Translation, Copyrighted 1971 by Cistercian Publications

The translation presented here is based on the critical text prepared by John Morson OCSO and Hilary Costello OCSO and published by Editions du Cerf, Paris, in their collection, Sources chrétiennes.

First published in 1971.
First paperback edition 1999.

cistercian publications

Editorial Office and Customer Service
Institute of Cistercian Studies
Western Michigan University
Kalamazoo, Michigan 49008

Warehouse and Website Orders
Saint Joseph's Abbey
Spencer, Massachusetts 01562

UK and European Customer Service
97 Loughborough Road
Thringstone, Coalville, Leics. LE67 8LQ

The work of Cistercian Publications
is made possible in part by support from Western Michigan
University to The Institute of Cistercian Studies

ISBN 0 87907 208 3

Printed in the United States of America

CONTENTS

The First Sermon for St Benedict	1
The Second Sermon for St Benedict	9
The Third Sermon for St Benedict	17
The Fourth Sermon for St Benedict	24
The First Sermon for the Annunciation	32
The Second Sermon for the Annunciation	39
The Third Sermon for the Annunciation	47
The First Sermon for Palm Sunday	55
The Second Sermon for Palm Sunday	59
The Third Sermon for Palm Sunday	66
The Fourth Sermon for Palm Sunday	73
The First Sermon for Easter	80
The Second Sermon for Easter	86
The Third Sermon for Easter	92
Sermon for Rogation Days	98
The Sermon for the Ascension	104
The First Sermon for Pentecost	109
The Second Sermon for Pentecost	116
The First Sermon for St John Baptist	123
The Second Sermon for St John Baptist	129
The Third Sermon for St John Baptist	134
The Fourth Sermon for St John Baptist	141

The First Sermon for Saints Peter and Paul	147
The Second Sermon for Saints Peter and Paul	153
The Third Sermon for Saints Peter and Paul	160
The First Sermon for the Assumption	167
The Second Sermon for the Assumption	173
The Third Sermon for the Assumption	179
The Fourth Sermon for the Assumption	186
The First Sermon for Our Lady's Birthday	192
The Second Sermon for Our Lady's Birthday	198
Sermon for the Feast of All Saints	204
A Sermon for Arousing Devotion at Psalmody	213
Analytic Index	219

SERMON 22

THE FIRST SERMON FOR ST BENEDICT

"HAPPY IS THE MAN who shall abide in wisdom and shall meditate on holiness and shall be mindful of the all-seeing eye of God."[1] How fittingly these words may be sung in praise of St Benedict each of you will easily recognize; his words and teaching are not unknown to any of you. How aptly they may be applied to the improvement of our own lives is obvious from the words themselves. Promising the reward of happiness, they commend to us wisdom, holiness, and the fear of God; nothing in life is of greater benefit than these.

"Happy is the man who will abide in wisdom." In other words, this is happiness, this is wisdom, if you continue in wisdom, holding fast to it to the end. For man becomes happy not immediately upon finding it, but only by holding it fast.[2] Scripture does indeed say: "Happy is the man who finds wisdom." But it does not finish there. On the contrary it adds: "And who is rich in prudence."[3] This it does lest a man think that merely to have found wisdom is enough for happiness. The truth is that when you have found it, you must continue with it and in it, and, making it your intimate companion, take your delight in it. Nor must you depart from its schooling until, by meditating on holiness and being mindful of the all-seeing eye of God, you have made it possible for prudence

---

1. Sir 14:22. This text is found in a third-nocturn canticle, sung on all feasts of Confessors.
2. Prov 3:18.   3. Prov 3:13.

to abound in you. Solomon certainly found wisdom. But prudence did not greatly abound in him and he did not guard himself with sufficient prudence, in that he did not protect himself from the pagan women. For that reason not only did he lose wisdom but he fell into the extreme opposite of wisdom, idolatry.[4] And so also with the wise men of the world who clearly saw the invisible things of God from the creation of the world through their knowledge of things created;[5] they seemed to have found wisdom. But because prudence did not abound in them and because when they knew God, they did not glorify him as God, they did in fact become fools and their foolish hearts were given over to evil thoughts and shameful lusts.[6]

2. Others, also, like these have rejected the wisdom they had found because of their proud hearts. Some like Solomon have been enticed away by the lusts of the flesh. Others because of inconstancy and frivolity of mind abandon it as soon as they meet the slightest set-back. These are they who believe for a while and in the time of temptation fall away. But why do they fall away? Because they have no roots that can hold them.[7] And how can they take root unless they stay in one place? What plant ever takes root unless it is left in the place where it was planted? Just so, the good man, planted in the house of the Lord,[8] cannot take root nor be founded in charity unless he abides there with stability of place.[9] And if he does not become rooted, he will never flower nor bear lasting fruit.[10] Even if he should give some sign of hope by flowering at the beginning, it may be said of him: "Before the harvest it was flourishing but it has budded without coming to ripe maturity."[11] And another Prophet says in like manner: "If it should yield fruit strangers shall eat it."[12]

---

4. 1 Sam 11:1ff. 5. Rom 1:20. 6. Rom 1:21ff.
7. Lk 8:13. 8. Ps 91:14.

9. Quite aptly does Guerric speak of stability on the Feast of St Benedict since this was one of the more significant contributions he made through his *Rule for Monasteries*, the emphasis on local stability, including it among the solemn promises the new monk was to make. See RB 1:10ff.; 4:78; 58:17.

10. Jn 15:16. 11. Is 18:5. 12. Hos 8:7.

But do you want to know why stability of place is so necessary if you are to continue in wisdom, take root and eventually bear fruit? Ask your holy Father Benedict and he will tell you[13] that "the cloister of the monastery and stability in the community" is the proper place to cultivate nearly all the virtues.[14] He gives a long catalog of them.[15] And what does Solomon say of instability? "As a bird that wanders from her nest, so is the man who leaves his place."[16] A turtledove finds a nest where she can put her chicks;[17] she begins to warm it and be warmed by it until the chicks are about to come to birth.[18] Then, lo and behold, she flies away and leaves the work thus begun unfinished. Why, whence or whither she flies she will understand either when she comes to make good the many losses she suffers in the meantime, or when she offers some reason to excuse her violation of her first commitment.[19] For myself, I would not think it a wise plan to suffer certain loss for a hope that is uncertain even if the progress of some individuals bids me refrain from too hasty a judgment.[20]

3. Most certainly there is a great difference between those who become discontented out of love for wisdom and those of whom I have just spoken, who, made restless by some light and frivolous matter, recoil from wisdom. Just as one must remain patiently under the discipline of wisdom in order to learn wisdom, so they who readily lose patience, we read,[21] lose little time in casting wisdom from them. But what the Scriptures say just before this might strike them: "She shall be to them as a mighty stone of trial."[22] For they have stumbled over the stumbling stone and the rock of scandal.[23] It was a heavy trial that rebuked and taught the unwise and tested their hearts. They considered the might of wisdom

13. Deut 32:7.   14. RB 4:78.   15. RB 4:1ff.   16. Prov 27:8.
17. Ps 83:4.   18. Is 37:3.   19. 1 Tim 5:12.
20. This advice is similar to that of Bernard of Clairvaux; see, e.g. *Monastic Obligations and Abbatial Authority: St Bernard's Book on Precept and Dispensation*, nn. 44ff., trans. C. Greenia, in *The Works of Bernard of Clairvaux*, vol. 1 (Cistercian Fathers 1), pp. 138ff.; *Cistercians and Cluniacs: St Bernard's Apologia to Abbot William*, nn. 7, 30f., trans. M. Casey, *ibid.*, pp. 42, 67ff.
21. Sir 2:16.   22. Sir 6:22.   23. Rom 9:32f.

to be the hardness of stone and they maintained that everything was hard: its discipline, its appearance, its teaching.

"This teaching," they said, "is hard."[24] Yes, this teaching is hard. Does that mean it is not true? The stone is hard. Does that mean it is not precious? But why is truth hard for you? Is it not because your hearts are hard?[25] If your heart were to be softened by love, the rigor of truth would please you more than the emptiness of falsehood or the oil of adulation. "This saying is hard," they said, because the testing time for wisdom was to them like a mighty stone. For that reason they lost little time in casting it from them and returning to their former state. They did not reject this precious stone chosen by God for any other reason save that they thought it was hard.

Now the fact is that the stone was Christ,[26] a stone of might, but without hardness. He was the rock, but a rock that could be changed, and indeed is changed, into pools or fountains of water[27] whenever he finds faithful hearts that are softened and humble. Into them he pours himself. For if they who drew back so quickly at the mere appearance of hardness[28] had remained with the Apostles they might well have drunk with them from the Rock which followed after them.[29] They might have drunk of the streams of living water[30] flowing copiously from the Rock who was struck on the Cross so that today also "the people and their cattle may drink."[31] They might even have sucked honey out of the rock and oil out of the hardest stone."[32]

4. Blessed are you, Simon Bar-Jona, the Father revealed to you[33] the sweetness of the mystery, so that it was seen hidden under the hardness of the saying. When the Twelve were asked if they too

24. Jn 6:61.
25. The "hard heart" is a biblical theme beginning from the time God hardened the heart of Pharaoh (Ex 7:13; 8:19). St Bernard describes it graphically in his *Advice to a Pope: St Bernard's Treatise on Consideration*, bk. 1, n. 3, trans. J. Anderson and E. Kennan, in *The Works of Bernard of Clairvaux*, vol. 7 (Cistercian Fathers 19).

26. 1 Cor 10:4.	27. Ps 113:8.	28. Jn 6:67.
29. 1 Cor 10:4.	30. Jn 7:38.	31. Num 20:11.
32. Deut 32:13.	33. Mt 16:17.	

wanted to go away you answered firmly: "Lord, you have the words of eternal life; to whom shall we go?"[34] You are indeed blessed. You decided to abide with Wisdom and to be nourished with the Bread of the Sacrament at his own table along with the members of his household, until, after you had progressed from faith to full knowledge, he might feed you with the Bread of Life and understanding and give you to drink of the waters of the wisdom of salvation.[35] And blessed are you also my brethren, who have enrolled in the study of wisdom, the school of Christian philosophy. But you will be blessed only if you persevere, so that when his teaching seems very hard because commands are difficult and corrections stern, there will be in none of you the evil spirit of unfaithfulness to take you away from the living God.[36] Instead with all steadfastness you will say with the Apostle: "You have the words of life; to whom shall we go?"[37]

You might imagine there is weariness in his precepts,[38] hardness in his teaching; but we know how great is the multitude of your sweetness, Lord, which you have hidden from those that fear you and will grant in abundance to them who hope in you.[39] And I shall always hope, even if you were to kill me.[40] Indeed I shall hope all the more when you scourge, lash, burn, kill all that lives in me, so that not I but Christ may live in me.[41] Most certainly we do not depart from you, for you give us life[42] even as you slay, heal us even as you strike[43] Blessed indeed is the man who continues in wisdom with this steadfast faith; who bears trial patiently and with all confidence becomes obedient even unto death;[44] who never leaves his place no matter how often the spirit of him who has power may come upon him. He knows that the cure of discipline will heal the greatest sins.[45]

5. Now to achieve this wisdom of continuing in wisdom, it is most important, I think, not readily to allow restlessness or any

34. Jn 6:68f.
35. Sir 15:3.
36. Heb 3:12.
37. St Peter, Jn 6:69.
38. Ps 93:20.
39. Ps 30:20.
40. Job 13:15.
41. Gal 2:20.
42. Ps 79:19.
43. Hos 6:2; Job 5:18.
44. Phil 2:8.
45. Eccles 10:4.

kind of slight provocation to keep you away from any of the exercises of wisdom: the divine office, private prayer, *lectio divina*,[46] the appointed daily labor or the practice of silence. For the praises of wisdom are sung at the completion of the office. "My lips will rejoice," says the Holy Man, "when they shall have sung to you."[47] And in another psalm you have it in so many words: "You make the outgoings of the morning and the evening joyful."[48] As for private prayer, you know from daily experience that it too is better at the end than it is at the beginning.[49] This is so that you may have confidence in the advice of the Lord, given so often and recommended by so much example, to be persevering in prayer.[50] Again when you sit down to read and you do not really read, or if before you even begin to read you put the book down again, what good do you think that will do you? If you do not continue with the Scriptures so as to become familiar with them through assiduous study, when do you think they will open themselves to you? He who has love of the word, we are told, to him shall understanding be given and he will abound; but he who has not, what knowledge he may have by way of natural endowment, will be taken away from him[51] because of his negligence. Then with regard to manual work, surely you have learned enough about this, have you not, to know that, like the wage given to the workers,[52] consolation is often reserved to the end of the work? And of course when we come to silence a promise is given by the Prophet when he says: "In silence and in hope shall your strength be."[53] For if you cul-

---

46. It is difficult to find a suitable English equivalent for the expression *lectio divina* as it is understood in monastic tradition. It is not simply reading. Its nature may vary from quite serious study to little more than holding an open book in one's hand. What is distinctive about it is that it is directly ordered to and wholly impregnated by the quest for God, contact with him, experience of him. Sometimes it is rendered in English as "sacred reading" but this still needs explanation.

47. Ps 70:23.

48. Ps 64:9. The Latin words of the text are those directly associated with the names of the hours of the Office: *exitus matutini et vespere*.

49. Eccles 7:9. 50. Lk 18:1ff. 51. Mt 13:12. 52. Mt 20:10.

53. Is 30:15.

tivate holiness in silence and, following the advice of Jeremiah, you wait in silence for the salvation of the Lord,[54] then secretly in the midst of the silence the all-powerful word of God will leap down to you from his royal throne.[55] The waters of Siloe which flow silently[56] will inundate the valley of your quiet and peaceful heart like a gently flowing stream. And this you will experience not once but many times, if only your silence is the cultivation of holiness,[57] that is, if you meditate on holiness so that you may continue in the Scriptures as I have suggested and in your mind consider the all-seeing eye of God.[58]

6. Meditate on these things, continue in them so that your progress may be made manifest.[59] For if you devise iniquity on your bed,[60] evil thoughts that the Evil One sends or imaginings that your own heart devises or empty philosophies or deceptive theories[61] which are no more than the dreamings of a sick mind, then surely is not your silence more the cultivation of unholiness than of holiness?[62] If therefore you want to continue in wisdom meditate diligently on holiness. "You have desired wisdom," he says, "keep holiness and God will give her to you."[63]

But if horrible thoughts rush in on you as if by force, set a strong and trusty guard on yourself, one that will guard your heart with all care.[64] I mean the fear of God, which overlooks nothing[65] and allows nothing to enter without careful examination, often questioning even an angel of light: "Are you one of ours, or from our adversary?"[66] It looks about on all sides as though it were aware at every moment of the all-seeing eye of God whom it contemplates without respite and it takes care to search the hearts of men.[67] It is well said: "He shall be mindful of the all-seeing eye of God,"[68] for obviously that man has no mind nor heart who neglects to keep the fear of God before him, who does not feel the weight of such great majesty and of the judgment that hangs over him.

54. Lam 3:26.
55. Wis 18:15.
56. Is 8:6.
57. Is 32:17.
58. Sir 14:22.
59. 1 Tim 4:15.
60. Ps 35:5.
61. Sir 34:5f.
62. Is 32:17.
63. Sir 1:33.
64. Prov 4:23.
65. Eccles 7:19.
66. Josh 5:13.
67. Prov 15:11.
68. Sir 14:22.

It is also well said that God is all-seeing; all things, past as well as future, are present to him so that he does not look backwards to the one or forward to the other, but sees both in the same way, for he sees all in one simple glance. For him eternity is as a moment, the center of all time; to his unchangeable simplicity the whole wheel of time as well as its moving finger is always equally present. Fear of the Lord which turns away from evil, not only in deed but in thought also, is ever aware of this eternal eye that sees without ceasing and judges all things; it spurs itself on by its own reflections, teaches us to meditate more on holiness, restrains us so that we will continue with wisdom.

So gradually it comes about that a man who at first was held back by the fear of judgment and punishment is afterwards upheld by the love and meditation of holiness and at last finds his rest and delight in the intimacy and embrace of wisdom. This not only casts out fear from the soul through an outpouring of love, but weariness and distress also through an inpouring of gladness. As one man who dwelt with wisdom[69] said to her: "When I go into my house I shall find repose with her; for her conversation has no bitterness nor her companionship any tediousness but only joy and gladness."[70] May he make us partakers in all these things who deigned to become partaker of our nature,[71] the Wisdom of God, Jesus Christ, who lives and reigns for ever and ever. Amen.

---

69. Wis 8:3.   70. Wis 8:16.

71. Guerric is here perhaps drawing his inspiration from a prayer said by the priest at the offertory of the Mass: *eius divinitatis esse consortes, qui humanitatis nostrae fieri dignatus est particeps.*

SERMON 23

THE SECOND SERMON FOR ST BENEDICT

"BLESSED IS THE MAN who trusts in the Lord."[1] Our holy Father Benedict, blessed alike in grace and in name,[2] whose memory is in benediction,[3] was indeed a man who trusted in the Lord. For the man whom God met with goodly blessings[4] so that he might have confidence in the Lord, is now blessed in Christ with every spiritual blessing in the heavenly places[5] because he trusted in the Lord. And not only has the Lord given him in the heavenly places the blessing of all the angels, but also on earth he has given him the blessing of all nations.[6] For where among the nations is Benedict not praised today as the Blessed of the Lord? Certainly the blessing of the Lord is on the righteous;[7] the grace of God has loaded him with so many blessings of both heaven and earth.

The blessing of Esau was in the fatness of the earth and the dew of

---

1. Jer 17:7.
2. *Gratia Benedictus et nomine*: this beautiful phrase is repeated frequently in the Office of St Benedict, e.g., first nocturn, first antiphon and first responsory; first antiphon of second vespers. It is taken from the opening sentence of Gregory the Great's second *Dialogue*, which is devoted to the life of St Benedict.
3. Sir 45:1. Taken from the lesson read at first vespers, lauds, tierce and second vespers.
4. Ps 20:4.   5. Eph 1:3.
6. Sir 44:25. Extraordinarily so was this blessing of the nations when in recent years Benedict was named the Patron of Europe.
7. Prov 10:6.

heaven;[8] not so Benedict's. His blessing is in the fruitfulness of the Spirit and the Author of Heaven, who speaks through the Prophet: "I will be as the dew."[9] Of him also it is said: "Your dew is the dew of light."[10] And certainly in Christ is the blessing of the Father, for the Father proclaimed of him: "Blessed be every one who blesses you."[11] In very truth therefore the man who trusts in the Lord is blessed in the Lord, because whoever puts his trust in the Lord inserts himself into him. The tree drinks in the sap of life and the waters of fertility from wherever its roots have penetrated. And surely he has sent out his roots to the waters[12] who—I use the words of our master, Benedict—"has put his hope in God"[13] and from the very Source of All Good drinks in the waters of life[14] full of blessings and grace.

2. Through this loving and devoted confidence sins are forgiven, healing obtained for bodily ills and more especially for ills of the soul, dangers averted, fears despised, the world overcome; all things are possible to the one who believes, there is no doubt about it. To those in sin Christ says: "Take heart, my son; your sins are forgiven you;"[15] to those to whom he gives health of body or soul: "According to your faith be it done to you,"[16] and: "Your faith has made you well;"[17] to those terrified and in danger of shipwreck: "Have faith in God,"[18] and: "Why are you afraid, O men of little faith?"[19] to those whom he was arming against the cruelty of the world and the violence of the devil: "Be of good cheer, I have overcome the world."[20]

And of course this is the victory that overcomes the world, our faith[21] but only if it is not tepid or timorous but confident, a faith unfeigned,[22] a hope unshaken. Not only is the world overcome by it but heaven is won. By it man is established forever, is rooted and established in the Lord by charity.[23] Those who trust in the Lord are like Mount Sion. Nor can he be moved forever[24] who is

8. Gen 27:39f.   9. Hos 14:6.   10. Is 26:19.   11. Gen 27:29.
12. Jer 17:8.   13. RB 4:41.   14. Rev 21:6.   15. Mt 9:2.
16. Mt 9:29.   17. Mt 9:22.   18. Mk 11:22.   19. Mt 8:26.
20. Jn 16:33.   21. Jn 5:4.   22. 1 Tim 1:5. 23. Eph 3:17.
24. Ps 124:1.

founded in the Eternal. For just as the Eternal cannot perish so neither can the man who unites himself with the Lord and so becomes one spirit with him.²⁵ Who has hoped in the Lord and been confounded; continued in his commandments and been forsaken?²⁶ If a man without faith should say: "He was forsaken because on the cross he cried: 'My God, my God, why have you forsaken me?'"²⁷ I would say God did not really abandon him, for God was in him reconciling the world to himself.²⁸ O what consolation to be thus forsaken, what love to be thus abandoned that you might merit to be associated with the Only-begotten, Well-beloved of the Father in his sufferings.

3. O Lord, open the eyes of this child²⁹—I tell you he is inexperienced and a novice—who whenever he is afflicted thinks he is abandoned. It would be something altogether new and unheard of were I to see any just man abandoned, for the Church says: "I have been young and now am old, yet I have not seen the righteous forsaken."³⁰ O Lord, I pray you, open the eyes of this child so that he may see that those who are with us are more numerous than those who are with our adversaries.³¹ If the Lord of Hosts is with us,³² and in his train all the might and hosts of heaven, then indeed the goodwill of every creature, obedient to the slightest command of its Creator, is ours too. If God is for us, who is against us?³³ And who is there to harm us if we are zealous for what is right?³⁴ The envious can rage, but this will only be to our advantage; he can annoy, buffet, cut to pieces, but in doing so he will only be making crowns for us to wear.

I love you, O Lord, my strength;³⁵ through you every hostile power yields to me, worm that I am, and the guile of the ancient Serpent is laughed to scorn by the angels you send to minister to us,³⁶ so that his desire to hurt is turned to our advantage instead. I love you, Lord, my powerful defender, wise guide, gentle con-

25. 1 Cor 6:17.
26. Sir 2:11f.
27. Mt 27:46.
28. 2 Cor 5:19.
29. Cf. 2 Kings 6:17.
30. Ps 36:25.
31. 2 Kings 6:16.
32. Ps 45:8.
33. Rom 8:31.
34. 1 Pet 3:13.
35. Ps 17:2.
36. Heb 1:14.

soler, generous rewarder. Confident, I cast all my care on him[37] whose strength cannot be overthrown, whose wisdom cannot be led astray, whose loving kindness cannot be exhausted in fulfilling my every need. How much better, how much safer, it is to have him caring for me than to be looking after myself. How much better it is to take refuge in the Lord than to put confidence in man.[38] How justly cursed is the man who, trusting in man, makes flesh his arm, whose heart turns away from the Lord.[39] Indeed I am poor and needy[40] but if the Lord takes thought for me[41] I am rich and blessed; no mistake, everything works for good in me.[42]

Therefore let those who know your name put their trust in you, for you, O Lord, do not forsake those who put their trust in you.[43] Let your people, as it is written, abide in the beauty of peace, in secure dwellings and in luxurious rest, in security forever.[44] It is a supremely beautiful peace and everlasting security to dwell in the shelter of the Most High, to abide in the shadow of the Almighty.[45] And it is altogether luxurious rest to sit at ease under the true vine, the fig-tree[46] and the olive, and after eating to repletion of the various fruits, to delight oneself with songs of love and to say: "I sat down under his shadow whom I desired and his fruit was sweet to my palate."[47] Certainly the fruit must have been sweet to the palate since it causes so sweet an utterance.

4. These then are the secure dwellings in which the true Israel dwells in safety, grazes and lies down, and there is none to make it afraid.[48] As Wisdom promises, resting without terror, it enjoys "abundance without fear of evils."

That phrase, "without fear of evils," is well put. It does not say, however," without fear of God," lest you may feel that negligence would arise from the confidence and security we are commending. Strong confidence lies in nothing else but the fear of the Lord.[49] For fear, in avoiding offense, preserves grace and protects the

37. 1 Pet 5:7. 38. Ps 117:8. 39. Jer 17:5.
40. Ps 69:6. 41. Ps 39:18. 42. Rom 8:28.
43. Ps 9:11. 44. Is 32:17f. 45. Ps 90:1.
46. 1 Kings 4:25. 47. Song 2:3. 48. Zeph 3:13. 49. Prov 4:26.

grounds of confidence, so long as you are not conscious of having offended God. From this it follows that you should have only chaste fear of him; apart from him you should have no fear at all of anyone. Only a good conscience gives rise to such confidence and gives support to our hearts before the Eternal Judge.

If a man thinks he is loved by another only a little, how can he expect much from him? But the man who loves never lacks confidence, knowing that he whom hearts cannot deceive loves all who love him[50] even when he reproves and corrects them.[51] If you only train your heart in wisdom[52] the discipline of the Father does not lessen confidence but increases it. You know what is written: "Happy is the man whom God reproves,"[53] and: "Those whom I love I reprove and chasten."[54] Therefore when his wrath is quickly enkindled blessed are all who take refuge in him, all, that is, who can take comfort in the consciousness of their own love, since in his wrath he remembers mercy.[55] When they say: "I will give you thanks, O Lord, for you were angry with me," they add immediately: "but your anger turned away and you comforted me,"[56] because not only is his wrath quickly enkindled but just as quickly it is appeased by humble confession of guilt.

5. For this reason Jeremiah quite rightly compares the blessed man who trusts in the Lord to a tree planted by the waters.[57] Because he sends out the roots of his heart to the stream of love, he will not fear when the heat of anger and distress comes, and in the time of drought, when for a long time the heavens are closed and neither the dew nor the showers of grace have fallen on him,[58] he will not be anxious as if God had forsaken him. He knows by experience that he is planted in faith, rooted in charity by the waters of life, which according to Ezechiel flow from the sanctuary and bring life to all things; and on the banks, on both sides of the river, there grow all kinds of trees for food. Their leaves do not wither nor their fruit fail.[59] Why therefore should that blessed tree

50. Prov 8:17.
51. Prov 3:12; Rev. 3:19
52. Ps 89:12.
53. Job 5:17.
54. Rev 3:19.
55. Hab 3:2.
56. Is 12:1.
57. Jer 17:8.
58. 2 Sam 1:21.
59. Ezek 47:12.

fear the heat or be anxious about the drought? The living water, the grace of the Spirit, does not cease to bring it secretly the life-giving sap of hope and charity. And so its leaves are green, that is, its words are full of grace and truth,[60] and it does not at any time cease to bring forth fruit of every kind of good work.

Certainly the spring-like peace and joy that God has set aside for his inheritance[61] is very welcome, the rain he willingly gives very desirable. But if it is necessary, the heat of adversity burns up all things and again all that Jeremiah has prophesied about spiritual dryness comes about. Still the man who trusts in God, who has rooted himself by the refreshing waters[62] of the grace of the Holy Spirit, will not fear. Even if grace does not openly shower on him so that he feels it entering into him, yet, secretly and interiorly, it gives life and fecundity, all the time keeping him faithful to his purpose, strengthening him to persevere and giving him sound speech[63] and steadfastness of action.

6. Let this be your consolation, my dear brethren, whenever other consolations, spiritual as well as material, have been withdrawn from you, not because of your own negligence but by Divine Providence.

And perhaps that hidden grace of the Spirit we have spoken of is the lower spring with which Achsah would not be content until she had been given the upper spring as well,[64] so that the Spirit may be poured down from on high, the heavens shower from above and the angelic clouds rain down righteousness,[65] justifying the Word of God and speaking to the heart of Jerusalem.[66] It seems right to compare the hidden graces to the lower spring; flowing as it were to the roots, it fosters humility. And the other grace is certainly the upper spring; pouring itself from above, it elevates the mind by hope and joy. Therefore, my brethren, if you long for the high spring, your desire is certainly to be praised. But if you have not yet attained to that, to send out your roots meanwhile to the waters that are below is a wholesome medicine. Whoever then

---

60. Jn 1:14. 61. Ps 67:10. 62. Ps 22:2. 63. Tit 2:8.
64. Josh 15:19. 65. Is 45:8. 66. Is 40:2.

is not successful in capturing the joys of the contemplative life, let him consider the holiness of the active life.[67] And so let him enlarge the roots of his good desires, make his conduct more agreeable and control every circumstance of his life until his leaves do not wither or fall, that is, his words are not uttered lightly or unprofitably, and his life does not cease to produce fruit. Blessed indeed is the tree whose leaves are for healing[68] and whose fruit is for life, that is, whose words bring grace to the listener and whose actions bring life to himself performing them.

7. It is for this, my dear brethren, that the divine rebirth or the change of the right hand of the Most High[69] has transplanted you next to refreshing waters, after carnal birth or worldly customs had planted you in the parched places of the wilderness[70] in an uninhabited salt land.[71] As a result you, who were marked down for the axe and the fire because of the unfruitfulness of your lives, now that you have been planted in the house of the Lord, in the courts of our God,[72] can flourish and bring forth fruit and your fruit will abide.[73] These refreshing waters, are they not the Holy Scriptures on which we meditate day and night?[74] Are they not the tears of compunction which become our food day and night?[75] Are they not the Sacraments and the other aids to salvation which we eat and drink at the altar? The fountain of wisdom that springs up in the middle of Paradise[76] flows outward in all these things as in so many tiny streams to scatter its waters on the streets.[77] "Like an aqueduct," says Wisdom, "I came out of Paradise. I said: 'I will water my garden of plants, I will water abundantly the fruits of my begetting.'"[78] There you have from the mouth of Wisdom

---

67. "Active life" here must be understood in the medieval sense, which was received from the Fathers, namely that life which was devoted primarily to the acquisition of the virtues, and distinguished from the more perfect state, or contemplative life, where one who had been prepared by the active life and had acquired the virtues could concentrate on the contemplation of God and his mysteries. See especially Gregory the Great's *Fourteenth Homily on the Book of Ezekiel*.

68. Ezek 47:12.	69. Ps 76:11.	70. Ps 62:3.	71. Jer 17:6.
72. Ps 91:14.	73. Jn 15:16.	74. Ps 1:2.	75. Ps 41:4.
76. Gen 2:10.	77. Prov 5:16.	78. Sir 24:41.	

herself who gives birth and plants, the assertion that the garden of plants is the community of her children. "Shall not I bring to birth who cause others to bring forth?" says the Lord.[79] He brings forth when he generates goodwill; he plants when he brings to life; he waters when he floods the mind with grace; he tills when he imposes discipline on conduct.

"Hear me, you divine offspring, and bud forth as the rose planted by brooks of water."[80] Sink your roots into the waters of life, that is to say, into the love of the land of the living, not into the love of this earth in which all things grow old and decay. The tree cannot bring forth fruit that will abide unless it fastens its roots above in the heavenly places, so that it seeks and tastes the things that are above, not the things that are of earth.[81] Doctors say that man is an inverted tree because the nerves of the body have their root and beginning in the head.[82] For myself, I prefer to say that he is so because the roots of his love and desire must be fixed in heaven, in the highest of all things, our Head Jesus Christ.[83] Whosoever sends his roots there and from that eternal source drinks in continually the sap of life and grace will not fear when the heat of the judgment comes; instead he will bring as offering the many fruits he has produced and will receive the reward of flowering forever before the Lord. To him is honor and glory for endless ages. Amen.

---

79. Is 66:9.   80. Sir 39:17.   81. Col 3:2.
82. Plato, Timaeus 90A. Known perhaps through Saint Augustine, Commentary on Psalm 48, 2:3.
83. Col. 2:6; Eph 3:17.

SERMON 24

THE THIRD SERMON FOR ST BENEDICT

"BELOVED OF GOD AND MEN."[1] In these few words Scripture describes the good and blessed man, and certainly Benedict was one of their number; he was beloved of the Lord. These few words, I might well say, are a summary of the whole of perfection; they describe the fullness of grace and virtue. They are also both a promise of eternal happiness in the life to come and an assurance of consolation here below. For what can be wanting to the eternal joy of one who is beloved of God; and what to the present consolation of one who is beloved of men? Even if something might seem to be wanting to a person who is beloved by God, it is lacking for no other reason than that he may want for nothing, that through what may be considered a defect he may be the more perfect. "For power is made perfect in weakness." "Paul," said the Lord, "my grace is sufficient for you."[2] To a man for whom God's grace is sufficient the lack of some particular grace is no serious loss but instead a great gain. For his very lack and weakness bring to him power; the diminution of a particular grace produces in him more fully and more firmly the grace of God, the greatest gift of all.

Keep far away from your servant, Lord, any grace, whatever it may be, which might destroy or lessen the gift of yourself: any

---

1. Sir 45:1. These are the opening words of the lesson read at vespers, lauds and tierce on this Feast.
2. 2 Cor 12:9.

grace which might make him more glorious in his own eyes, more displeasing in yours. Such a thing is not a sign of your favor but of your wrath. It is to those with whom you are angry because of their deceit that you give these things, casting them down when they are exalted,[3] "dashing them down mightily when they are walking on air."[4] In order that the one grace, without which no one can be loved by you, may remain securely with us, let your grace take all other gifts away from us, or at least let it give us at the same time the grace of using them rightly. And so possessing that grace through which we may offer a pleasing service in awe and reverence, by the right use of the gift, we may deserve to receive the Giver. The more anyone has been favored, so much the more may he be grateful.

2. Truly it is with wonderful art, but even more wonderful love, that the kindness and wisdom[5] of God takes care of the salvation of mankind. Even though he loves all men he does not allow them to be easily certain or secure about his love. He hides the great multitude of his sweetness from those who fear him[6] for this one reason: that by keeping them always humble he may make them always worthy of his love. There are just and wise men, and their works are in the hand of God. Yet none of them knows whether he is worthy of love or hate; everything is kept uncertain for the time to come.[7] The Ruler of all things so distributes the grace of his gifts and works that by means of the gifts he grants he gives the consolation that they are deserving of his love and by means of those he withdraws he instills uncertainty and fear that they deserve his displeasure. He brings consolation when he visits at dawn; he strikes terror when suddenly he puts them to the test.[8] Now he kills, now he brings to life. Now he leads down to Sheol, now he raises up. At one moment he makes poor, then he makes rich. Now he brings low, now he exalts.[9] And in all these changing circumstances the more uncertain we are of our salvation and the more we cooperate with him in

---

3. Ps 72:18.   4. Job 33:22.
5. The Latin is much richer here: *prudens clementia clemensque prudentia Dei.*
6. Ps 30:20.   7. Eccles 9:1ff.   8. Job 7:18.   9. 1 Sam 2:6f.

great fear and trembling, so much the more certainly does he bring it about.

I know that Paul said: "I am certain nothing can separate me from the love of God."[10] But this was Paul speaking, not you or I; for us it is right that everything in the future should remain uncertain. Paul said it, and he was also quite competent to say: "I live, now not I but Christ lives in me."[11] He was so completely united to the love of God in his heart that, being thus joined to the Lord, he had become one spirit with him.[12] But Paul himself, who at one moment was so certain, at another was anxious and full of cares, and chastised his body lest perhaps while he had preached to others he himself might become a castaway.[13] He was also buffeted by Satan lest perchance he become puffed up.[14] So even in Paul you can see how certitude was at one time strengthened and grew by the consolation of the spirit and in like manner was enfeebled and disappeared under the onslaught of temptation.

And so I, wretched and unworthy as I am of even life itself, by what consolation, by what confidence can I presume to be worthy of love? Everything, inside and outside, denounces me as deserving wrath. My life is not a striving and a warfare against sin; on the contrary it is a veritable slavery to sin.[15] I am a slave to the law of sin in mind and body. I seem to have made an unholy alliance with prudence of the flesh[16] and friendship of this world, both of which are enemies of God.[17]

What is this but a league with death, a covenant with hell? But I know very well who he was who said: "Your league with death will be abolished, your covenant with hell will not stand."[18] Indeed nothing can be friendly with the enemy of God; his zeal will arm not only death and hell but even every creature for the downfall of his enemies.[19] On that day how happy will the man be who is loved by God. How worthy of praise will they be whom God will praise,[20] to whom he will say on the manifest proof of their actions:

10. Rom 8:38f. 11. Gal 2:20. 12. 1 Cor 6:17. 13. 1 Cor 9:27.
14. 2 Cor 12:7. 15. Rom 7:25. 16. Rom 8:6. 17. Jas 4:4.
18. Is 28:18. 19. Wis 5:18. 20. 1 Cor 4:5.

"You are my friends because you have done the things I have commanded you."[21] To be deserving of God's friendship: this is the supreme virtue, the best gift of grace, the choicest fruit of life, because it is the surest pledge of happiness. Others may set themselves up as the enemies of such a man, but "the enemy shall have no advantage over him nor the sons of iniquity power to harm him."[22]

3. And if after and because of this, the sum total and cause of all grace, you should merit that further grace, so that, beloved of God, you become beloved of men as well,[23] what a consolation that would be amid the miseries of this life, what peace, what joy, what delight. And all the more so if you learn from human applause not to grow lukewarm but to be on fire to love God the more, for whose sake you are loved by men.

Caused by anything else, referred to anyone else, human favor is a consuming wind, a breeze laden with sickness and pestilence, a pillaging robber, a sly lurking murderer, a serpent in the way, a viper on the path that bites the horse's heels so that the rider falls backwards.[34] The vain man is lifted up in pride,[25] and by the vanity of his senses he is brought to ruin just like the stumbling horse. The Serpent strikes and sows confusion in his path, and, patting him on the head as it were, praises his first tender efforts in the spiritual life. Unless I am very much mistaken this is what happens to the man who, before he knows how to love, desires to be loved too much, and before he has learned to be a friend to himself seeks to draw all to himself in friendship. He gathers riches unjustly and in the prime of life he will abandon them and at the end he will become a fool.[26] He will be abandoned by all his friends,[27] for whose sake he himself abandoned God. Then the words of Scripture will be fulfilled: "God has scattered the bones of them that please men; they have been confounded because God has despised them."[28]

4. The most important thing of all to be sought therefore is the love of God which is the beginning and end of all things. As a

21. Jn 15:14. 22. Ps 88:23. 23. Sir 45:1. 24. Gen 49:17.
25. Job 11:12. 26. Jer 17:11. 27. Lam 1:2. 28. Ps 52:6.

reward for this we may become worthy to be loved also by men; and by striving to grow in the love of God we may learn how to make use of the love of men. And when you do have the matter safely under control, that is, when you have the firm intention of being loved only in God and for his sake, then I sincerely hope that your pleasant behavior, your gracious humility, your genuine zeal, will commend you to the goodwill of all men. So that the love of all men may be yours and you may receive the esteem of all insofar as the holy way of life which commends you to them becomes through you, by a just reversal of roles, worthy of commendation by them. Thus in you also, the son by adoption, will be fulfilled the prayer of the Only-begotten Son: "Father, glorify your Son so that your Son may glorify you."[29] Seeing the splendor of your actions men will glorify your Father.[30]

Now I am not saying that between the love of God and the love of the neighbor there must be any order of time, although there must be an order of intensity. From the very beginning it is necessary to pay attention to the one and not to neglect the other, since God cannot be loved without the neighbor nor the neighbor without God. But if the heart is right a man cannot be unaware which of these two loves should be the stronger, which of them should determine the form and expression the other should take and the limits that should be put on it.

But I do say that it is one thing to love and quite another thing to strive to be loved. And certainly that striving, just as it is pursued at their peril by those who seek to please more out of vanity than charity, so it is neglected at their peril by those who are reserved more out of pride than wisdom. For this reason I would call blessed the man who can hold to the royal road of truth[31] that lies between the two vices of silly amiability on the one hand and proud aloofness on the other. The man who is filled with true charity does not pursue his efforts out of vanity nor disdain the struggle out of pride.

5. For it is the power and nature of true love that even when it does not feel affection it nevertheless contrives to make itself loved

---

29. Jn 17:1.   30. Mt 5:16.   31. Num 21:22.

in return. Truth readily commends itself to everyone's goodwill even without any other support, unless it meets with the opposition of an evil and wicked mind, ever ready to put a wrong interpretation on everything. For the commending of this holy love some have their own special gift from God,[32] who makes their faces bright with oil,[33] floods them with a gentle and pleasing graciousness, makes their every word and action agreeable in the sight of all. At the same time many who perhaps love not less but even more do not easily acquire that grace.

But the obligation is the same for everyone. Taking thought for what is good not only in God's sight but also in men's[34] you must neglect neither a clear conscience through love of a good name nor the esteem of men through too much trust in a clear conscience. How can you possibly flatter yourself about this clear conscience unless you are without complaint among your brethren? Unless you show that you really are a brother among brothers in all your dealings with them? Do you think it is enough not to scandalize them? The fact is that you do scandalize if you do not edify, that is, if you do not glorify God everywhere according to your own proper role in the community, with your own conscience and your brethren bearing witness to your goodness.[35]

However, if you find that you do not please evil men, know that nothing pleases them except what is itself evil and even the sight of a just man is painful to them. If your failure is not due to your own negligence, seeing that you love all your enemies, but to their bad will, because they return evil for good and hatred for your love,[36] then be consoled. Take courage from him who said: "Blessed are you when men hate you,"[37] and by him also who said that if anyone please such men as these he cannot be Christ's servant.[38]

6. But there is another evil that is really grievous and one to be lamented with an abundance of tears, an evil that is experienced not only by superiors but by subjects also who are jealous of their brethren with the jealousy of God.[39] I mean the evil of good men

32. 1 Cor 7:7. 33. Ps 103:15. 34. Rom 12:17.
35. 1 Tim 3:7. 36. Ps 37:21; 108:5. 37. Lk 6:22.
38. Gal 1:10. 39. 2 Cor 11:2.

(not of course insofar as they are good) who are found to be at enmity with other good men. They hate him that rebukes at the gate.[40] "A man's enemies are those of his own household."[41] Even Paul laments that he has become the enemy of his sons and friends because he told them the truth.[42] And so he experienced what the poet[43] said: "Truth begets hatred." And of course what the Spouse speaks of: "The sons of my mother have fought against me[44] when I would have fought for their salvation." O triumphant Queen, wonderful Victor, go on fighting, do not yield, do not run away, do not grow fatigued. Be not overcome by evil but rather overcome evil by good.[45] Wisdom conquers evil.[46] How much more will it conquer weakness or ignorance? Not that the charity of a spiritual man can look on the contradictions of worldly men as malice; it considers them rather as ignorance or weakness hampering a man. Yet we must not look on it as an insult to the Apostles that they were called evil by our Lord.[47]

Now why am I talking like this to you, my brethren, who are beloved alike of God and me? Is it because I feel that this evil is to be found in one of you, an evil I and his brethren have to contend with? Is it because one of you is, I would not say rebellious, but hard of heart and self-willed? No, I speak to you like this not because this kind of evil is to be found among you now, but so that it may not be found among you in the future; so that if some weakness should overcome one of you at any time, he may receive whatever correction charity may give in a like spirit of charity. Then it will come about that not only the one who makes the correction, but also the one who receives it, will be beloved of God and men and the memory of both will be held in blessing.[48] Through the merits of our blessed Father Benedict may he who is the singularly Blessed of God the Father deign to grant this, Jesus Christ, who is blessed for ever and ever. Amen.[49]

---

40. Amos 5:10. 41. Mt 10:36; Mic 7:6. 42. Gal 4:16.
43. *Comicus*, i.e., Terence in *Andria*, I, i, 41. 44. Song 1:5.
45. Rom 12:21. 46. Wis 7:30. 47. Mt 7:11.
48. Sir 45:1. 49. Rom 1:25.

SERMON 25

THE FOURTH SERMON FOR ST BENEDICT

"HE SANCTIFIED HIM through his faith and meekness."[1] Moses is the real subject of this verse, but today I think it can be applied very well to Saint Benedict. Filled as he was with the spirit of all the saints,[2] he must be considered much more to have not a little of the spirit of Moses. For if the Lord drew from the spirit of Moses and inspired with it every one of the supporting band of elders who shared his ministry,[3] how much more must it rest on him who more truly fulfilled on a more spiritual level the fullness of his whole ministry? Moses was the leader of those making their way out of Egypt; Benedict of those turning their backs on the world. They have both given a law. But the one was the minister of the letter that kills, the other, of the spirit that gives life.[4] Moses, owing to the hardness of the hearts of the Jews,[5] apart from a few guides to behavior, left no prescriptions adequate to the task of justification; Benedict however has handed on the unique purity of the Gospel teaching and the simplicity of its way of life. So many of the things about which Moses writes

1. Sir 45:4. This follows upon the text used as the opening for the previous Sermon; see above, note 1.

2. This phrase was probably inspired by the *Dialogues* of Gregory the Great: *Ut perpendo, vir iste spiritu justorum omnium plenus fuit.* "This man must have been filled with the spirit of all the just."—Dialogue 2, c. 8, trans. O. Zimmerman (New York: Fathers of the Church, 1959), p. 72. Aelred also employs it in his Third Sermon for the Feast of St Benedict, n. 3, trans. M. B. Pennington in *Cistercian Studies*, 4 (1969), p. 84.

3. Ex 18:24ff.   4. 2 Cor 3:6.   5. Mt 19:8.

Sermon 25:1-2

are difficult to understand, impossible or useless to perform.⁶ Benedict on the other hand wrote a most excellent Rule of life remarkable both for the lucidity of its style and for its discretion.⁷ Finally although Moses was the leader of the children of Israel when they left the land of Egypt he did not lead them into their promised resting-place; whereas our leader, like the standard-bearer of the army of monks, has today gone before us along the straight path, the path stretching eastwards, into the kingdom of heaven. Therefore it is not absurd to consider his merits equal to those of Moses, whose ministry he is found even to have surpassed.

It will not be unfitting therefore to apply to him what we read was written about the other: "He sanctified him through his faith and meekness," especially since it is of these two virtues, faith and meekness, that he is our teacher; he could never have lived otherwise than as he taught.

2. What could be more notable than his faith? While still a mere youth he scorned the world that smiled upon him. He trampled on the flowers of the world and of his own body as if they were already withered.⁸ He desired to suffer the hardships of the world for the sake of God rather than to make merry in it for the moment. What could be more like the faith of Moses, which the Apostle praises in the words: "By faith Moses, when he was grown up, denied himself to be the son of Pharaoh's daughter, rather choosing to be afflicted with the people of God than to have the pleasure of sin for a time."⁹

And what could be holier than the meekness of our Father? He even refused to be provoked by the spite of those who were plotting to kill him, offering poison instead of wine.¹⁰ Moses indeed, so the Scripture tells us, was a man exceedingly meek, above all men

---

6. Acts 15:10.

7. This description of the Rule of St Benedict is taken from the *Dialogues*, though Guerric inverts the order. See Zimmerman, *op. cit.*, Dialogue 2, c. 36, p. ¯07.

8. See Gregory's Dialogue Two, intro.; c. 1f.; Zimmerman trans., pp. 55ff.

9. Heb 11:24f.

10. See Gregory's Dialogue Two, c. 3; Zimmerman trans., pp. 61f.

that dwelt upon earth.[11] But does it deny that his spirit was ever provoked? Does it not tell us that he was not only annoyed but terribly enraged against all who stood in his path? As for the gentleness of our teacher, I remember reading that it was remarkable not only toward those who spoke against him, but also toward those who tried to do him harm. Of his wrath I have no recollection. It must not however be considered prejudicial to the praise of holy meekness in either him or Moses if the just man burns with zeal against sinners, since this is the zeal without which meekness would sink to the level of tepidity or timidity. How could that kind of meekness, which brought a curse on Heli despite his other virtues,[12] sanctify anyone? "Brethren, have peace among you,"[13] commands the Master, so meek and peace-loving. But before this he gives an admonition: "Have salt in you." For he realized without a doubt that the meekness of peace is the nurse of vice unless a demanding zeal first sprinkles it with searing salt, just as warm weather causes meat to decay unless it is salted. Therefore have peace among you, but a peace that is seasoned with the salt of wisdom. Seek after meekness, but a meekness that burns with faith.

3. You also will be sanctified through faith and meekness. And your meekness will remain unblemished, if faith precedes it. But it must be a faith that is true and unfeigned;[14] a faith not dead but living and vigorous.[15] And not only living and vigorous; it must be the constant and fearless faith of Moses of which St Paul writes: "By faith he left Egypt, not fearing the fierceness of the king."[16] Kings are fierce but faith is fiercer, for it sees that their power has no foundation. Because of this it scorns all the folly of those who persecute it, secure in its own superiority. It is more ready and strong to endure to the end than their fury is to persecute.

On the reading of today's lesson we have said we must compare the faith of our holy Father Benedict with that of Moses. Now there are two points in his faith, it seems to me, especially singled out by

11. Num 12:3.	12. 1 Sam 2:27ff.	13. Mk 9:49.
14. 1 Tim 1:5.	15. Jas 2:17.	16. Heb 11:28.

the Apostle for commendation. It is quite clear that Moses, whom he sets before us as an example of faith, despised the favors of this world and had no fear of its hardships. He despised the world's favors, esteeming abuse suffered for Christ greater riches than the treasure of the Egyptians. He had no fear of hardships, not fearing the fierceness of the king. To both these points the Apostle adds the reason why our faith is weak. He considered abuse suffered for Christ greater riches than the treasure of the Egyptians because, the Apostle says, he looked to the reward. He feared not the fierceness of the king, because, the Apostle adds, he endured as seeing him that is invisible.[17] From this it is clear that things temporal are considered as nothing if things eternal are kept before our eyes, and that human power is easily ridiculed if divine power is feared as if it were constantly about to strike.

Faith alone does these two things. For its eyes are so vigorous and penetrating that with regard to the future it provides a lively foresight, and with regard to the hidden present it gives a keen perception. The faith which the eternal Spirit enlightens neither the passage of time nor the drag of the body can blemish, because it goes ahead of time by laying hold of the future and rises above the body by contemplating the things of the spirit. For the virtue of faith, contemplating not what is visible but what is invisible, is twofold, just as the concept of things invisible is twofold. Things are not seen either because they are not present, or because even though present they are spiritual entities. The good things to come that have been promised are not yet present. God himself, he who promises or threatens, is present, but owing to his spiritual nature[18] he lies hidden. Now because faith is the substance of things to be hoped for[19] it lays hold of the good things to come that are the object of its hope as if they were already present, and makes them as it were already exist in the heart of the believer. In the same way, because it is the evidence of things that appear not,[20] it exposes, examines and demonstrates to itself the presence of God, even though he appears not. To him who said: "He it is

17. Heb 11:26f.   18. Jn 4:24.   19. Heb 11:1.   20. *Ibid.*

who has raised us up together and has made us sit together in the heavenly places through Christ Jesus,"[21] faith was indeed the substance of things to be hoped for. To him who endured as seeing him that is invisible[22] faith was the evidence of things that appear not. For he who said: "We are saved by hope,"[23] did he not clearly show that through faith the object of his hope and enduring expectation already abode in his heart? And is not he who holds God constantly in his sight[24] persuaded by the evidence of faith that he is present even though he appears not?

4. To this kind of faith the words of Scripture are directly applicable: "The just man lives by faith."[25] For this is the faith which makes him just and keeps him just and, so that he may live for ever, feeds him in the meantime with the joy of hope. For what can recall a man from the path of sin and save him so well as the faith which endures and preserves, seeing him that is invisible? What makes a man rejoice with hope so well as the faith which always looks to the reward? Why is it, brethren, that we are negligent? Is it not because we pay too little attention to the presence of our Judge? And why is it that we almost wallow in sadness? Is it not because we do not duly consider our promised reward? In these two faults, negligence and sadness, our lack of faith struggles pitifully. Either we are remiss about what has been commanded, or if we are forced out of our negligence by fear, there is no joy in our work nor, as faith demands, are we consoled in our toil by the hope of the reward. The Apostle said: "They that come to God must believe that he is, and rewards them that seek him."[26] If we do not dodge the fact that he is, we have the protection of fear; if we hold fast to "he rewards those that seek him," we have the consolation of hope. Where there is the protection of fear, negligence has no place; where there is the consolation of hope, sadness has no abode.

And just as the faith by which we believe that God is gives rise to salutary fear, so also when we do not believe it or hide the fact the curb is released from every kind of sin. For why are they cor-

---

21. St Paul, Eph 2:6.   22. Moses, Heb 11:27.   23. St Paul, Rom 8:24.
24. Ps 15:8.   25. Rom 1:17.   26. Heb 11:6.

rupted and become abominable in iniquities if not because the common fool has said in his heart: "There is no God."[27] Or if he does not admit that he has no knowledge of God, certainly there is no fear of God before his eyes. In his sight he has acted deceitfully, denying that he knows what he does know yet does not want to know, so that "his iniquity may be found to be hatred."[28] Rightly indeed does deceit turn to hatred in him who is not ignorant of God but has hatred of him. For how can he not hate God if he ignores his presence, scorns his authority and has no wish for his judgment? The man who does not know God will not be known by him; and the one who hates God will earn his hatred in return. The first will be condemned by the truth of the judgment; on the other the severity of hatred will take its vengeance.

5. And so, brethren, feigned faith, faith full of deceit which denies its own existence, is more fraught with danger than no faith at all. It is the complete lack of faith that speaks through the fool who says in his heart: "There is no God." It is feigned faith that, through malice, acts deceitfully in his sight. With this faith a man pretends he does not know God and that God has no knowledge of him. Making himself out to be learned and prudent, he is on the contrary reckless and impertinent[29] and sins in God's presence. I do not know how this can be called faith, seeing that it makes men hypocrites and deceivers rather than faithful. I know indeed that the earth rings with the confession of faith, but on the other hand I hear the Prophet lamenting that faith has perished out of all the earth.[30] Do you think that if the Son of Man were to come now, he would find faith over the earth?[31] Would he consider this is faith, this feigned faith of the negligent and the contemptuous? He deals less harshly with the blindness of the unbelievers, holds the credulity of the demons to be better. Even the demons believe, and shudder.[32] Men believe but do not tremble. The devils hold in awe the One they believe in; men since they have no fear

27. Ps 52:1f.   28. Ps 35:2f. (Vulgate).
29. The Latin here is a play on words: *dum sciens et prudens immo imprudens et impudens.*
30. Mic 7:2.   31. Lk 18:8.   32. Jas 2:19.

or awe of him in whom they believe are condemned all the more because of their scorn.

Let us not be fooled, brethren, by the common use of the word faith, as if every kind of faith is reckoned as justice.[33] But let us be mindful of the definition of that faith which is pleasing to God given to us by the Teacher of the Gentiles in faith and truth:[34] "Faith is the substance of things hoped for, the evidence of things that appear not."[35] This is the faith that works through love.[36] From it hope is born at the realization of our merits. Again faith is laid down as the groundwork and foundation upon which those everlasting goods we hope for are to rest. Without this faith it is impossible to please God,[37] with it it is impossible to displease him. "Your eyes, O Lord, are upon faith," said he who forever stood in your sight through faith.[38] And indeed it is only right and fitting, in fact you owe it to us, that your eyes, Lord, should return the gaze of faith, because my eyes are always upon the Lord[39] who replies in all sincerity: "You understand what faith is."

6. And we, brethren, if we push God behind our backs as if we had no faith, so that putting aside fear of him we fix our attention rather on empty things, in what way do we think he will look on us? He will look on us, but with what sort of gaze? The face of the Lord is against evil-doers.[40] How angry, how dreadful, how terrible will he be known then at the last day when those who hate him flee from before him.[41] And where shall they flee to from before you, O Lord, save into the exterior darkness,[42] into that chaos and abyss of fire and gloom? Then they shall say to the mountains: "Fall upon us," and to the hills: "Cover us,"[43] considering it more endurable to be swallowed up in the depths of hell than to face the anger of God. On that day the just will stand in great constancy.[44] The faith which now stands before God anxious to behold his will, will then stand before him serenely to behold his

---

33. Rom 4:5.
34. 1 Tim 2:7.
35. Heb 11:1.
36. Gal 5:6.
37. Heb 11:6.
38. Jer 5:3.
39. Ps 24:15.
40. Ps 33:17.
41. Ps 67:2.
42. Mt 8:12; 22:13; 25:30.
43. Lk 23:30.
44. Wis 5:1.

glory. Be watchful, brethren, stand firm in your faith.[45] The man whom faith arouses with fear is not able to slumber through negligence; the one whom faith establishes in hope cannot falter through lack of confidence. But let all that you do be done in love[46] so that meekness is joined to faith until it may be said of each one of you: "The Lord sanctified him through his faith and meekness." May the Holy of Holies grant you this, who lives and reigns through endless ages. Amen.

---

45. 1 Cor 16:13.   46. 1 Cor 16:14.

SERMON 26

THE FIRST SERMON FOR THE ANNUNCIATION

IN THESE DAYS OF LENTEN observance the solemnity of our Lord's Annunciation provides us with a welcome interlude, so that men who are wearied by bodily affliction may be revived by spiritual joy, and men brought low by the grief of repentance may be consoled by the annunciation of him who takes away the sins of the world.[1] For so it is written: "Grief in a man's heart will bring him low and he will be gladdened by a good word."[2] Truly it is a good word, a trustworthy word and worthy of all acceptance,[3] the glad tidings of our salvation which the angel sent by God[4] announced to Mary today. Day unto day announced the joy;[5] the angel brought to the Virgin the joyful word concerning the incarnation of the Word. That utterance, while it promises the Virgin a Son, promises the guilty forgiveness, prisoners redemption, captives liberty and the buried life. That word, while it proclaims the kingdom of the Son, announces also the glory of the just, strikes fear into hell, gladdens the heavens and seems to have increased the perfection of the angels by knowledge of mysteries and by new kinds of joy. Who then is not gladdened by that word in his affliction? Who is not consoled by that utterance in his humility? "Be mindful," says

---

1. Jn 1:29. The Feast of the Annunciation although sometimes postponed until after the celebration of Easter is ordinarily observed on March 25th during the Lenten season.
2. Prov 12:25.   3. 1 Tim 1:15; 4:9.   4. Lk 1:26.
5. Ps 18:3.

David, "of your word to your servant by which you gave me hope. For this has consoled me in my humility."[6] He had received only the word of promise, but as yet there was no sign of the fulfillment. He was afflicted by the delay in the answering of his prayer but he was consoled by the certitude of hope arising from the fidelity of him who had made the promise.

2. If David then fed his spirit with the mere hope of this salvation which was reserved for us, what a joy, what a delight should the fulfillment be for us? O the happiness of these times, O the unhappiness of these times. Shall we not speak of the happiness of the times in which there is such a plenitude of grace and of all good things? Shall we not speak of the unhappiness of the times which are marked by such ingratitude on the part of the redeemed? For, behold, the fullness of time has come in which God sends his Son[7] to become the Son of Man and men's Savior; and behold the ingratitude of the times, that sinful man should be weary of his Savior. Salvation is announced to the lost and they scorn it; life is promised to those in despair and they neglect it; God comes to men and they do not rise to meet him.

He rises who bestirs himself with some devotion to give glory to the grace of God, who welcomes at least with joy the word of his own salvation. Now I know who it is who is gladdened by those good tidings. Without doubt it is he whom a holy heartfelt sorrow has previously brought low,[8] sorrow over his pilgrim state and exile, sorrow over the bonds of death and the perils of hell;[9] the man who grieves daily and laments that the snares of death have encompassed him and the perils of hell have found him.[10] To this man today's message from heaven brings joy, this man receives with exultation the tidings of God's Son. To this man, I say, as he grieves and mourns that he is the prey of such evils surrounding him, the Liberator is not announced without gladness, the Liberator who is to give the oil of gladness for mourning, a mantle of praise for the spirit of grief,[11] who will bring wretchedness to an end but

6. Ps 118:49f.   7. Gal 4:4.   8. Prov 12:25.
9. Ps 17:6.   10. Ps 114:3.   11. Is 61:3.

give to the wretched happiness without end. Blessed therefore are they who mourn, for they shall be consoled.[12] Blessed are they whom a holy heartfelt sorrow has brought low, for they shall be gladdened by a good word.[13]

A good word indeed and consoling is your almighty Word, Lord, which today has come from a royal throne[14] into the Virgin's womb. In it also he has made for himself a royal throne in which, although he sits even now as a king in the heavens surrounded by a host of angels, he is nonetheless the comforter of those who grieve on earth.

3. The Virgin was chosen from a royal race,[15] noble scion of a royal stock, but more nobly endowed with royal virtue, in order that the royal honor of the eternal King, the King's Son, should be defended also by his Mother's nobility, and he who comes from his Father's royal throne should be welcomed also by a royal throne in the virginal court of his queenly Mother. In her and from her Wisdom built himself a house;[16] in her and from her he prepared a throne for himself[17] when in her and from her he fitted a body to himself.[18] It was so made and adapted to all things that it might be for him both a house in which to rest and a throne for judgment, after first serving him as a tent for fighting and a chair for teaching. Consider if it be not the throne of David his father which the angel promises will be given him,[19] not because David had sat on it, but because it was taken and fashioned from the seed of David. And certainly if it is not David's throne, your throne, God, is for ever and ever.[20] If it is not David's throne, certainly it is a throne raised aloft[21] above every creature.

If however anyone wishes to interpret that great throne which Solomon made himself of ivory[22] as the very body which our

---

12. Mt 5:5. 13. Prov 12:25. 14. Wis 18:15.

15. Guerric uses here an expression drawn from an antiphon which is sung at both vespers and tierce on the Feast of the Nativity of the Blessed Virgin Mary.

16. Prov 9:1. 17. Ps 9:8. 18. Heb 10:5.
19. Lk 1:32. 20. Ps 44:7. 21. Is 6:1.
22. 1 Kings 10:18.

Peacemaker took today from the Virgin, he would not seem to be far from the truth since what follows ". . . and he overlaid it with gold exceeding bright,"[23] applies well enough to the same body which the Lord now clothes in the beauty of unbearable splendor. He overlaid it with gold exceeding bright. Indeed if you question the eyes of the apostles who saw him transfigured on the mountain they will confess that the gold is exceeding bright, that the splendor of his body was too great for them to bear—although Scripture is accustomed to use the word "exceeding" for "very."[24] The rest of what Scripture has to say about the magnificence of that throne, if anyone wishes to treat of it, will be more aptly applied, if I am not mistaken, to the Body of Christ which is the Church.[25]

4. For my part, I prefer now to wonder at that ivory of virginal chastity, so precious or rather priceless, of which he who sits above the cherubim[26] chose to make a seat for himself, saying: "This is my resting place for ever and ever, here will I sit, for I have chosen it."[27] How brilliant is that ivory which pleased the eyes of so great and so rich a king, in whose days silver was of no account;[28] how cool—it did not know the heat of passion even in conception; how solid—even childbirth did not violate it; how white and at the same time how ruddy—it was filled by the whiteness of eternal light[29] and the fire of the Holy Spirit with all their plenitude. Mary to be sure is herself whiter than snow, more ruddy than old ivory;[30] chastity conferred on her, as we know, an incomparable whiteness and charity, or indeed martyrdom, a ruddiness brighter than that of all the elect of old. For her own soul was pierced by a sword,[31] so that the Mother of the supreme Virgin and Martyr might be herself too a virgin and a martyr, white and ruddy just as her Beloved is white and ruddy.[32]

Finally, just as Solomon had nothing among all his treasures and vast wealth so precious that he judged it preferable to ivory for

---

23. Ibid.
25. Col 1:24.
28. 1 Kings 10:21; 2 Chron 9:20.
30. Lam 4:7.
24. Mt 17:1ff.; Lk 9:28ff.; Mk 9:2ff.
26. Ps 98:2
31. Lk 2:35.
27. Ps 131:14.
29. Wis 7:26.
32. Song 5:10.

that magnificent work of art, the throne of his glory; so did Mary find before the Lord a grace all her own, above that of all of the elect, angels and men, the grace to conceive and bear God's Son and to have a throne of glory carved from the ivory of her body by the power of the Most High[23] without the labor of hands. Glorious indeed is that throne and wonderful, of which Scripture says that no such work of art was produced in any other kingdom.[34] That could easily be proved by the witness of the angels who desire always and insatiably to look upon the glory and beauty of our Lord's body.[35] For, since no such work of art was produced in any other kingdom, whatever has been produced bends the knee to it in all the kingdoms of heaven, of earth and of the infernal regions.[36] How blessed then is that womb of ivory from which the Redeemer's flesh of ivory was taken,[37] the price of souls, the wonder of angels, the seat of supreme majesty and the throne of power, the food of immortal life, the medicine of sin, the restoration of health. "All those," we read, "who touched him were healed of their infirmities, for power went out from him and healed everyone."[38]

5. Blessed is the womb that bore you,[39] Lord Jesus; happy is the chastity of the virginal womb which provided the material for this work of art. Happy indeed, my brethren, is the brilliance of that ivory, that is, the whiteness of chastity, in preference to which our Solomon chooses neither the gold of worldly wisdom nor the silver of eloquence nor again the gem of any outstanding grace; provided that chastity is commended by humility, for the Lord has looked upon the humility of his Handmaid.[40] Therefore when Solomon in his canticle of love proclaimed the Virgin's chastity—the chastity, that is, of both Bride and Bridegroom, since the same words of praise befit for the most part those who share the same spirit and the same flesh—in order to show that their chastity was adorned and ours must be adorned with other virtues too, he said: "His body is of ivory studded with sapphires."[41]

33. Lk 1:35.
34. 1 Kings 10:20.
35. 1 Pet 1:12.
36. Phil 2:10.
37. Lk 11:2; Song 5:14.
38. Mt 6:56; Lk 6:18f.
39. Lk 11:27.
40. Lk 1:48.
41. Song 5:14.

Sermon 26:5–6

That you may know that chastity is a receptacle for other virtues or graces, the cupboards in which our Solomon stores his scents and ointments are but houses of ivory, as David sang in that nuptial canticle, whose title, *Canticle for the Beloved*,[42] shows that it is to be applied to the Church's Bridegroom. "Myrrh," he says, "and aloes and cassia are wafted from your garments, from houses of ivory, with which king's daughters have delighted you, paying you honor."[43] The ivory bodies of the saints are the house of Christ, they are Christ's garment, they are Christ's members,[44] they are a temple of the Holy Spirit.[45] From these garments of Christ, from these houses of ivory, is wafted to him all the fragrance of the virtues and spiritual gifts with which the daughters of the apostles and prophets delight and honor the King of kings.

You have experienced yourselves, my brethren, since each one of you began to control his own body as something holy and to be held in honor (not yielding to the promptings of passion as the heathen do in their ignorance of God[46]) what ointments, what scents have been poured into it by God's generosity. The body that was a sink filled with dirt is now the venerable sanctuary of the Holy Spirit; what was an abyss of iniquity is now a reservoir of graces.

6. "Myrrh," we read, "and aloes and cassia are wafted from your garments, from houses of ivory."[47] We dwell to be sure in houses of clay,[48] but what are of clay by reason of their material, come to be of ivory through the virtue of continence; and if myrrh first begins to be wafted from them through the mortification of pleasures, other fragrant scents will follow in due course, breathed forth by the manifold grace of the virtues.[49] They will be breathed forth also far and wide to our neighbors as Christ's good odor in every place.[50] As soon as Isaac smelled the fragrance of these garments of Christ he exclaimed: "Behold, the odor of my son is like the odor of a field which the Lord has blessed."[51]

---

42. Ps 44:1. 43. Ps 44:9. 44. Eph 5:30. 45. 1 Cor 6:19.
46. 1 Thess 4:4f. 47. Ps 44:9. 48. Job 4:19. 49. 1 Pet 4:10.
50. 2 Cor 2:15. 51. Gen 27:27.

The Bridegroom too speaks to the Bride, who is also his Body and his garment, in the words: "The odor of your garments is like the odor of incense."[52] This odor of incense, so pleasing to the Bridegroom, your heartfelt devotion will breathe forth, brethren, if it is so ardent and dedicated that your prayer rises like incense in the sight of the Most High[53] and goes up before him like a column of smoke perfumed with myrrh and frankincense.[54] And indeed myrrh is wafted to him from your bodies; it is wafted to me also. Would that incense were so wafted from your hearts, that the Bridegroom, finding you as dedicated as you are chaste, would honor you more frequently with his visits and say: "I will go to the mount of myrrh and the hill of incense."[55]

That utterance however seems to be a prophecy of this day, spoken of old by Solomon and fulfilled today by Jesus. For today he came to that highest mount of mountains, mount not only of myrrh and incense but also of all perfumes. I mean the Virgin of virgins, full of all graces,[56] among which, if I am not mistaken, the Bridegroom took special pleasure in the myrrh of chastity and the incense of devotion. This odor, my brethren, is above all perfumes. This odor attracts the Lord of majesty from on high and invites him to incline the heavens and come down.[57] This is seen today when the Most High, after sending an angel from heaven, himself too came down into his Mother's womb, he who always remains in the Father's bosom, with whom he lives and reigns for ever and ever. Amen.[58]

---

52. Song 4:11.   53. Ps 140:2.   54. Song 3:6.
55. Song 4:6.   56. Lk 1:28.   57. Song 4:10; Ps 143:5.
58. See above, Sermon 11, note 65, vol. 1, p. 75.

SERMON 27

THE SECOND SERMON FOR THE ANNUNCIATION

TODAY THE WORD was made flesh and began to dwell among us,[1] according to the rule of sound faith which has been handed down to us by the definition of the Church's dogmas. For the Church holds most firmly and has not the least doubt that Christ's flesh was not conceived before the Word took it to himself: the Word of God himself was conceived by taking flesh to himself and the flesh was conceived by the incarnation of the Word.[2] So today Wisdom began to build himself the house of our body in the Virgin's womb, and for the building up of the Church's unity hewed out the corner-stones[3] from the mountain without the labor of hands.[4] Without the intervention of man he fashioned for himself from a virginal body the flesh of our redemption. From this day the Lord of hosts is with us, the God of Jacob is our champion,[5] because today we are exalted in the Lord[6] so that glory may dwell in our land.[7]

1. Jn 1:14.
2. Guerric here refers to one of the errors which was attributed to Origen, which substantially held that the incarnation or the union of the Word with the sacred humanity took place only some time subsequent to the conception. In the *Liber adversus Origenem* of Emperor Justinian, which was published in 543, the third canon reads: "If anyone says or thinks that the body of our Lord Jesus Christ was first formed in the womb of the Blessed Virgin and afterwards united by him to the Word of God and the soul, as though it were something that previously existed, let him be anathema." According to Cassiodorus (*De inst. div. litt.*, chap 2 [PL 70:1111]) these canons of Justinian were confirmed by Pope Vigilius.
3. Eph 2:20. 4. Dan 2:34. 5. Ps 45:8, 12. 6. Ps 88:19. 7. Ps 84:10.

Indeed today, Lord, you did bless that earth of yours,[8] blessed among women.[9] Today you did bestow the kindness of the Holy Spirit, so that our earth might yield the blessed fruit of its womb[10] and as the heavens dropped down dew from above a virginal womb might bring forth a Savior.[11] Accursed is the earth in the work of the sinner, bringing forth as it does, even when cultivated, thorns and thistles to the heirs of the curse.[12] But now blessed is the earth in the work of the Redeemer, for it brings to birth the remission of sins and the fruit of life to all men, and frees the sons of Adam from the doom with which their origin was cursed. Indeed that earth is blessed which, wholly untouched, not dug nor sown, from heaven's dew alone brings forth a Savior and provides mortal men with the Bread of angels[13] and the Food of eternal life. So this earth, which was not cultivated, seemed to be derelict but it was full of rich fruit; it seemed to be a lonely waste but it was a paradise of happiness. Truly the waste was a garden of God's delights, since its fields brought forth a sweet-smelling seed, truly a full desert from which the Father sent forth the Lamb, the Lord of the earth.[14]

"Send forth," we read, "the Lamb, Lord, from the rock of the desert,"[15] that is, hew out a rock from the rock, let a holy and inviolable rock be brought forth by a holy and inviolate virginity. To be sure in this very respect Christ's setting corresponds quite aptly with his rising, his burial with his conception. A lamb is sent forth from the rock of the desert to be laid in the rock of the sepulcher. He for whose body a sepulcher was to be hewn out in the rock, from the beginning of his conception hewed out for himself a body from the rock and for his body a place in the rock, no more lessening the integrity of the rock when he was sent forth from it than he broke the seal of the sepulcher's rock when he came forth from it.

2. If the rock is Christ, as St Paul says,[16] then the Son does not belie his origin from a Mother who herself is also called a rock. Is

8. Ps 84:1.	9. Lk 1:28.	10. Ps 84:13; Lk 1:42.
11. Is 45:8.	12. Gen 3:17.	13. Ps 77:25.
14. Is 16:1.	15. *Ibid*.	16. 1 Cor 10:4.

she not rightly styled a rock who for love of integrity was firm in her resolve, solid in her affections, in her feelings wholly without feeling and like a stone against the enticements of sin? Is not that virginal integrity a rock which gives birth to nothing by its own natural power, and when it does give birth by the power of God's dew is able to remain unopened both when it admits conception and when it brings forth a child?

"If the earth is to be opened," says Isaiah, "let it be opened and bring forth a Savior."[17] O holy Isaiah, you who say: "Let it be opened," what are we to make of the Lord's declaration to Ezechiel: "This door shall be closed, it shall not be opened"?[18] Or is it that only the plan to bring about the mother's fertility was revealed to you, while the mystery of her integrity for ever closed was a closed book to you? "Not at all," he says, "no one is more aware of this secret than I. How should the mystery of perpetual virginity have been hidden from me who so long before made the prediction: 'Behold a virgin shall conceive and bear a son'?[19] Do you ask then how, while I say: 'Let it be opened,' Ezechiel can say: 'It shall not be opened'? It shall not be opened to a man, but it shall be opened to the Lord, as Ezechiel is told in the same place: 'No man shall pass through it, for the Lord God of Israel has entered through it.'[20] And what shall be opened to the Lord is not the integrity of the Virgin's body, for, as Ezechiel added: 'This shall be closed even to the prince himself,'[21] but the ear and the door of the heart, since it was through the Virgin's ear that the Word entered to become incarnate and through the closed door of her body that he came forth incarnate." Although the almighty Word of God took upon himself our weakness he did not lessen in any way his own omnipotence. Contrary to the nature of flesh and exceeding our understanding he was able to make his body in all its solidity pass through members that remained closed and entire, just as when he came into the disciples through closed doors he demonstrated to their eyes what is beyond reason's grasp.

17. Is 45:8.
20. Ezek 44:2.
18. Ezek 44:2.
21. *Ibid.*
19. Is 7:14.

3. Free from fear then, unspotted Virgin, door of the sanctuary forever closed, free from fear, open to the Lord God of Israel, who for a long time has been calling to you: "Open to me, my sister, my beloved."[22] There is no reason why you should fear for your integrity. It is not God's wont to violate what is integral, but to restore the integrity of what has been violated. If you have been opened to the Word of God, then indeed you have been not only closed but also sealed. "Put me," we read, "as a seal upon your heart, as a seal upon your arm."[23] For Jesus, leaving his impression in the heart, his expression in her work, is a seal and a bulwark of his Bride's inviolable chastity, and by the very fact that he leaves the impression of a pattern for imitation he sets also a guard which preserves from corruption. If then, faithful Virgin, your ear is open to hear and your mind to believe, with your ear hearken to the angel's word, with your heart receive the Word of the Most High and with your body conceive the Son of God. Do you also say, you who are blessed at once in your humility and in your fidelity, say: "The Lord has opened my ear and I was not rebellious, I turned not backward.[24] Behold the handmaid of the Lord. I am ready to do his will, indeed I will help him with my prayers if I can; be it done to me according to thy word."[25] To say this, so to offer one's devotion, is indeed to open one's breast to the Lord and also to open one's mouth and attract the Spirit.[26] Thus to be sure the earth was opened, that it might receive the dew which the heavens dropped from above and bring forth a Savior.[27]

A noble bud, a just bud,[28] a sweet-smelling bud, the bud of the Lord which is already in magnificence and glory,[29] since the same fruit of the earth is on high above all things, raised aloft above the heavens as God, and his glory is over the whole earth.[30] It makes no difference whether you call it a bud or a fruit or a flower, since the one Christ is all these things and an infinite number of others; grace is one reality but manifold, and virtue that is one acts in many

22. Song 5:2.
23. Song 8:6.
24. Is 50:5.
25. Lk 1:38.
26. Ps 118:131.
27. Is 45:8.
28. Jer 23:5.
29. Is 4:2.
30. Ps 107:2.

ways. The poverty of human understanding and language endows this one reality with an infinite number of names to bring out its various aspects, but it will not be able to convey its full meaning.

Rightly however is he called at once bud and flower and fruit who, without having to make progress by degrees, from the beginning of his conception possessed in himself the perfection of all virtue and grace. For in us he is at first a bud, when faith breaks forth into confession or manifest activity; afterwards a flower when God's sanctifying action blooms upon the man who is making progress by making visible the beauty of his virtues; finally a fruit, when beatitude satiates the man who has reached his consummation. Now God's economy preordained most aptly and most watchfully not only mysteries but also the foreshadowings of mysteries, so that the place in which earth brought forth a Savior who was the just bud, and a flower arose from the shoot and root of Jesse,[31] was called Nazareth, that is, holiness, bud, flower, shoot. Thus by an apt choice of words the event vouched for the place and the place for the event, while at one and the same time the name of the place proclaimed what was to take place and what took place indicated the reason for the name.

4. Forgive me, my brethren, for, while I should have been providing instruction to guide your behavior, I have lingered longer perhaps than was necessary in wonderment at and praise of that unspeakable mystery.[32] What cause for wonder is there, if I

31. Is 11:1.
32. The Cistercian Fathers were alike in this that they all conceived their sermons and writings to be geared primarily toward a practical living out of the Christian monastic life rather than speculating on the wonders of the creation or revelation. As Bernard of Clairvaux tersely expressed it: "My purpose is not so much to explain words as to move hearts."—*On the Song of Songs*, Sermon 16:1 (Cistercian Fathers Series 4), p. 114. See also Sermon 80:1 (Cistercian Fathers Series 40). The value of speculations on things natural and supernatural was judged by them in the light of their utility in the spiritual life: "But I am of the opinion that knowledge of these matters will not contribute greatly to your spiritual progress."—Bernard of Clairvaux, *ibid.*, Sermon 5:7, p. 29. Dogmatic or speculative considerations are always to lead into moral instruction and action: "And now that we have gotten past through the shadow land of allegories, it is time to explore the great

wonder at what causes the angels amazement, if I am eager to proclaim the glory of God which the heavens tell forth?[33] What cause for wonder, if I am delighted by what gladdens the spirits of the blessed, what justifies sinners and glorifies the just? I do not know if there can be any more efficacious and pleasing moral edification than the faithful and devout consideration of this mystery, that is, of the Word Incarnate. For what can so stir up man to the love of God as the love which God first bestows on man, a love for man so ardent that he wills to become man for the sake of man? What so nourishes love of one's neighbor as the likeness and nature of one's neighbor in the humanity of God? As for an example of humility, surely none greater can be imagined than God humbling himself and taking on the form of a servant[34] and a servitude below that of a servant. What can commend chastity as much as chastity itself bringing forth a Savior? Or what exhibits more plainly the power and merit of faith as that the Virgin conceived God by faith, by faith deserved to have all that God had promised her fulfilled? "Blessed," we read, "is she who believed, for what was told her by the Lord shall be brought to fulfillment."[35]

Now that you may know more fully that the Virgin's conception has not only a mystical but also a moral sense, what is a mystery for your redemption is also an example for your imitation, so that you clearly frustrate the grace of the mystery in you if you do not imitate the virtue of the example. For she who conceived God by faith promises you the same if you have faith; if you will faithfully receive the Word from the mouth of the heavenly messenger you too may conceive the God whom the whole world cannot contain, conceive him however in your heart, not in your body. And yet even in your body, although not by any bodily action or outward

---

plains of moral truths. Our faith has been strengthened, let our lives reveal its influence; our intellects have been enlightened, let them prescribe the right behavior. For they have sound sense who do this...."—*ibid.,* Sermon 17:8, p. 132; see also Sermon 39:1 (Cistercian Fathers Series 7) and the Editor's Note in T. Merton, *The Climate of Monastic Prayer* (Cistercian Studies Series 1), pp. 6f.

33. Ps 18:2.   34. Phil 2:7.   35. Lk 1:45.

form, nonetheless truly in your body, since the Apostle bids us glorify and bear God in our body.[36]

Pay careful attention then to your hearing[37] as it is written, for "faith comes from hearing, while hearing comes through the word of God,"[38] which without any doubt the angel of God proclaims to you when a faithful preacher treats with you of the fear or the love of God. You can be quite certain that such a preacher is called and is in fact an angel of the Lord of hosts. How blessed are they who can say: "For fear of you, Lord, we have conceived and given birth to the Spirit of Salvation,"[39] which indeed is no other than the Spirit of the Savior, the Truth of Jesus Christ. Behold the unspeakable condescension of God and at the same time the power of the mystery which passes all understanding. He who created you is created in you, and as if it were too little that you should possess the Father, he wishes also that you should become a mother to himself. "Whoever," he says, "does the will of my Father he is my brother and sister and mother."[40] O faithful soul, open wide your bosom, expand your affections, admit no constraint in your heart,[41] conceive him whom creation cannot contain. Open to the Word of God an ear that will listen. This is the way to the womb of your heart for the Spirit who brings about conception; in such fashion are the bones of Christ, that is the virtues, built up in the pregnant womb.[42]

5. Thanks be to you, Spirit, who breathe where you will.[43] By your gift I see not one but countless faithful souls pregnant with that noble offspring. Preserve your works, lest anyone should suffer miscarriage and expel, shapeless and dead, the progeny he has conceived of God.

You also, blessed mothers of so glorious an issue, attend to yourselves until Christ is formed in you.[44] Be careful lest any violent blow coming from without should injure the tender foetus, lest you should take into your stomach, that is your mind, anything

36. St Paul: 1 Cor 6:20.
37. Sir 13:16.
38. Rom 10:17.
39. Is 26:17f. (Septuagint).
40. Mt 12:50.
41. 2 Cor 6:12.
42. Eccles 11:5.
43. Jn 3:8.
44. Gal 4:19.

which might extinguish the spirit you have conceived. Spare, if not yourselves, at least the Son of God in you; spare him not only from evil deeds and utterances but also from harmful thoughts and deadly pleasures which obviously stifle the seed of God.[45] Guard your heart with all vigilance, for from it life will come forth,[46] that is, when the offspring is ready for birth and the life of Christ which is now hidden in your hearts[47] will be made manifest in your mortal flesh.[48] You have conceived the spirit of salvation,[49] but you are still in labor, you have not yet given birth. If there is labor in giving birth, great consolation comes from the hope of offspring. A woman in childbirth feels the distress of labor; but when she has borne her child she will not remember the distress any longer, so glad will she be that a man, Christ, has been born into the outer world of our body,[50] which is accustomed to be called a world in miniature.[51] For he who is now conceived as God in our spirits, conforming them to the Spirit of his charity, will then be born as man in our bodies, conforming them to his glorified body, in which he lives in majesty, God, for ever and ever. Amen.[52]

---

45. Mt 13:22.   46. Prov 4:23.   47. Col 3 3.
48. 2 Cor 4:11.   49. Is 26:18.   50. Jn 16:21.
51. *E.g.* in "The Life of Pythagoras." *Bibliotheca Photii*, ed. Bekker, 440, 23. Rupert of Deutz says exactly the same thing in his commentary on Ecclesiastes, ch. I, v. 4 [PL 168, 1200–1201].
52. The theme of the soul's motherhood with regard to Christ is found as early as Origen, and is constant in christian tradition. See vol. 1, pp. xxxvii and xxxviii, and patristic places recorded in note 171.

SERMON 28

THE THIRD SERMON FOR THE ANNUNCIATION

"LISTEN, HOUSE OF DAVID. Behold, the Lord himself will give you a sign. Behold, a virgin shall conceive."[1] Today this prophecy is fulfilled in your ears.[2] For today you have heard the fulfillment, as you had heard the promise, of that unspeakable mystery, the virginal conception. The Virgin conceived today. And this sign, unheard of in past ages, the Lord has given to our age, as Jeremiah foretold in the same spirit and with the same meaning: "The Lord has created something new on earth, for a woman has encompassed a man."[3] For what is: "The Lord will create something new on earth: a woman shall encompass a man" that Jeremiah says, if not what Isaiah says: "The Lord will give a sign, a virgin shall conceive a son"? By "will encompass" is meant that she will not receive from intercourse with a man but will conceive alone, of herself, within herself and will clothe him in the wrappings of her maternal body alone.

Otherwise let the Jews say, if they can, what sign the Lord gave in this if it was not a virgin but a young woman, as they mistranslate,

---

1. Is 7:13f. This is taken from the first reading of the mass for the Feast of the Annunciation.

2. Lk 4:21. At the mass on this Feast the second reading tells of the Annunciation itself, the accomplishment of the prophecy of Isaiah.

3. Jer 9:32. This version, with its interpretation, is fairly constant in the Latin tradition, but it is due only to the Vulgate translation: *Circumdabit*. The Hebrew means: "The wife seeks her husband," and refers to the love which Israel has for her God.

who conceived. What new thing did the Lord create if a female encompassed in her womb a male received from a male? Iniquity may indeed lie to itself,[4] but in the greatness of your power, Lord, your enemies shall lie to you,[5] so that your power, repudiated by a few dishonest Jews, may be confessed the more gloriously and abundantly by the faith of all peoples. "May the peoples confess to you, God, may all peoples confess to you, for the earth has given its fruit,"[6] the Virgin has conceived Jesus. Whether the Jews like it or not, the Lord has created the novelty of this miracle as a sign for their refusal to believe, as a sign indeed which is gainsaid[7] up to the present day, more, if I am not mistaken, through a hateful stubbornness than through an ignorance that could be pitied.

2. Yet it is not foreign to the origin and customary behavior of the serpent brood[8] if the same people deny this sign after it has come to pass who, from the beginning in their father and king, Achaz, rejected it lest it come to pass. For the Lord spoke to Achaz saying: "Ask a sign for yourself." "I will not ask," said he, "and I

---

4. Ps 26:12. The animosity which Guerric seems to show here toward the Jews is characteristic of the spiritual writers of his period. However, it is not indeed an expression of a personal enmity toward the Jewish people as such. For these writers, the "Jews" are rather a type of the person who knowingly rejects Christ, those who "through a hateful stubbornness" refuse to believe. In actual fact there are beautiful examples of occasions where the Cistercians came to the defense of the Jewish people. Perhaps the most notable is that which took place during the time when Bernard of Clairvaux was preaching the Second Crusade. A zealous but rather ill-educated religious by the name of Raoul while preaching the Crusade began to incite the Christians in the Rhineland to begin their expedition by exterminating the Jews right there. Bernard's intervention and especially his very strong letter to the archbishop of Mainz (Letter 365; James trans., Letter 393, pp. 465f.) is to this day not forgotten by the Jews of that district. In an encyclical letter sent both to the English people and to the hierarchy, clergy, and people of Eastern France and Bavaria (Letter 363; James trans., Letter 391, pp. 460ff.) Bernard again spoke up for the Jewish people: "The Jews are not to be persecuted, killed or even put to flight. . . . It is an act of Christian piety . . . to spare the subjected, especially those for whom we have a law and a promise, and whose flesh was shared by Christ, his name be forever blessed." Guerric could also appreciate the goodness that was to be found among the Jews, see below, Sermon 32:3, p. 76, where he praises their faith.

5. Ps 65:3.   6. Ps 66:6f.   7. Lk 2:34.   8. Lk 3:7.

will not tempt the Lord."⁹ O worldly-wise religiosity, O detestable piety, O deceitful humility. In order not to tempt the Lord, as you say, you scorn the Lord. How would you be tempting him if you obeyed him faithfully? But now how do you not tempt him the more seriously whom you provoke with manifest scorn? So we know, we know the deceit and the envy of the Jewish stock which even before Christ was born began to envy his glory. For this Achaz too, as far as can be deduced from the manner of his life (he worshipped idols),¹⁰ was inspired by no sentiments of religion or reverence in his refusal to ask for a sign when he was bidden but only sought to prevent the Lord's being glorified.

Truly amazing and clearly deserving the anger of God and men is this stubborn perversity of the Jews, who when they are bidden to ask for a sign refuse, not as they pretend, in order not to tempt the Lord, but in order not to glorify him. Yet when they are not bidden, they do tempt him and they do ask.¹¹ For as if by second nature and force of habit the Jews look for signs,¹² and if they are produced they bring false charges against them and strive to demolish them. Thus they confess openly that they were tempting when they asked and had no intention of believing in him who worked the sign. O sinful nation, O wicked seed, O criminal sons, says Isaiah,¹³ is it too little for you to be troublesome to men, to me and the other prophets, indeed to the whole race of men, that you must be troublesome to my God also? Therefore the Lord himself will give you a sign.¹⁴ Because you walk perversely in opposition to him, he too, as he says, will walk perversely with you.¹⁵ You do not wish for a sign to be given lest the author of the miracle should be glorified. But he will provide a sign for this reason, that he may be glorified and you confounded. "Work, Lord, work a sign with me for good, so that they who hate me may see and be confounded";¹⁶ so speaks the Son to the Father concerning the Jews.

3. The first sign which the Father and the Son worked to the

---

9. Is 7:10ff. 10. 2 Kings 16:2ff.; 2 Chron 28:19ff. 11. Mt 12:38.
12. 1 Cor 1:22. 13. Is 1:4. 14. Is 7:13f. 15. Ps 17:27.
16. Ps 85:17.

confusion of the faithless, in witness of their own power and to effect our salvation, I consider to be the virgin's conception on this day. For after first declaring of it: "The Lord will give a sign," the Prophet, in the language of an evangelist, goes on, as if answering the question: what sign? "Behold a virgin shall conceive and bear a son," so that either the two statements have no connection and are false or, what is more probable, the lie of the Jews loses all semblance of truth.

Deservedly, therefore, when a wicked and unfaithful generation asks for a sign, no sign shall be given it except the sign of Jonah,[17] so that those who through perversity of mind are not edified by the sign of power may be scandalized by a sign of weakness, the death and burial for three days. For the word of the Cross and of death is a scandal to the Jews who court their own ruin while to those who are on the way to salvation, that is, to us, it is the power of God.[18] The Son of Man in the heart of the earth[19] is not any less or any weaker for us than when he is seated at the Father's right hand. The sign which they refused either in the depths of Sheol or in the heights above[20] we receive with full faith and devout veneration, recognizing the Son whom the Virgin conceives to be for us in the depths of Sheol a sign of liberation and pardon, in the heights above a sign and a hope of exultation and glory. For he who first went down into the lower regions of earth[21] so that in the blood of his covenant he might set the captives free from the pit in which there is no water,[22] is no other than he who has gone up high above all the heavens to fill creation with his presence.[23] The Lord has now lifted up an ensign, first on the gibbet of the Cross, afterward on the throne of his kingdom, and he has raised the ensign on high for the Gentiles[24] because he has been rejected by the Jews, and day by day he gathers around this ensign the disciples of the true Israel from the four winds.[25]

O Root of Jesse, who are established as an ensign for the peoples,

---

17. Mt 12:39; 16:4.
18. 1 Cor 1:23, 18.
19. Mt 12:40.
20. Is 7:11.
21. Eph 4:9.
22. Zech 9:11.
23. Eph 4:10.
24. Is 11:12.
25. Mt 24:31.

Sermon 28:3-4

because of whom kings shall shut their mouths, may the mouths of those who speak evil also be shut,[26] the mouths[27], that is, of the blaspheming Jews, who still reject the sign of your spotless conception and do not believe even the angel Gabriel when he says that nothing is impossible for God.[28] Blessed is she who believed,[29] satisfied with this argument. When she asked how she could receive a Son since she had no knowledge of man [30] her belief set her free thenceforth concerning her integrity and her offspring.

4. Whatever the impious pratings of the infidels, we believe that the Virgin conceived and bore a Son; we have as an assuring sign both the Mother and the Son. For us the Mother is wholly a miracle, she who extraordinarily and without any precedent is mother and virgin. For us the Son is wholly a miracle, who not only extraordinarily but also incomprehensibly is God and man. The Virgin Mother conceiving and giving birth is a sign for us that he who is conceived and brought forth is God and man. The Son doing the things of God and suffering the things of man is a sign for us that he raises up to God man for whom he is conceived and brought forth and for whom also he suffers.

Of all the human weaknesses or injuries which God deigned to bear for us, the first in time and, one might say, the greatest in humility, was, I think, that the majesty which knows no bounds allowed itself to be conceived in the womb and to be confined in the womb for the space of nine months. Where else did he so empty himself out, or when was he seen so completely eclipsed? For so long a time Wisdom says nothing, Power works nothing that can be discerned. The majesty which lies hidden and enclosed is not betrayed by any visible sign. He was not seen so weak on the Cross. What was weak in him immediately appeared stronger than all men, when he glorified the thief as he died;[31] and with his last breath breathed faith into the centurion.[32] The sorrow of the hour of his passion not only made the elements of creation suffer with him[33] but also subjected the opposing powers to a passion of

26. Is 11:10; 52:15.   27. Ps 62:12.   28. Lk 1:37.   29. Lk 1:45.
30. Lk 1:34.   31. Lk 23:40ff.   32. Lk 23:47.   33. Mt 27:45, 51.

timeless sorrow. On the other hand in the womb he is as if he were not.³⁴ Almighty power lies idle as if it could do nothing. The eternal Word constrains himself to silence.

5. But to you, brethren, to you that silence of the Word speaks, to you it cries out, to you to be sure it recommends the discipline of silence. For "in silence and hope shall be your strength"³⁵ as Isaiah promises, who defined the pursuit of justice as silence.³⁶ As that Child in the womb advanced towards birth in a long, deep silence, so does the discipline of silence nourish, form and strengthen a man's spirit, and produce growth which is the safer and more wholesome for being the more hidden. Mere man with his natural gifts, who does not take in the thoughts of God's Spirit,³⁷ does not know the way of the Spirit and how bones are built up in the womb of a woman with child.³⁸ But "my frame was not hidden from you," the Holy Man tells God, "the frame you made for me in the mind's hidden depth"³⁹ under the pall of silence. Neither from you is this mystery hidden, my brethren. You have shared your experience with me and have told me how a quiet and disciplined spirit is strengthened, grows fat and flourishes in silence, and how on the contrary by speaking it is broken up and dislocated as if by paralysis, grows thin and withers and dries up. If there was not strength in silence Solomon would not have said: "Like an open city without any encompassing walls, so is the man who cannot restrain his spirit from speaking."⁴⁰

Moreover, if you ask with what business the mind is to be occupied in silence we do not impose anything burdensome on you; eat your bread, as the Lord himself shows you by the example of his conception. For what did the Prophet say of him when he was speaking of the eastern gate in the Lord's house, the one that was always closed, which yet let in and let out the God of Israel? "The prince himself," he said, "shall sit in it, to eat bread before the Lord."⁴¹ "He shall sit in it," he said, for he will rest in that of which he also said: "This is my resting-place."⁴² He shall sit in it

34. Is 40:17.   35. Is 30:15.   36. Is 32:17.   37. 1 Cor 2:14.
38. Eccles 11:5.   39. Ps 138:15.   40. Prov 25:28.   41. Ezek 44:1f.
42. Ps 131:14.

Sermon 28:5-6

as on the great throne, which, as I said on another occasion, King Solomon made himself out of ivory.⁴³ If you consider the confines of the womb, the place is indeed confined; if you consider the breadth of the heart, the throne is great on account of which the womb too was made adequate to receive such majesty. In it then the prince sat and ate bread, for "if anyone," he says, "will open to me, I will come into him and sup with him and he with me."⁴⁴

6. This supper is not without bread, since he who sups is the Bread of Life, the Bread which today comes down from heaven and gives life to the world.⁴⁵ But it is a matter for wonder if he who eats and that which is eaten are one and the same, and he who eats is himself the Bread which is eaten by him. Truly a matter for wonder, but it is very truth, for Christ does not feed on any bread other than himself. For he is wholly bread: the Word on his own account, the flesh on account of its union with the Word. For the rest, the flesh is of no advantage since it is the spirit which gives life,⁴⁶ neither does man live by bread alone but by every word which comes forth from the mouth of God.⁴⁷ Every word coming forth from the mouth of God is the one and only-begotten Word of the Father, which although it is simple contains in itself the reason and form of every divine word. So the Word feeds on the Word, the Son lives on himself, for as the Father has life in himself, so he has given to the Son to have life in himself.⁴⁸ In another way, but yet with unspeakable beatitude and incomparable happiness, that Prince, sitting in the gate of the virginal womb, ate the bread of the Word before the Lord.⁴⁹ That will be the occupation, if you are wise, which will keep you busy in your silence: to eat the bread of God's Word before the Lord, preserving like Mary what

---

43. 1 Kings 10:18. See above, Sermon 26:3f., pp. 34ff.   44. Rev 3:20.
45. Jn 6:33ff.   46. Jn 6:64.   47. Deut 8:3; Mt 4:4.   48. Jn 5:6.
49. Ezek 44:1ff Some theologians were unhappy about this sentence so a long interpolation is found in the later MSS. See vol. 1, p. xxi, note 73 (however, note that in the note the original text and the emended text have gotten inverted). This sentence is theologically very significant and is discussed at length in a volume soon to be published in the Cistercian Studies Series: J. Morson, *Christ in the Sermons of Guerric of Igny*.

is said about Christ and pondering it in your heart.⁵⁰ Christ will take pleasure in eating this bread with you, and he who feeds you will himself be fed in you. The more the bread itself is eaten the more it will abound for eating, since grace is not lessened by use but increased.

7. There is a further way in which Jesus, conceived and carried in the womb, should be an example to you. As that light and pleasant burden made Mary's womb pregnant without being a heavy weight, so the womb of the Church should not feel you heavy or troublesome. The Church is pregnant, brethren, not as Mary was, with Jesus alone, but as Rebecca was with Jacob and Esau,⁵¹ that is, not only with those who are good and well-behaved but also with those who are ill-tempered and undisciplined.⁵² However, these too, for the sake of Jesus or perhaps because they possess the principle by which they are grounded in him,⁵³ the womb of the Church receives and enfolds. But when the two infants struggled and fought in Rebecca's womb she, who previously had prayed to conceive, was grieved that her womb ached with pain, trouble and sorrow.⁵⁴ She was almost sorry that she had conceived. "If it was to be thus with me," she said, "why should I have conceived?"⁵⁵ If it should happen, brethren, that the bowels of our mother should complain thus of any one of us, I am afraid that it would have been better if that man had not been conceived,⁵⁶ except that even for such we are not allowed to despair. He who even from stones raises up sons to Abraham will not allow it.⁵⁷ If there be any such, may he soften the stony heart in them so that their mother's womb will not ache, and may he comfort their mother's womb, so that she will not grow weary of carrying them, however ill-behaved they may be, until Christ is formed in them,⁵⁸ he who as perfect God and perfect man lives and reigns for ever and ever. Amen.

50. Lk 2:19.
51. Gen 25:24ff.
52. 1 Pet 2:18.
53. Heb 3:14.
54. Ps 106:39.
55. Gen 25:22.
56. Mt 26:24.
57. Mt 3:9.
58. Gal 4:19.

SERMON 29

THE FIRST SERMON FOR PALM SUNDAY

"LET THIS MIND BE IN YOU which was in Christ Jesus, who, although he was by nature God. . . ."[1] This is for the hearing of the wicked and runaway slave, man I mean, who although he was by nature and rank a slave and bound to serve, refused to serve and tried to appropriate freedom and equality with his Lord. Christ was by nature God; equal to God not through robbery but by birth because he shared omnipotence, eternity and divinity. He nevertheless dispossessed himself and not only took the nature of a slave, fashioned in the likeness of men,[2] but also carried out the ministry of a slave, lowering his own dignity and accepting an obedience to the Father which brought him death, death on a cross.[3]

But reckon it as too little for him to have served the Father as a slave although his Son and co-equal unless he also served his own slave as more than a slave. Man was made to serve his Creator. And what could be more just than that you should serve him by whom you were created, without whom you cannot exist? And what could be more blessed or more sublime than to serve him? To serve him is to reign. "I will not serve,"[4] man says to his Creator. "Then I will serve you," his Creator says to man. "You sit down, I will minister, I will wash your feet.[5] You rest; I will bear your

---

1. Phil 2:5f. This is a central theme in the liturgy for Palm Sunday. It is read not only at both vespers, lauds, and tierce but also at the first reading of the Mass.

2. Phil 2:7.   3. Phil 2:8.   4. Jer 2:30.   5. Jn 13:4f.

weariness, your infirmities.⁶ Use me as you like in all your needs, not only as your slave but also as your beast of burden and as your property. If you are tired or burdened I will carry both you and your burden, so that I may be the first to keep my own law. 'Bear one another's burdens,' we read, 'and so you will fulfill the law of Christ.'⁷ If you are hungry or thirsty and have nothing better at hand perhaps, and no other calf so well fattened is available, behold I am ready to be slaughtered that you may eat my flesh and drink my blood. Neither need you fear that through the death of your slave you will suffer the loss of his service; even eaten and drunk you will still have me whole and alive and I shall serve you as before. If you are led into captivity or sold, here I am, sell me and redeem yourself at my cost, or with myself as the price. I may seem to be a worthless serf, but although I am put up for auction by night and in secret like stolen property, although I am bought by the most avaricious of the Jews, the priests, yet I shall be able to fetch a price of at least thirty silver pieces.⁸ With this price given for me a burial place for strangers can be bought, with myself as price the life of those who are buried there. If you are ill and afraid to die I will die for you so that from my blood you may make yourself medicine that will restore life."

2. Well done, good and faithful servant.⁹ You have served indeed, you have served with all loyalty and trustworthiness, you have served with all patience and endurance.¹⁰ Not lukewarmly, for you have exulted as a giant to run the course of obedience;¹¹ not fictitiously, for after so many and so great exertions you have gone further and spent your soul too; not complainingly, for you did not open your mouth when, innocent, you were scourged. It is written and it is justly so: "The slave who knows his master's will and does not act worthily will be beaten with many stripes."¹² But what has this Slave done, I ask, that is not worthy? What is there he ought to have done and has not done? "He has done all things well," those who observed what he did exclaim, "he has

6. Is 53:4.   7. Gal 6:2.   8. Mt 27:9.   9. Mt 25:21.
10. Col 1:11.   11. Cf. Ps 18:6.   12. Lk 12:47.

made the deaf hear and the dumb speak."[13] He has done everything that was worthy of himself; how is it then that he has suffered thus everything unworthy? He bared his back to scourging and was flogged with stripes that were neither few nor gentle, as is shown by the streams of blood that flowed from so many parts of his body. Put to the question with insult and torture, he was like a slave or a thief laid under interrogation to extort a confession of his crime.

O detestable pride of man who scorns to serve, pride that could not be reduced to humility by any other example than the servitude, and such servitude, of its Lord. And would that it could so be humbled, that even now it would feel and show gratitude for such great humility and goodness. But I seem still to hear the same Lord in Isaiah complaining of the ingratitude of his worthless slave in the words: "I have not made you serve me with offerings, I have not made you toil to provide me with incense. Yet you have made me serve with your sins, you have made me toil with your iniquities.[14] And what toil? Even to exhaustion, hunger and thirst. Yes, even to sweat, a sweat of blood which ran down on to the earth;[15] yes, even to death, death on a cross.[16] Not to repeat everything now, I was struck in the face, covered with spittle, crowned with thorns, pierced with nails, transfixed by the lance, given vinegar and gall to drink. This winepress I have trodden alone and from the peoples there was not a man with me.[17] You then, who stand idle the whole day,[18] attend and see if there is any toil like my toil."[19]

3. Indeed you have toiled hard, my Lord, in serving me. It were only just and fair that at least for the future you should rest and your slave, if only because it is his turn, should serve you. At what a price, my Lord, you have bought back for yourself my useless service, you who do not need even the ministry of the angels. With how sweet and kind an art of love you have recovered for yourself and subjected to yourself your stubborn servant, over-

---

13. Mk 7:37. 14. Is 43:23f. 15. Lk 22:44. 16. Phil 2:8.
17. Is 63:3. 18. Mt 20:6. 19. Lam 1:12.

coming evil with good,[20] shaming pride with humility, overwhelming ingratitude with benefits. So it is indeed, so it is that Wisdom overcomes wickedness,[21] so it is you have heaped coals of fire on the head of stubborn man[22] to kindle him to penance. You have conquered, Lord, you have conquered the rebel; behold I surrender to your bonds, I put my neck under your yoke. Only deign to let me serve you, suffer me to toil for you. Accept me as a slave forever, useless as I am, unless now also your grace always going before and following on be with me and toil with me.[23] It goes before us by first showing examples of humility and patience; may it follow us by helping us to imitate what it has shown us.

How happy we shall be, O my brethren, if in this we listen to St Paul's advice: "Let this mind be in you which you have known to have been first in Christ Jesus."[24] That is, let no one be lifted up above himself, but rather brought down below himself. Let him who is greater serve others; if anyone is injured let him be the first to make satisfaction in common; let everyone obey even to death. These are the footsteps, brethren, in which we may follow Christ in the form of a slave, and come in the end to see him in the form of God, in which he lives and reigns for ever and ever. Amen.[25]

20. Rom 12:21.   21. Wis 7:30.   22. Prov 25:2; Rom 12:20.
23. Wis 9:10.   24. Phil 2:5f.
25. See above, Sermon 11, note 65, vol. 1, p. 75.

SERMON 30

THE SECOND SERMON FOR PALM SUNDAY

IF PAUL, OUR TEACHER in faith and truth, were to come to us today he would not, I think, consider himself to know anything among us except Jesus Christ and him crucified.[1] In these days in which the yearly remembrance of the Lord's passion and cross is solemnly celebrated, nothing, I think, is more suitable for preaching than Jesus Christ and him crucified. For even on all other days what can ever be preached that is more conducive to faith, what can be heard that is more wholesome, what can be thought that is more fruitful? What so kindles the affections of the faithful, what medicine is so good for their morals, what is there that so does sins to death, crucifies vices, nourishes and strengthens virtues as the remembrance of the Crucified? Let Paul then speak among the perfect the wisdom that is hidden in mystery;[2] to me, whose imperfection is obvious even to men's eyes, let him speak of Christ crucified, who is to those who court their own ruin foolishness, but to me and those who are on the road to salvation truly God's power and God's wisdom.[3] For me this is the loftiest and most noble philosophy, enabling me to laugh at the stultified wisdom of both the world and the flesh.

How perfect I would consider myself, how advanced in wisdom

1. 1 Cor 2:2.   2. 1 Cor 2:6f.   3. 1 Cor 1:18.

if I were to be found capable to hear about the Crucified, who was made for us by God not only wisdom but also justice and sanctification and redemption.[4] Truly if you are fastened to the Cross together with Christ[5] you are wise, you are just, you are holy, you are free. Or is not he wise who together with Christ is raised up from the earth and tastes and seeks the things that are above?[6] Is he not just in whom the living power of sin has been annihilated so that he is no longer the slave of sin?[7] Or is he not holy who has showed himself to be a living sacrifice, holy and pleasing to God?[8] Or is he not truly free whom the Son has freed, who in the freedom of his conscience confidently makes his own the Son's proclamation of freedom: "The prince of this world is coming but he has no hold over me"?[9] Indeed with the Crucified there is mercy and abundant redemption, with him who thus redeems Israel from all its iniquities[10] so that it may be able to escape the false accusations of the prince of this world.

2. But whoever is that blessed and true Israel should know that this is not due to his own perfection but is God's free gift of redemption—not, that is, because he committed no sin and no treachery was found on his lips[11] but because he to whom this commendation is proper has freed him from his sins. Through the blood of his cross[12] making atonement for sins,[13] he achieved the greatest triumph over princedoms and powers there where his strength was hidden.[14] It was hidden, but not lost, for crucified through weakness he was alive by God's power. It was hidden, but it was not idle, because by his crucifixion he crucified the old man in all the elect. He crucified the world to Paul and Paul to the world.[15] Finally he crucified the tyrant of this world and all the ministers of his long-standing tyranny.

To be sure he concealed the hook under the bait by hiding his strength under weakness. Therefore that murderer who from the beginning thirsted for human blood, rushing blindly upon weak-

4. 1 Cor 1:30.	5. Gal 2:19.	6. Col 3:1f.	7. Rom 6:6.
8. Rom 12:1.	9. Jn 14:30.	10. Ps 129:7f.	11. 1 Pet 2:22.
12. Col 1:20.	13. Heb 1:3.	14. Heb 3:4.	15. Gal 6:14.

ness encountered strength; he was bitten in the act of biting, transfixed as he grasped at the Crucified.[16]

3. Thanks be to your cross and your nails, Lord Jesus. I behold the jaws of that serpent pierced through, so that those who had been swallowed may pass through them. And he who was confident that the Jordan would flow into his mouth[17] is in a frenzy of anger because the river which he had swallowed has to a great extent ruined him. Forth from those jaws have come to us the men who today sing with us the noble and magnificent triumph of the Cross. Truly they have been freed from the lion's mouth,[18] or rather they have come back from the depths of hell.[19] Well may he be angry, roar and waste away, for the prey has been snatched from his teeth. As for Christ, he will rejoice that he was not crucified in vain.

Let hell and death lament, the one bitten, the other dead.[20] The heavens are glad and the Church exults because Christ despoils hell and triumphs over death. In the conversion of these men he has renewed the triumph of his passion and resuscitated the wonders of his cross. In these men the Cross has flowered once again. Now the tree of life has borne again this precious fruit. How should it remain barren when it has been not only watered but also made life-giving by the Savior's blood? He will not regret now that he climbed up into the palm tree, since he has gathered so much fruit, such precious fruit from it. He foresaw this fruit among others when he was hastening of his own free will to the Passion. "I said," we read, "I will climb up into the palm tree and take hold of its fruit."[21] He sums up in a few words that he suffered freely, that he was raised on high by the passion, that his suffering was not without

---

16. This idea, rather crude as it is, of hiding the godhead from the devil, so that he might exceed his rights over man and so lose them, with the metaphor of the bait and the hook, is generally received until the scholastics accept Saint Anselm's juridical theology of the Redemption. It can be traced back to Origen and even to Saint Ignatius of Antioch, but Guerric had probably learned it from Saint Gregory the Great: Twenty-fifth Homily on the gospels, n. 8 [P.L. 76: 1194–5].

17. Job 14:18. 18. 2 Tim 4:17. 19. Jon 4:3.
20. Hos 13:14. 21. Song 7:8.

fruit for us. When he sets forth his purpose in the words, "I said," he expresses the freedom of his will; the climbing up shows forth the value of redemption. You senseless Jews cried out: "Climb up, baldpate! Climb up, baldpate!"[22] but your fury could only serve the purposes, wholly free from constraint, of him who of his own will had decided to climb up. He climbed the cross by his will, he triumphed on it by his power, he gathered fruit from it by his loving kindness. By one and the same work he mocked the Jew, destroyed the devil and redeemed the Christian.

4. Let those then say who have been redeemed by the Lord, those whom he has redeemed from the power of the enemy (behold he has assembled them from this land and that)[23] let them say with the voice and the mind of their Master: "God forbid that I should glory in anything, except the cross of my Lord Jesus Christ,"[24] in which God's wisdom turned evil counsel into folly, God's justice destroyed him who had power over death, God's mercy set the captive free. Rightly indeed, you who wisely glory, glory in your Lord's cross; its triumph has set you free, its mystery has brought you life, its example has justified you, its sign fortifies you. For consistency and right reason seem to demand that those who mark their foreheads with the sign of the cross to fortify themselves should mark their behavior with the example of the Crucified to justify themselves, living by the law of the cross as they are armed by faith in it. Otherwise it is mockery for the soldier to wear the badge of a king whose command he does not follow; it is wrong for him to protect himself with the sign of him whose bidding he does not obey.

Consider what perversity it is and what an abuse that the enemies of Christ's cross should wish to protect themselves with the sign of Christ's cross. As long as they are free from fear, they live wantonly, in total disloyalty to the cross; when they are threatened by danger, they are eager to be defended by the power of the cross. Truly the enemies of Christ's cross are the friends of their own belly; their God is their belly,[25] their idol is money. Whoever now makes a

---

22. 2 Kings 2:23.   23. Ps 106:2.   24. Gal 6:14.   25. Phil 3:18f.

mockery of the Crucified by using his sign should indeed know that he will not be able to protect himself with it in that final distress. Then, no longer at the choice of men but by the judgment and ministry of angels, the sign of a cross will be marked on the foreheads of men who sigh and groan, to distinguish those who are to be saved from the multitude of the lost.

5. Paul too, that energetic leader, the faithful standard-bearer of the Christian army, who carried the marks of the Crucified on his own body,[26] gave us a clear sign to distinguish true soldiers from false now when all are mixed together. He said: "Those who belong to Christ have crucified their flesh together with its vices and evil desires."[27] A guarded definition indeed and carefully phrased; it derives a model as it were from the pattern marked out by Truth himself. What is marked in a man's life is expressed more articulately by his tongue. He then who was nailed with Christ to the cross drew forth this model from the pattern of his own conscience: "Those who belong to Christ have crucified their flesh with all its vices, all its evil desires." Man of knowledge and much experience as he was, he knew that there were or would be many who would crucify the evil desires of the flesh while giving free rein to the heart's vices, many on the other hand who, confident in the tranquillity of their heart, would neglect to mortify their body. But just as divine justice sometimes scourges a spirit which is not subject to it with the revolt of the flesh even though it has been mortified, so a pampered body often rebels and stirs up fresh conflicts against a spirit that has been set at rest. Therefore the Apostle wishes that both interior vices and exterior evil desires should be crucified and so we should cleanse ourselves from every defilement of flesh and of spirit, achieving the work of our sanctification in the fear of God.[28]

The fear of God, like nails driven deep,[29] fastens us to the cross and keeping us as it were attached to justice makes us continent, so that we may not make our bodily powers over to iniquity but to justice and, although it may be present, sin may not reign over our

26. Gal 6:17.   27. Gal 5:24.   28. 2 Cor 7:1.   29. Eccles 12:11.

perishable bodies.³⁰ That the fear of God may be compared to nails firmly fixed, David says in the words: "Fasten (as if with nails) my flesh with fear of you, for I have feared your judgments."³¹ So if you have not yet prevailed over your vices so as to extinguish them, St Paul would have you find consolation in crucifying them. He does not say: "Those who belong to Christ have extinguished their vices," for this is the achievement of the few, but: "have crucified them," without which there is no salvation, just as apart from Christ's cross there is no redemption. For our Redeemer chose this way of suffering to work out our salvation and give it its form, to the end that the mystery of redemption should provide a pattern of justification. As he crucified the likeness of sinful flesh, condemning sin with sin,³² in the same way, and indeed to a much greater extent, we should mortify sinful flesh, crucifying sin in it if we cannot yet extinguish it.

6. Here you can recall that Moses, in order to placate the anger of the Lord, crucified the princes of the Israelites,³³ while Joshua, who is also Jesus, crucified the five kings of the Amorrhites.³⁴ For if we want to placate the anger of the Lord which we have deserved we must needs mortify ourselves by continence. But our Jesus, who is to lead us into the Promised Land, will crucify the vices of the five senses in us, indeed he will extinguish them, provided that we as we have been commanded hang on our gibbets till evening.³⁵ Our Savior took care to give us an example in himself of this perseverance on the cross. He wished to reach his consummation only on the cross and would not be taken down from the cross before evening, both of that day and of his life.

Balaam said: "May my soul die the death of the just." But do you say: "May my soul die the death of my Lord Jesus Christ and may my end be like his,"³⁶ that is, "May I hang on the voluntary cross of penitence until the end of my life." With what trust you will commend your spirit into the hands of the Father³⁷ from the

---

30. Rom 6:12f.   31. Ps 118:120.   32. Rom 8:3.
33. Num 25:4.   34. Josh 10:26f.   35. *Ibid.*
36. Num 23:10.   37. Lk 23:46.

cross of his Son. And even more with what clemency will the Father welcome him whom the Son commends. For the Son, who once undertook the defense of your soul upon the cross, never ceases to defend it, but is always interceding with the Father.[38] Go to him free from fear, go gladly where your judge is your advocate. Only let your spirit take with it the sign of the cross, the dying state of Jesus which you carry around in your body.[39] May the Lord of glory who suffered for you, brethren, and is glorified in you, deign to have you as the companions of his passion and glory. May he glorify those who find their glory in the Cross with that splendor which he had with the Father before the beginning of the ages[40] and will have for ever and ever. Amen.

38. Heb 7:25.   39. 2 Cor 4:10.   40. Jn 17:5.

SERMON 31

THE THIRD SERMON FOR PALM SUNDAY

THE DESIRE OF OUR SOUL,[1] the most comely among the sons of men,[2] is presented to the sons of men by the present day now in one form, now in another.[3] In both forms he is remarkable, in both desirable and lovable, because in both the Savior of men. Nevertheless in the one he is sublime, in the other lowly; in the one glorious, and in the other suffering; in the one an object of veneration, in the other an object of compassion—if indeed he should be called an object of compassion who compassionately took misery upon himself so that from his misery he might show compassion to the miserable. For it is not for him to beg for compassion from the miserable; he is his own beatitude. So where he willed to seem an object of compassion, there he is all the more venerated. But "I waited," he says, "for one who would share my sorrow and there was no one; one who would comfort me, and I did not find anyone."[4] So he who freely willed to become miserable in his compassion for all, met with compassion in almost no one.

But where, you will say, is he seen today as sublime and glorious,

---

1. Ps 41:1; Is 26:8f.
2. Ps 44:3.
3. Guerric is here referring to the two highlights of this day's liturgy, the procession of the palms and the chanting of the Passion at the mass, as he brings out further on in the Sermon.
4. Ps 68:21.

where lowly or suffering? Look at the procession;[5] listen to the passion.[6] In these you will be able plainly to recognize what Isaiah says: "As many were astonished at him, so will his countenance be lacking in glory among men and his form among the sons of men."[7] Many were astonished at his glory, when like a triumphant conqueror he made his entry into Jerusalem, but nonetheless a little later his countenance was lacking in glory and despised when he suffered. "When he entered Jerusalem," says Matthew, "the whole city was in a stir; 'Who is this?' they said."[8] When he suffered, confusion covered his face, so that he truly confessed: "After being exalted, I have been brought low and confounded."[9] To be sure when he says here that he was confounded it is to be understood of what elsewhere he says of his bodily face: "Confusion has covered my face,[10] because they did not hesitate to spit in my face, to veil it, strike it and mock me." For the face of his mind, which always and without moving dwelt with God's countenance, could be neither disturbed nor confounded. "The Lord God," he says, "is my helper, therefore I have not been confounded; therefore I have set my face like the hardest of stones and I know that I shall not be confounded.[11] For in you, Lord, have I hoped: may I not be confounded for ever.[12] Rather may they be confounded while I am not confounded; may they be afraid, while I am not afraid."[13]

2. If then, as I began to say, today's procession and passion are considered together, in the one Jesus is seen as sublime and glorious, in the other as lowly and suffering. In the procession he is thought of as receiving the honor of a king, in the passion he is seen undergoing the punishment of a thief. In the one he is surrounded by glory and honor, in the other he has no form or comeliness.[14] In the one he is the joy of men and the glory of the people, in the

---

5. This was one of the three feasts on which the Cistercians in their simplified liturgy retained the procession. For details of this procession see the *Consuetudines*, Section I, *Officia Ecclesiastica*, c. 17 in *Nomasticon Cisterciense*, ed. Séjalon (Solesmes, 1892), p. 97.

6. The Passion was chanted at mass on Palm Sunday. 7. Is 52:14.
8. Mt 21:10. 9. Ps 87:16. 10. Ps 68:8. 11. Is 50:7.
12. Ps 30:2; 70:1. 13. Jer 17:18. 14. Is 53:2.

other he is scorned by men and despised by the people.[15] In the one he receives the acclamation: "Hosanna to the Son of David. Blessed is he who comes as the king of Israel."[16] In the other he is disclaimed as guilty of death and mocked for having made himself king of Israel. In the one he is met with palm branches, in the other he is hit in the face with blows of the palm and his head is struck with a reed. In the one he is raised on high with praise, in the other he is overwhelmed with insults. In the one men compete to lay their garments in his path, in the other he is stripped of his own garments. In the one he is welcomed to Jerusalem as a just King and a Savior,[17] in the other he is cast out of Jerusalem as a criminal and condemned for stirring up sedition. In the one he is seated on an ass, and accorded every mark of attention; in the other he hangs on the wood of the Cross, torn by whips, pierced with wounds and abandoned by his own.

Behold one greater than Job here,[18] whose fortunes God once reversed so suddenly and so violently. "You have heard of Job's endurance and you have seen the end of the Lord," says the Apostle James,[19] as if to say: "Job's endurance lasted until the restoration of his wealth, the Lord's endurance lasted to the end of his life." Job bore patiently with his losses, but soon received twofold in his own land; Christ, filled with wretchedness and inebriated with bitterness,[20] went forth from the world. So there is one greater than Job here: cast down suddenly and once for all from what was thought to be supreme good fortune, he came to an end in the worst and most painful of calamities. "And these things," he says, "I have suffered although there is no iniquity in my hands, and my prayers to God are pure"[21]—even for his crucifiers that he may forgive them.

3. Will not he, the Son, troubled by so sudden and complete a reversal of fortune, be seen to call upon the Father in those tearful accents: "God, my God, why have you forsaken me?[22] Certainly

---

15. Ps 21:7.
16. Mt 21:9; Jn 12:13.
17. Zech 9:9.
18. Cf. Mt 12:41.
19. Jas 5:11.
20. Job 14; Lam 3:5.
21. Job 16:17.
22. Mt 27:46; Ps 21:1

it was your hands that made me, in your will you have led me on." And, a little before: "With glory you have borne me up, and so do you suddenly cast me down?[23] After raising me up you have thrown me away.[24] You lifted me up on the wind, you hurl me down with all your strength.[25] After being exalted I have been brought low and confounded,[26] and all the more confounded the more I was then raised aloft and am now brought down to the greater depths; the higher I was then lifted up the more grievously am I now cast down.

"It is just, Father, that he who raises himself up should be brought down[27] and that the exaltation of the unworthy should be punished by a worthy humiliation; but was it likewise just that he whom you had raised up should be brought down in such utter confusion and that the glory which humility had deserved should be followed by such ignominy? Were you angry with me, Father, because I allowed myself to be honored here even for a passing moment? Did I have to pay for that trifling amount of this world's goods which I had received, pay for it in pain and ignominy, lest afterward the objection should be brought against me: 'My son, you received good things in your life'?[28] But the Son's honor was your honor, Father; he who does not honor the Son does not honor the Father who sent him.[29] Behold your enemies revile, Lord, behold they revile the downfall of your Christ.[30] Behold they glory in my ignominy and my torment, they who a little before writhed at my glory and honor. Shall I not give a word in answer to those who revile me,[31] that they may know at length by what dispensation you have brought about the downfall of your Christ, what is your purpose in thus raising him up to bring him down immediately, or bringing him down when he was raised up?"

4. You will give a word, Lord Jesus, you will give a word in answer to those who revile you, and a sharp word it will be when their arrogance answers them to their face and their ill will accuses

---

23. Ps 72:14; Job 10:8 24. Ps 101:11. 25. Job 30:22.
26. Ps 87:16. 27. Lk 14:11. 28. Lk 16:25.
29. Jn 5:23. 30. Ps 88:52. 31. Ps 118:42.

them,[32] when they look upon him whom they have pierced through.[33] For when they see the Son of Man coming on the clouds with great power and majesty,[34] then they will know what now they refuse to believe, that the previous glory of today's procession was a portrayal in mystery of that later glory, just as the ignominy of the passion was its meritorious cause. Then they will understand that Christ, now honored, now mocked, was made a stumbling-block and a cause of offense to those who court their own ruin, as he brings resurrection and wisdom to those who are on the way to salvation. For what is a sign of redemption serves at the same time to teach and edify. This was called for by the desserts of the proud: Christ's honor should be a stumbling-block to their pride and his death should cast them down headlong; his triumphal glory should stir up the envy of men who were justly on the road to perdition, while his suffering and death should be their condemnation.

But for those who are on the road to salvation, that is for us,[35] it was altogether necessary that as Christ traversed the paths of this world he should trace out a path for his followers, through prosperity as through adversity. First raised up, then brought down, he should teach by his own example how moderation is to be preserved in honor, patience adhered to in ignominy or pain. For while he could be honored he could not be puffed up; he willed to be despised, but he could not be cast down by despondency or embittered by anger. On another occasion when men sought to carry him off and make him king he fled[36] and thus taught by example what he had prescribed by word of mouth, that we should be unwilling to be raised aloft. So now by another dispensation he allowed himself to be honored for a passing moment, preserving in the midst of that honor his habitual and inborn meekness, and thus he gave a model to those who have been entrusted with power. Yet in order that these should learn to combine their meekness and humility with a discretion that would allow them to act energetically

32. Hos 5:5; Jer 2:19. 33. Zech 12:10; Jn 19:37.
34. Mt 24:30; Lk 21:27. 35. 1 Cor 1:18. 36. Jn 6:15.

Sermon 31:5

when the occasion demanded, the Lord, as soon as he went into the temple, made a whip of cords and avenged the wrong done to his Father.[37] He chose to stir up the wrath of the priests to his own destruction rather than pass over in silence the profanation of the temple.

5. In order then, brethren, that we may follow our leader with untroubled step both through prosperity and through adversity, let us consider him honored in the procession, undergoing ignominy and pain in the passion. In such reversal of fortune he never changed in his mind, although he assumed another appearance in the presence of Abimelech,[38] that is, in the presence of the kingdom of the Jews, a change in Christ which is reviled by the blind folly of the faithless.[39] That his mind remained unchanged we have the assurance of Scripture: "The holy man remains steadfast in wisdom like the sun; but the fool changes like the moon."[40] Of the change in his face it says elsewhere: "The wisdom of a man shines in his countenance and the most powerful will change his face."[41]

Truly in your countenance, Lord Jesus, however it may seem to be changed, whether it appears glorious or lacking in glory, wisdom shines; from your countenance the brightness of eternal light[42] sends forth its rays. Would that the light of your countenance, Lord, would shine upon us.[43] Your countenance, alike in sorrow and in joy, is restrained, serene, all bright with the hidden light of the heart; cheerful and pleasant to the just, merciful and kind to the repentant. Look, brethren, upon the countenance of your august king. "There is life in the cheerfulness of the king's countenance," says Scripture,[44] "and his graciousness is like the late rain." He looked upon our first father and he was at once given

---

37. Mt 21:12f.

38. 1 Sam 21:13, where the name is not Abimelech but Achis. The name was changed by some error in the title to Ps. 33. Jerome and Augustine accepted the change and gave it an allegorical justification. Guerric is basing himself on Saint Augustine's commentary on Ps. 33, Serm. 1, no. 7; CCL 38: 278.

39. Ps 88:52. 40. Sir 27:12. 41. Eccles 8:1. 42. Wis 7:26.
43. Ps 4:7. 44. Prov 16:15.

a soul and drew the breath of life;[45] he looked upon Peter and he was immediately moved to repentance and drew the fresh breath of forgiveness.[46] For as soon as the Lord looked upon Peter, Peter received from the graciousness of his most loving countenance the late rain, tears after sin.

This light of your countenance, O eternal Light, as Job assures us, does not fall upon the earth.[47] For what has light in common with darkness?[48] Rather let the souls of the faithful receive its rays; let it bring joy to men of good conscience, medicine to the wounded. Truly the countenance of Jesus in triumph, as it is to be seen in the procession, is gladness and jubilation; the countenance of Jesus in death, as it is to be thought of in the passion, is healing and salvation. "They who fear you will see me and be glad," he says,[49] "they who mourn over themselves will see me and be healed," like those who looked upon the snake hung upon the pole after they had been poisoned by snakes.[50] May you then, the Joy and the Salvation of all, whether they see you seated upon the ass or hanging on the cross, receive the praises of all, so that when they see you reigning upon your throne they may praise you throughout all ages: to you be praise and honor for ever and ever. Amen.

---

45. Gen 2:7.
48. 2 Cor 6:14.
46. Lk 22:61f.
49. Ps 118:74.
47. Job 29:24.
50. Num 21:8f.

SERMON 32

THE FOURTH SERMON FOR PALM SUNDAY

"HOSANNA TO THE SON OF DAVID."[1] This is the voice of exultation and salvation,[2] the voice of gladness and devotion, the voice of faith and love, rejoicing in the arrival of the Savior and proclaiming with a Prophet's gladness the joy of redemption long desired. "Hosanna to the Son of David," says David's family; salvation belongs to him who has been made of David's seed that he may save those who are of David's faith. Praise the Lord, you sons, praise the name of the Lord. Say: "May the name of the Lord be blessed.[3] May he be blessed who comes in the name of the Lord."[4] From the mouth of these you have brought forth, O Father, the praise of your Son, so as to destroy by the uncorrupted witness of simple innocence the enemy and the avenger,[5] the Pharisee and the High Priest. He is not the avenger of God's law, as iniquity has lied to itself;[6] he is rather the avenger of his own envy and fury. But his mischief shall return upon his own head, and upon his own pate shall his iniquity come down.[7] "God, be not silent in my praise," says the Son to the Father," for the mouth of the sinner and the mouth of the deceiver is opened against me."[8] The Father cannot deny the Son anything; the Father's voice, often heard from heaven, did not keep silent the Son's praise.[9] Creation did not keep it silent, in so many signs and

---

1. Mt 21:9. This is the text, of course, which marks out most characteristically the celebration of Palm Sunday as such.
2. Ps 117:15.   3. Ps 112:1f.   4. Ps 117:26.   5. Ps 8:3.
6. Ps 26:12.   7. Ps 7:17.   8. Ps 108:2.   9. Lk 3:22; 9:35; Jn 12:28.

prodigies confessing him as the author of nature. The angels bore him witness, devils confessed him, the ranks of the prophets and of the apostles sang of him, answering one another with harmonious voice. This finally is perfect praise, which cannot be repressed by little ones who know nothing of flattery and cannot dissimulate what the Spirit suggests.

For what could be more obvious than the fact that that age neither said nor did of itself things so new and so unaccustomed? The Holy Spirit according to his wont bore witness to the Son by speaking through the mouths of the simple.

2. Surely the Holy Spirit, aware of Christ's works, aware, that is, of what Christ's coming would cause, aware of the joy and the salvation which his passion would bring forth, stirred up prophetic joys in the hearts of the innocent. For foretelling to the world the gladness of redemption he made his own the ministry of simple minds. It was to these that the Spirit spoke, calling "those who are not as if they were,"[10] when through his prophet he foretold what today has taken place. He gave the command then, and now they have been created.[11] "Exult," he says, "exult greatly, daughter of Sion; be jubilant, daughter of Jerusalem. Behold your king shall come to you, just and a Savior; poor he will be and seated upon an ass."[12] Now, he says: "Exult greatly, you who hitherto were in sadness; now satiate yourself, if indeed you can be satiated, with unspeakable joy, which satiates desire in such a way as to cause greater and happier hunger. Let your mouth and your tongue be filled with exultation,[13] and if neither mouth nor tongue can contain it, let jubilation pour forth with the overflow of your affections. Be jubilant, daughter of Jerusalem; for blessed is the people which is acquainted with jubilation."[14] Truly blessed is the people which knows and understands that today it must rejoice unspeakably, when the Savior has come to it who was promised and awaited from the beginning of the ages. Blessed is the people which goes to meet him today with all the eagerness of devotion, crying at once

10. Rom 4:17.   11. Ps 148:5.   12. Zech 9:9.
13. Ps 125:2.   14. Ps 88:16.

with heart and voice: "Blessed is he who comes in the name of the Lord."[15] For in this the Son has been blessed by the Father, that he who blesses is filled with blessings,[16] not with one, but with many. The blessing which a man lends to the Lord on interest, returns upon his head with manifold interest.

Woe to the sinful nation, the worthless seed, the criminal sons,[17] to whom that terrible complaint of the Lord applies: "I have not lent nor have I borrowed, yet all of them curse me, says the Lord."[18] This was the Jewish people, who scorned to have dealings with the Lord on the basis of give and take, refusing to bless him who was blessed by God the Father in order to be blessed by him. They called him a Samaritan possessed by the devil,[19] they inveighed against God with insane and blasphemous curses. "Let them curse," we read, "but you will bless,"[20] for the blessing which they have refused will depart from them and be transferred to the nations. "Bless our God, you nations,"[21] for he who first lent to you, anticipating you in blessings of sweetness,[22] will pay back interest in blessings of happiness to those who lent to him.

3. Yet I am afraid, my brethren, that perhaps these lukewarm and faithless times are the object of the Lord's complaint: "I have not lent nor have I borrowed"; because grace is offered and is not welcomed, work is promised its reward and scarcely anyone works to obtain the reward. The Lord lends when he distributes talents to his servants,[23] bestowing skill in speaking or the grace of any office for a man's benefit. But the generous man, who has compassion and lends,[24] is the one who lends to the Lord—as Scripture says: "He lends to the Lord who shows compassion to his neighbor."[25] Indeed whoever does anything in the hope of a reward from God lends to the Lord, so that he can say: "I know in whom I have trusted.[26] I know who it was that said: 'If you spend anything further I will pay you back when I return.' "[27] We either lend him

---

15. Jn 12:13. 16. Cf. Gen 21:29. 17. Is 1:4.
18. Jer 15:10f. 19. Jn 8:48. 20. Ps 108:28.
21. Ps 108:18. 22. Ps 20:4. 23. Cf. Mt 25:14ff.
24. Ps 111:5. 25. Prov 19:17; Sir 29:1. 26. 2 Tim 1:12. 27. Lk 10:35.

nothing or are so timid and cold about it that we treat him as an untrustworthy debtor or one who has not the wherewithal to pay us back.

The Jewish people showed great faith when they saw him poor, seated upon an ass and that not his own, and yet lent to him with all assurance and devotion. They not only spread out their garments in his path, but spent themselves too as far as they could in his honor. But they certainly understood this poor and needy man,[28] for the Prophet had given them a sign enabling them to recognize the Savior: that poverty which impoverished pride. "He will be poor," he said, "and riding on an ass."[29] "By this sign," he said, "you will be able to recognize your king when he comes, him whose kingdom is not of this world.[30] In order to vanquish the pride which reigns in the world he will proclaim poverty and humility both by word and by example."

4. Blessed then is the daughter of Sion, who has learned to venerate Christ's humility as heavenly armor, as the insignia of his kingship. A wretched mother and faithless was that Sion which turned away from him in disgust when it saw him humble, envied him when it saw him honored. Blessed, I say, was the Church of the first generation which recognized with such faith and welcomed with such gladness him who came in the name of the Lord. Unhappy the Synagogue of the faithless which, ready to welcome one who would come in his own name,[31] writhed at the honor paid to him who sought his Father's glory. "Rebuke," they say, "your disciples,"[32] as if their simplicity was capable of flattery or his own purity could take pleasure in empty praises. "I tell you," he says, "that if these are silent the stones will cry out,[33] for God will not keep my praise silent."[34] So indeed it is: "If these are silent, the stones will cry out," for at the time of the passion these were silent, but the stones cried out when in witness to and praise of the dying Christ the rocks were split and tombs were opened.[35] So indeed it is, for while now the Synagogue is silent according to the text: "In

28. Ps 40:2. 29. Zech 9:9. 30. Jn 18:36. 31. Jn 5:43.
32. Lk 19:39. 33. Lk 19:40. 34. Ps 108:2. 35. Mt 27:51.

the night I made your mother keep silent,"³⁶ the Church of the Gentiles cries out from living stones. The stones cry out from which he who is powerful has raised up sons to Abraham.³⁷ "Give praise," the Prophet says, "you that dwell on the rock; from the summit of the mountains they shall cry out."³⁸ Behold today in the clefts of the rock, in the hollows of the wall,³⁹ the voice of the dove echoes, crying out and saying: "Hosanna to the Son of David. Blessed is he who comes in the name of the Lord."⁴⁰

5. Blessed is he who, in order that I might be able to build a nest in the clefts of the rock,⁴¹ allowed his hands, feet and side to be pierced and opened himself to me wholly that I might enter "the place of his wonderful tent"⁴² and be protected in its recesses.⁴³ The rock is a convenient refuge for the badgers,⁴⁴ but it is also a welcome dwelling-place for the doves. These clefts, so many open wounds all over his body, offer pardon to the guilty and bestow grace on the just. Indeed it is a safe dwelling-place, my brethren, and a tower of strength in the face of the enemy,⁴⁵ to linger in the wounds of Christ, the Lord, by devout and constant meditation. By faith in the Crucified and love of him a man keeps his soul safe from the heat of the flesh, from the turmoil of the world, from the attacks of the devil. The protection this tent affords surpasses all the world's glory. It is a shade from the heat by day, a refuge and a shelter from the storm and the rain,⁴⁶ so that by day the sun shall not scorch you with prosperity,⁴⁷ nor the storm move you with adversity.

Go into the rock, then, man; hide in the dug ground.⁴⁸ Make the Crucified your hiding-place. He is the rock, he is the ground, he who is God and man. He is the cleft rock, the dug ground, for

---

36. Hos 4:5.   37. Lk 3:8.   38. Is 42:11.   39. Song 2:14.
40. Mt 21:9.

41. Song 2:14. Bernard of Clairvaux in his commentary on the Song of Songs (Sermon 61:7f.), also sees the "clefts of the rock" as the wounds of Christ the Savior, a place of refuge for sinful man; trans. K. Walsh, *The Works of Bernard of Clairvaux,* Vol. 11 (Cistercian Fathers Series 31).

42. Ps 41:5.   43. Ps 26:5.   44. Ps 103:18.   45. Ps 60:4.
46. Is 4:6.   47. Ps 120:6. 48. Is 2:10.

"they have dug my hands and my feet."[49] Hide in the dug ground from the fear of the Lord,[50] that is, from him fly to him, from the Judge to the Redeemer, from the tribunal to the Cross, from the Just One to the Merciful, from him who will strike the earth with the rod of his mouth[51] to him who inebriates the earth with the drops of his blood, from him who will kill the godless with the breath of his lips[52] to him who with the blood of his wounds gives life to the dead. Rather do not fly only to him but into him, go into the clefts of the rock, hide in dug ground, hide yourself in the very hands that were cleft, in the side that was dug. For what is the wound in Christ's side but a door in the side of the Ark for those who are to be saved from the flood.[53] But the one was a figure, the other is very truth, in which not only is mortal life preserved but immortal life is recovered. For in his loving kindness and his compassion he opened his side in order that the blood of the wound might give you life, the warmth of his body revive you, the breath Of his heart flow into you as if through a free and open passage. There you will lie hidden in safety until wickedness passes by.[54] there you will certainly not freeze, since in the bowels of Christ charity does not grow cold. There you will abound in delights.[55] There you will overflow with joys, at least then when your mortality and that of all the members of his body have been swallowed up by the life of the Head.

6. Rightly then the dove of Christ, Christ's fair one, for whom his wounds have provided clefts so safe, so good for the building of a nest, sings his praises everywhere today with rejoicing. From the remembrance or the imitation of his passion, from meditation on his wounds, a pleasing voice sounds in the ears of the Bridegroom[56] as if from the clefts of the rock. Now you, my brethren, have built your nests the more deeply within the clefts of the rock the more

---

49. Ps 21:17.   50. Is 2:10.   51. Is 11:4.   52. *Ibid.*

53. Gen 6f. Guerric must have learned this interpretation from Saint Augustine, Commentary on John, Tract 120, no. 1; CCL 36:661 or possibly from the Venerable Bede, Hexaemeron, book 2; PL 91:90A.

54. Ps 56:2.   55. Song 8:5.   56. Song 2:14.

secretly you live in Christ and your life is hidden with Christ in God.⁵⁷ So it is for you surely to see that the more tranquil and protected your life is, the sweeter your devotion is, especially today when the recurrence of the anniversary and the performance of the liturgy make us present as it were at the festival joy with which he was welcomed into Jerusalem. Blessed is he who comes as king in the name of the Lord.⁵⁸ To him be blessing, kingship and empire. who rules as God over all things, blessed for ever and ever.⁵⁹ Amen,

57. Col 3:3.   58. Lk 19:38.   59. Rom 9:5

SERMON 33

THE FIRST SERMON FOR EASTER

THEY TOLD JACOB: "Joseph is still alive." When he heard it his spirit revived and he said: "It is enough; Joseph my son is still alive. I will go and see him before I die."¹ Perhaps you will say to me: "Very good, but what is the point of that? Has this any connection with today's joy and the triumph of Christ's resurrection? Remember that it is Paschal time. Are you going to feed us with Lenten fare again? Our soul hungers for the Paschal Lamb, the one for whom it has prepared itself by fasting all this time. Our heart is burning within for Jesus.² It is Jesus we desire even if we do not yet merit to see him or listen to him. It is Jesus we are hungering for, not Joseph; the Redeemer, not the dreamer; the Lord of heaven, not of Egypt. Not the one who fills the belly, but he who nourishes the mind, the hungry mind. Your sermon will at least help us in this way; it will make us even more hungry for him whom we already desire. For we read: 'Blessed are they who hunger, for they shall be filled.'³ When we hear this we hunger yet more. One who praises the banquet sharpens the hunger of his hearers. If we hear about Jesus it will be joy and happiness for us to listen. Our very bones, humbled in the dust,⁴ will be exalted to the skies. Our bones have been humbled by the penance and mourning of Lent, more indeed by the sorrows

---

1. Gen 45:25ff. Quoted in a responsory on the third Sunday of Lent. The scriptural readings were concerned with Joseph at that time; this is the meaning of "Lenten fare" a few lines later.

2. Lk 24:32.   3. Mt 5:6.   4. Ps 50:10.

of his passion, but they will rejoice even more at the news of his resurrection. Why then do you continue to feed us on Joseph? No subject you speak of, unless it be Jesus, will hold any satisfaction for us, especially today when the Paschal Lamb is eaten, when Christ our pasch has been sacrificed."[5]

2. What I have placed before you, brethren, is like an egg or a nut; break the shell and you will find the food. Beneath the image of Joseph you will find the Paschal Lamb, Jesus, the one for whom you yearn. The great depth at which he is hidden and the diligence necessary in seeking him and the difficulty you will have in finding him will only make him all the sweeter to your taste. Again you insist: "What has Joseph to do with Christ? What has this story I have put before you got to do with today's feast?" Much in every way.[6] Run through the details, and the loving meaning of the mystery will reveal itself to you, provided that it is Jesus who expounds the mystery to you, who on this day of his resurrection discussed with his disciples on the road to Emmaus the letter that kills[7] and then expounded the Scriptures to them.[8] For which one of the Prophets or Patriarchs is more clearly and distinctly a type of the Savior than Joseph? "Give the wise man an opportunity," we are told, "and he will increase his wisdom."[9] And so here is the explanation in a nutshell. If we think with faith and reverence about the meaning of his name[10] and go on to consider that he was more handsome and good-looking than the rest of his brothers,[11] that his actions were blameless, that he was prudent in his judgments, that after he had been sold by his own he redeemed his own from death, that he was humbled even to imprisonment, then elevated to a throne, and was rewarded for his work by being given a new name among the nations—the Savior of the World[12]—if we think, I say, about all these things reverently and faithfully, we shall surely recognize how truly it was said by the Lord: "Through the Prophets I gave parables."[13]

---

5. 1 Cor 5:7.
6. Rom 3:2.
7. 2 Cor 3:6.
8. Lk 24:27.
9. Prov 9:9.
10. Gen 30:24.
11. Gen 39:6.
12. Gen 41:45.
13. Hos 12:10.

3. And now if we go back to the words I quoted at the beginning, I do not think they will need any further explanation. Rather they will inspire both wonder and joy because the resurrection of Christ is so plainly witnessed to by the Law and the Prophets.[14] The story from the Old Testament speaks so clearly of the mysteries of the New that when the prophecy is read it is almost as if we were listening to the gospel, apart from the change in names. "They told Jacob: 'Joseph is still alive.' "[15] What else can I take this to mean than:"They told the Apostles: 'Jesus is still alive.' "? Jacob I take to be none other than the band of the Apostles. Nor do I consider this explanation far fetched. Not only are they descendants of Jacob, not only have they been changed from Jacob into Israel when they passed from the wrestling of the active life to the vision and rest of contemplation,[16] but also they are the fathers of the multitude of those who believe, the true Israelites, just as he was father of the Israelites according to the flesh.[17] Thus they sorrowed just as he did and could not be consoled when they thought that their Joseph was dead. When they heard that he was alive they came to believe it only slowly and with difficulty. But when at length they realized it was true their joy was unbounded.

And they told Jacob: "Joseph is still alive." Jacob hearing this awoke as it were from a deep sleep, yet did not believe them.[18] This seems to me to be no more than a different presentation of the account that we read in the Gospels: "She (obviously Mary Magdalen) went and told those who had been with him as they mourned and wept. But when they heard that he was alive and had been seen by her, they would not believe it. After this he appeared to two of them as they were going along the road. And they went back and told the rest, but they did not believe them either."[19] And in Luke we read: "Returning from the tomb they told all this to the eleven and to all the rest, but their words sounded like madness to them and they did not believe them."[20] The obvious

14. Rom 3:21. 15. Gen 45:26. 16. Gen 32:23ff.
17. Gen 35:11. 18. Gen 45:26. 19. Mk 16:10ff.
20. Lk 24:9, 11.

reason for this is that they were only just awakening from the deep sleep of weariness and despair.

"But when Jacob saw all that Joseph had sent him," it goes on to say, his spirit revived and he said: 'It is enough, Joseph my son is still alive. I will go and see him before I die.' "[21] And so too with the Apostles. Words had no effect on them until they received the gifts. For when Jesus himself came and stood before them, he convinced them not so much by showing them his body as by breathing on them his Gift.

4. You know that when he came to them the doors were locked and he stood among them, but they were startled and frightened and supposed they saw a spirit.[22] But when he breathed on them saying: "Receive the Holy Spirit,"[23] and when later he sent from heaven the same Spirit with another gift, these gifts were indeed undeniable proofs and testimonies of resurrection and life.

It is the Spirit who bears witness in the hearts and on the lips of the saints that Christ is the truth,[24] the true resurrection and the life.[25] Thus the Apostles who had previously doubted even after seeing his living body, after tasting his life-giving Spirit with great power gave testimony to his resurrection.[26] So it is much more important to receive Jesus in our hearts than to see him with our eyes or hear him with our ears. The Spirit makes a much deeper impression on the interior man than material things make on the exterior senses. What room is left for doubt when he who bears witness and he who is the object of that witness are the one Spirit?[27] If the Spirit is one there must be a complete understanding, everything fits together.

Then indeed, as we read of Jacob, their spirit, almost dead from grief if not buried in despair, revived. Then, if I am not mistaken, each one of the Apostles said to himself: "It is enough for me that my Joseph is still alive, since for me to live means Christ and to die is gain.[28] I will therefore go into Galilee to the mountain where

---

21. Gen 45:27f. 22. Jn 20:26; Lk 24:36f. 23. Jn 20:22f.
24. Jn 14:6. 25. Jn 11:25. 26. Acts 4:33.
27. 1 Jn 5:6ff. 28. Phil 1:21.

Jesus told us to meet him[29] and I will see and adore him before I die, so that afterwards I may never taste death." For everyone who sees the Son and believes in him has everlasting life,[30] so that even though he die, yet shall he live.[31]

5. Now, my brethren, what witness to Christ's love does the joy of your hearts give you? I venture to judge, and rightly as you will see, that if you have ever loved Jesus alive or dead or risen from the dead, your heart rejoices within you today. As the tidings of his resurrection resound and re-echo again and again through the Church you will say to yourselves: "They have told me that Jesus my God is still alive. On hearing it my spirit, which was asleep through weariness, languishing through tepidity, disheartened through timidity, has revived." For the joyful voice of this happy message raises even from death those buried deep in sin. Otherwise, if Christ, coming up from hell, left them there in the depths, there would certainly be no hope for them; their fate would be buried in forgetfulness. By this token you may clearly know that your soul lives again fully in Christ if it echoes this sentiment: "It is enough for me that Jesus is still alive."

How faithful and worthy of a friend of Jesus is that voice, how pure that act of love which says: "It is enough for me that Jesus is still alive. If he lives, I live, for my spirit acts through his. Yes, he is my life, my all in all. For what can I lack if Jesus is still alive? Rather everything else may be taken from me, nothing else matters to me so long as he lives. If he wishes then, let him take no account of me. It is enough for me that he still lives even if he only lives for himself." When the love of Christ so absorbs all a man's affections that, unmindful and forgetful of himself, he has no feeling for anything but Jesus Christ and what pertains to him, then, I say, love has been made perfect in him. To a man who so loves, poverty is no burden, he feels no hurt, laughs at insults, disdains misfortunes, considers death as a gain.[32] In fact he does not think in terms of death, knowing that he passes from death to life. And he confidently asserts: "I will go and see him before I die."

29. Mt 28:16.   30. Jn 6:40.   31. Jn 11:25.   32. Phil 1:21.

6. Although, my brethren, we have not been endowed with such a great purity of conscience, let us, nevertheless, go to see Jesus journeying to the mountain of the heavenly Galilee, where he awaits us. On the way our love will increase, and on our arrival, at least, it will be perfected. On the way, the road, at first hard and difficult, will grow easier, and the strength of the weak will increase.[33] For to prevent Jacob or any of his household from excusing themselves from the journey there were sent to the poor old man besides other gifts, provisions and wagons in case anyone should plead poverty or weakness. The flesh of Christ is our food for the journey, his Spirit our means of conveyance. He himself is the food, he himself is the chariot and charioteer of Israel.[34] When you arrive, all the goods, not of Egypt but of heaven, will be yours. There, in the best place in the kingdom, at the bidding of your Joseph you will take your rest. He who first sent angels, women and apostles as witnesses and messengers of his resurrection, now cries from heaven: "Behold, I whom you have mourned as dead these three days did indeed die for you, but see, I live.[35] And all power in heaven and earth is given unto me.[36] Come to me all you that labor and are burdened with hunger, and I will refresh you.[37] Come you blessed of my Father, possess the kingdom prepared for you."[38] May he who calls you lead you to where he lives and reigns with the Father and Holy Spirit, through endless ages. Amen.

---

33. RB, Prologue 47f.
34. 2 Kings 2:12.
35. Rev 1:18.
36. Mt 28:18.
37. Mt 11:28.
38. Mt 25:34.

SERMON 34

THE SECOND SERMON FOR EASTER

"BLESSED AND HOLY IS HE who has a share in the first resurrection."[1] "I am the resurrection and the life," Jesus said.[2] He indeed is the first resurrection, he is also the second resurrection. For rising from the dead as the first-fruits of those who sleep[3] Christ both brings about for us the first resurrection by the mystery of his own resurrection and by the example of that same resurrection will bring about for us the second. The first is that of souls, when he raises them together with himself to newness of life;[4] the second will be that of bodies, when he forms this humbled body of ours anew, molding it into the image of his glorified body.[5] Christ does well then to proclaim himself the resurrection and the life since it is through him and into him that we rise in order to live according to him and with him; now according to him in holiness and justice, afterwards with him in happiness and glory. Now the first resurrection of our Head, the Lord Jesus Christ, is the cause and the proof of the second resurrection which will be that of his whole body. So also for each of us the first resurrection of the soul, by which it comes to life again from the death of sin, is the proof and the cause of its second resurrection, by which the body will be freed not only from the corruption of death but also from every tendency to corruption and death. That the one is proof and cause of the other St Paul shows clearly in

1. Rev 20:6.   2. Jn 11:25.   3. 1 Cor 15:20.   4. Rom 6:4.
5. Phil 3:21.

the words: "If the Spirit of Christ who raised Jesus from the dead dwells in you, he will give life also to your perishable bodies on account of his Spirit who dwells in you."[6]

2. It is well said then: "Blessed and holy is he who has a share in the first resurrection."[7] Holy, that is, on account of the first, which he has already obtained through the renewal of his soul; blessed on account of the second, which he happily awaits when his body is restored. The reason for his blessedness is indicated by the same passage of Scripture, which goes on: "Over these (who have a share, that is, in the first resurrection), the second death has no power,"[8] even if the first death has seemed to exercise its dominion over them for a passing hour. For death has reigned from Adam to Moses, even over those who did not sin according to the likeness of Adam's transgression.[9] But as with Christ so with the Christian; rising from the dead he dies no more, death has no more dominion over him.[10] So over those blessed neither has the second death any power nor will the first keep the power which it had for a time. For the one death of Christ triumphed over both of ours, setting free from the one those who were already its captives, from the other, those who would be its captives. It prevented us from falling into the one, from remaining in the other.

How true, how devout and at the same time how magnificent is that threat he uttered as he died: "I will be your death, O death."[11] How fittingly and wonderfully he triumphed who tasted death on behalf of all and so swallowed up both his own death and all the dying of all men. Truly death has been swallowed up in victory.[12] Free from fear he may mock at it, whoever that blessed man is who has a share in the first resurrection: "Where is your victory, death? Where is your sting, death?"[13] You have been conquered, you who conquered all things. You have lost even the arms in which you trusted. For where is your sting? The sting of death is sin,[14] which when it once pricked the roots of the human race spread death's

---

6. Rom 8:11.   7. See note 1.   8. Rev 20:6.
9. Rom 5:14.   10. Rom 6:9.   11. Hos 13:14.
12. 1 Cor 15:54. 13. 1 Cor 15:55.   14. 1 Cor 15:56

incurable poison throughout the whole stock. As St Paul says: "Through one man sin came and through sin death, and so it passed into all men."[15] Death reigned as conqueror then from the first Adam to the second; for just as by the law of its origin the whole human race was subject to the chains of sin, so also to the debt of death.

3. Thanks be to God who has given us the victory both over sin and over death, through our Lord Jesus Christ.[16] Wholly innocent of sin and therefore free from the debt of death, he yet paid it, dying of his own will on our behalf; and rising he has set us free from sin. For, as St Paul says, "Christ died for our sins and rose for our justification."[17] By dying he underwent the punishment due to our sins, and by rising he established for us the form and the cause of everlasting justification. Christ rising from the dead dies no more, death has no further dominion over him.[18] So also the Christian rising together with Christ, should no longer commit deadly sin nor should sin have any further dominion over him.

This is that blessed and holy one who has a share in the first resurrection, over whom the second death too will have no power; even the first death will be swallowed up in the victory of Christ's resurrection. This is the man who has not only recognized but has also taken hold of the power of Christ's resurrection and the fellowship of his sufferings. He has been molded into the pattern of his death, so that he may arrive at resurrection from the dead.[19] St Paul was not mistaken when for the sake of this gain he not only wrote down as loss everything which had been as gain to him, but also treated it as refuse, if only he might be found in Christ,[20] molded alike into the pattern of his death and of his resurrection. It is indeed profitable trading to despise the things which weaken and defile you in order to gain Christ, and, if need be, to spend in addition not only your property but also yourself in order to recover yourself with such a generous interest of immortality and glory. Who would hesitate to regard it as a profitable trade to sow

15. Rom 5:12.   16. 1 Cor 15:57.   17. 1 Cor 15:3; Rom 4:25.
18. Rom 6:9.   19. Phil 3:10f.   20. Phil 3:8f.

Sermon 34:3-4 89

a body, mortal, natural, unhonored, that it may rise immortal, spiritual, glorious;[21] to die to the world so as to be able to say: "For me to live is Christ and to die a gain":[22]

You who desire wealth, who devote your time and energy to making profits, why do you not learn the art of making true profit? Why do you not despise what is worthless, or rather loss and refuse, in order to gain Christ? Why do you spend your money for what is not bread and your work for what does not fill?[23] It seems to me that you regard as of less worth than your money that bread which comes down from heaven and gives life to the world.[24] But it is impossible to appreciate its value without tasting its quality. Would that the miser himself were more precious to himself than his money, and that he would not put his soul up for sale for the love of money, casting away his inner being while still alive.[25] It is a wise businessman and a trustworthy judge of the value of things—I mean St Paul—who does not consider even his soul, that is, his natural and sensitive life, to be more precious than himself, that is, than his spirit, in which he was joined to Christ and dwelt in union with him.[26] He was ready to lose his soul in order to keep it for eternal life.[27]

4. The owners of wealth will enter the kingdom of heaven only with difficulty,[28] and those who treasure up money weigh it in their hands more readily than they spend it for bread—I mean the unleavened bread of purity and honest intent[29] with which the Paschal Lamb should be eaten today. However, you who are blessed in your poverty, sons of the poor Crucified, who have no money, come quickly, buy and eat.[30] Those who have nothing buy these wares more readily and more easily than those who have great possessions.[31] When money is lacking goodwill is enough to buy it, and of that those who are poor in material possessions usually have the greater store. Scripture does well to invite them: "Come, buy, without money and without anything given in

---

21. 1 Cor 15:43ff.   22. Phil 1:21.   23. Is 55:2.   24. Jn 6:33.
25. Sir 10:10.   26. Acts 20:24.   27. Jn 12:25.   28. Lk 18:24.
29. Is 55:2; 1 Cor 5:8.   30. Is 55:1.   31. Cf. 2 Cor 6:10.

exchange, buy wine and milk."[32] See, O happy pauper, only goodwill is demanded of you, that alone is required for such profitable trading. Do not refuse ungratefully what is offered so freely; do not lose through an ungrateful will what you have already won by blessed poverty. Realize what a profit it is to have no share in the world's ruin in order to have a share in Christ's resurrection. Understand what happiness it is not to be drunk with the world's luxury and froth so that you may drink new wine with Christ in his Father's kingdom.[33] The Paschal Lamb himself invites his friends to the savory repast of his body and blood in the words: "Eat, friends, drink and be inebriated, my dearest ones."[34] That food and drink is a mystery of life, a medicine that bestows immortality, cause of the first resurrection and pledge of the second, because it is the principle by which we are grounded in him. As St Paul says, "We have been made sharers of Christ, but only on condition that we keep unshaken to the end the principle by which we are grounded in him."[35]

The man who returns to his vomit[36] after receiving grace will vomit forth the riches which he devoured and God will extract them from his belly.[37] Or certainly "his bread will be turned into the gall of asps in his stomach"[38]—because the grace that has been received is turned into remorse when the blood of the covenant by which a man was sanctified is reckoned as defiled and the Spirit that brought grace is mocked.[39] This is the contempt and the nausea which cause the riches which had been devoured to be vomited forth, so that it is said of such a man: "Nothing will remain of his food and therefore nothing of all his property will endure."[40]

5. This dreadful sentence may also apply perhaps to the man who is filled with the good things of God's house through the grace of devotion but keeps nothing at all of them in his memory so as to share with us the remembrance of God's abounding sweetness.[41] There is no flavor in his speech, like a taste in his mouth; no virtue

---

32. Is 55:1. 33. Mt 26:29. 34. Song 5:1.
35. Heb 3:14. 36. Prov 26:11. 37. Job 20:15.
38. Job 20:14. 39. Heb 10:29. 40. Job 20:21. 41. Ps 144:7.

in his behavior, like juice in his bowels, but vomiting the lot through foolishness or buffoonery, he turns grace into wrath against himself. Into wrath indeed, and frightful wrath, if there applies to him what this same passage of Scripture goes on to say: "When he has been satiated he will be in straits, all the force of misery will come upon him. Would that his belly were filled, so that God would send upon him his fierce anger and rain his warfare upon him."[42] Rightly the Prophet thought and agreed that warfare should rain upon sinners who have not brought forth the fruit of peace after receiving the rain of benediction, that fire, brimstone and a storm-wind should be the cup allotted to those who have drunk the Lord's cup unworthily.[43] For a piece of ground which has drunk in, again and again, the showers which fell upon it, has God's blessing on it if it yields a crop answering the needs of those who tilled it. If it bears thorns and thistles it has lost its value; a curse hangs over it, and it will feed the bonfire at last. But in you, brethren, we look with confidence for something better and more conducive to your salvation.[44]

Only, be grateful for God's grace; and as you have been transformed into a new creation by Easter's healing action, so walk always in newness of life.[45] You have been given a share in Christ through the fellowship of faith, by participation in his sacrament, by communion in the Holy Spirit. Strive not only to keep the principle by which you are grounded in him unshaken to the end[46] but also constantly to increase it. Thus may you who have begun to share in the first resurrection through the privilege of so many gifts, trusting in so great a pledge, on the day when you present it for recognition, make good your eternal right to the second resurrection. May our Lord Jesus Christ grant you this, he who is our resurrection and our life,[47] who on our account was dead for three days but now lives and reigns for ever and ever. Amen.

42. Job 20:22. 43. Cf. Ps 10:7; 1 Cor 11:27. 44. Heb 6:7ff.
45. Rom 6:4. 46. Heb 3:14. 47. Jn 11:25.

SERMON 35

THE THIRD SERMON FOR EASTER

"BLESSED AND HOLY IS HE who has a share in the first resurrection."[1] Christ is the first-fruits of them who sleep,[2] the firstborn from the dead,[3] who by his own resurrection, which is the first of all, consecrated for us both the first resurrection of our souls and the second of our bodies. In his own body which he raised from the dead he inaugurated for our souls the mystery of rising and gave our bodies a first example of it. For our souls Christ's single resurrection prepared a twofold grace of resurrection: day by day they come to life again from the death of sin through the working of this mystery, and today especially they arise from the torpor of sleep through the devotion which joy brings. For who is so slothful or lukewarm that when he hears today those words full of every joy: "The Lord has risen," he is not wholly aroused to exultation, does not wholly come to life again and recover his warmth of spirit? Indeed, we read, "my heart and my flesh have exulted in the living God,"[4] I who had fallen wholly into grief and despair when I looked upon the dead Jesus. It is with no mean profit to faith, no slight dividend of joy that Jesus comes back to me from the tomb; he is recognized as the living God who a little while before was mourned as a dead man. My heart was sorrowing for him as slain, but now he is alive, and not only my heart but also my flesh exults on his account, assured through him of its own resurrection and immortality. "O my soul,

---

1. Rev 20:6.   2. 1 Cor 15:20.   3. Col. 1:18.   4. Ps 83:3.

I have slept and I have risen,"[5] Christ says. Do you also arise who are asleep, rise from the dead and Christ will enlighten you[6].

Does he not, brethren, resemble a dead man who is still snoring when the Sun has risen, who is still sunk in negligence and sloth as if buried in despairing torpor when the grace of the resurrection sheds its glowing beams on all sides? The new Sun as it rises strikes the eyes of those who watch for it early in the morning,[7] disclosing the day of eternity. This day knows no evening, for its Sun will not set any more.[8] It set once, then rose once and for all, subjecting death to itself.

2. Brethren, this is the day which the Lord has made, let us exult and rejoice in it.[9] Let us exult in the hope it brings, that we may see and rejoice in its light. Abraham exulted that he might see the day of Christ and by this token he saw and rejoiced.[10]

You too, if you keep watch daily at the doors of wisdom, steadfast at its threshold,[11] if you stay awake through the night with Magdalen at the entrance of his tomb, if I am not mistaken you will experience with Mary how true are the words we read of the Wisdom which is Christ: "She is easily seen by those who love her and she is found by those who seek her. She anticipates those who desire her and shows herself to them first. He who, as soon as it is light, keeps watch for her will not have to toil, for he will find her seated at his doors."[12] So did Christ, Wisdom himself, promise in the words: "I love those who love me, and they who from early morning keep watch for me will find me."[13] Mary found Jesus in the flesh. For this she was keeping watch. Over his tomb she had come to mount guard while it was still dark. You, who no longer ought to know Jesus according to the flesh[14] but according to the spirit, will be able to find him spiritually if you seek him with a like desire, if he finds you likewise vigilant in prayer. Say then to the Lord Jesus with the desire and the affection of Mary: "My soul has longed for you during the night, my spirit too, deep within

---

5. Ps 3:6. 6. Eph 5:14. 7. Is 26:9. 8. Is 60:20.
9. Ps 117:24. 10. Jn 8:56. 11. Prov 8:34. 12. Wis 6:13ff.
13. Prov 8:17. 14. 2 Cor 5:16.

me; from early morning I will keep watch for you."[15] Say with the voice and the mind of the Psalmist: "God, my God, for you as soon as it is light I keep watch, my soul is athirst for you."[16] And see if it is not your lot to sing with him: "We have been filled early in the morning with your mercy, we have exulted and been delighted."[17]

3. Keep watch then, brethren, intent in prayer; keep watch and carefully guard your actions; especially since the morning of that day which has no sunset has already shone upon us. For already eternal light has come back to us from the nether regions, more serene and more pleasing, and the morning has given its welcome to the newly restored Sun. Indeed it is time now for us to arise from sleep; the night has passed away, while the day has drawn near.[18] Keep watch, I say, that the morning light may rise for you, that is Christ, whose coming forth has been made ready like the dawn,[19] ready to renew often the mystery of the morning of his resurrection in those who keep watch for him. Then you will sing with jubilant heart: "God the Lord has shone upon us. This is the day which the Lord has made; let us exult and rejoice in it."[20] For then he will give you a glimpse of the light which he has hidden in his hands, telling his friend that it is his possession and he can attain to it.

How long will you sleep, sluggard? How long will you slumber? "A little sleep, a little slumber, a little folding of the hands to rest."[21] And while you sleep, all ignorance, Christ rises from the tomb and you do not deserve to see even his back as his glory passes before you.[22] It will be too late to repent and bemoan, saying with the impious: "And so we have strayed from the path of truth, and the light of justice has not shone upon us, and the sun of understanding has not risen for us."[23]

But, we read, "for you who fear my name the sun of justice will rise."[24] And "he who walks in justice will see with his eyes the king

---

15. Is 26:9. 16. Ps 62:2. 17. Ps 89:14. 18. Rom 13:11f.
19. Hos 6:3. 20. Ps 117:27, 24. 21. Prov 6:9f. 22. Ex 33:22f.
23. Wis 5:6. 24. Mal 4:2.

in his beauty."[25] Now this is the beatitude of the life to come, but to a certain extent it is granted also for consolation in the present life, as Christ's resurrection clearly demonstrates. For by many proofs throughout forty days[26] Wisdom demonstrated to us that he goes around seeking men worthy of him, and in his way he shows himself to them with glad countenance, and comes to meet them with all discretion.[27] For in order that Jesus might show himself to be that Wisdom of which these things were written, and in order to manifest corporally on this day what he does not cease to do spiritually day by day—happily to show himself along the paths of justice—he came today to meet the women on their way as they were returning from the tomb,[28] and he showed himself along the way to the two disciples who were going to Emmaus.[29]

4. Let them hear and rejoice who walk in the ways of justice. Let them hear, I say, for Jesus deigns to meet and manifest himself not only to those who devote themselves to contemplation but also to those who justly and devoutly walk the ways of action. Many of you, if I am not mistaken, recognize what you have experienced; often Jesus whom you sought at the memorials of the altars, as at the tomb, and did not find, unexpectedly came to meet you in the way while you were working. Then you drew near and held on to his feet,[30] you whose feet slothfulness had not held back for desire of him. Do not then be too sparing of your feet, brother, in the ways of obedience and in the coming and going which work demands, since Jesus did not spare his feet on your account even from the pain of the nails, and he still allows the work of your feet to be rewarded or revealed by the embrace and kiss of his own feet. What a consolation it will be also if he joins you as a companion on the way and by the surpassing pleasure which his conversation gives takes away from you all feeling of toil, while he opens your mind to understand the Scriptures which perhaps you sat and read at home without understanding.[31]

I beseech you, my brethren, to whom God has on occasion given

25. Is 33:15ff. 26. Acts 1:3. 27. Wis 6:17. 28. Mt 28:9.
29. Lk 24:13f. 30. Mt 28:9. 31. Lk 24:45.

the experience of this: was not your heart burning in you on account of Jesus when he spoke to you on the way and opened the Scriptures?[32] Let them then who have experienced it remember it and let them sing in the ways of the Lord that great is the glory of the Lord.[33] Let those who have not experienced it believe and be eager to experience it, so that they too may sing of God's graces in the place of their pilgrimage and affliction.[34]

5. So let the spirit of us all rise and come to life again, whether to watchfulness in prayer or to constancy in work, so that by a certain revived and lively alacrity each may prove himself anew to have received a share in Christ's resurrection. The first sign of life's return to a man is energy and diligence in action, and his perfect resurrection, as long as he is in this mortal body, is to open his eyes to contemplation. This however the understanding only wins when the affections have been opened wide by frequent sighs and vehement desires, that they may be able to contain such great majesty.

This growth of resurrection as it were through certain stages was clearly portrayed, I think, in the child whom Elisha raised from death. When he began to return to life, first of all, we read, the boy's flesh grew warm, then he yawned seven times, and finally he opened his eyes.[35] The child's flesh is the fleshly heart of one who is little in Christ, whose first hope of life is to be able to say: "My heart has grown warm within me, and as I meditate fire blazes forth."[36] His garments too are warm, since there has blown over his land the south wind,[37] that is, the Holy Spirit whom the true Elisha is quick to breath into him as he revives. More fully however and more obviously does he advance towards resurrection when by desire and a certain hunger for justice he begins to yawn often, in the way in which he yawned who said: "I opened my mouth and drew breath, because I desired your commandments."[38] This yawning is a spreading wide of the affections that they may be the more able to contain the breath of life, so that after other spiritual

---

32. Lk 24:32. 33. Ps 137:5. 34. Ps 118:54. 35. 2 Kings 4:32.
36. Ps 38:4. 37. Job 37:17. 38. Ps 118:131.

gifts of the sevenfold grace the spirit of understanding and wisdom[39] may be infused and open the eyes to contemplate God.

First then there is the warmth of returning life when good works are performed; the second stage of resurrection is the extending of the affections through prayer; perfection is reached when the understanding is enlightened so as to contemplate. Strive, my brethren, to rise more and more by these stages of virtue, these increases in holiness of life, so that you may arrive, as St Paul says, at the resurrection of Christ,[40] who lives and reigns for ever and ever. Amen.

---

39. Is 11:2.   40. Phil 3:11.

SERMON 36

SERMON FOR ROGATION DAYS

"**GIVE ME THREE LOAVES.** Friends have come to us from their journey and I have nothing to set before them."[1] I am no physician and in my house there is no bread. That is why I said from the start: "Do not make me your leader."[2] It is not right for one to rule who cannot be of service. And how can he be of service who is not a physician and in whose house there is no bread? He has neither the art to heal souls nor the learning to feed them. I told you this but you would not listen. You made me your superior. There was only one course open to me. If I could not escape the burden, I had to look for a remedy. I listened to the advice of the wise man: "Have they made you ruler? Be among them as one of them."[3] But I cannot even do

---

1. Lk 11:5f. Guerric here takes his text from the Gospel pericope which is read at the mass on the Rogation Days. He uses it to enter into what is one of the most personal passages in his sermons and touches upon a matter which was probably most frequently the subject of his own personal prayer and asking of the Lord—his own insufficiencies as an abbot.

2. Is 3:7. Guerric uses this text to give voice here to his reluctance to accept the burden of the abbatial office at Igny to which he was elected while still a simple monk at Clairvaux. He makes it clear that the community freely elected him. See above: Introduction, vol. 1, p. xvii.

3. Sir 32:1. In these few lines Guerric sums up the role of the abbot in the community as he saw it. Above all it was one of service. He was to serve the community as a physician, healing souls, as a teacher, feeding them with sound doctrine, and as a brother, one in their midst sharing with them the common toils of a common life. Above all he was to be a humble man—"humble and helpful."

this. Lack of wisdom forbids my being put over others; lack of health prevents my being one among them. I have not the depth of soul for ministering the word, nor the strength of body for giving a good example. I am not fit to be a ruler over you nor am I fit enough to be among you as one of you. What is left to me then but to choose the last and safest place and be the servant of you all? And this I can do by thinking humbly, or rather truly, about myself. There is nothing to prevent me, in fact truth itself strongly urges me, to be subject in spirit to you all, even though I am compelled by my office to rule over you.

2. It is you yourself, Lord God, who warn me to be subject yet command me to rule. So, confident you will grant my plea, I beg you to make me humble and helpful in the ministry you have confided to me: humble in realizing the truth about myself, helpful by speaking the truth about you. Breathe the one truth into my heart, let the other be ever on my lips. You have told us: "Open your mouth and I will fill it."[4] Put into my mouth the appropriate word that pleases the ear,[5] so that this entire family of yours may be filled with blessings. Behold, friends have come to us, my friends certainly, but still more are they your friends. And I have nothing to set before them unless something is provided by another.

And who else is so rich and generous in his giving as the Lord of all, rich unto all who call upon him.[6] He opens his hand and fills with blessing every living creature;[7] he gives to all freely and ungrudgingly[8]—except perhaps to the man slow in asking or remiss in giving thanks for what he receives. How many hired servants[9] are there in that Father's house who have more bread than they can eat?[10] Because they are making Christ known, even though they

---

4. Ps 80:10.   5. Esther 14:13 (Septuagint).   6. Rom 10:12.
7. Ps 144:16.   8. Jas 1:5.

9. The Latin word used here is *mercenarii*—mercenaries. Guerric seems to have shared with most of the monastic reformers of his own and the preceding century a rather low estimation of many of the clergy and hierarchy. Cf. especially Bernard of Clairvaux: *Tenth Sermon on the Song of Songs*, II (Cistercian Fathers Series 4); *On Consideration*, bks. 2–3 (Cistercian Fathers Series 19); *To Clerics on Conversion*, 32 (Cistercian Fathers Series 43).

10. Lk 15:17.

do not do so wholeheartedly, the grace of teaching is not denied them. It is given them not on their own account but for the sake of others. And where hired servants have their fill, will children go short?

Then, Lord (I hesitate to call you, Friend, but readily acknowledge you as Lord), give me three loaves[11] that my friends may be refreshed. Otherwise if I send them away fasting they may grow faint on the way[12] and I shall be called to account for it. "The little ones have asked for bread," I shall be told, "and there was no one to break it unto them."[13] Give me, Lord, what will redound to your own profit. After all you can recover, when you will, whatever you send, and that with interest.[14] So I say: give me three loaves, if that is your good pleasure; if not give me what you will, however small it is. Even one slice will be enough to feed thousands and thousands, provided only that you bless it.[15] I know very well that you want us to be importunate in our asking. You may feign not to hear, make the excuses that you have returned to heaven and that your Apostles are with you in bed. Nevertheless we have to go on asking, seeking, knocking.[16] We know that to merit the ability to teach, it is not enough to live a blameless life whereby we become your friends; we must show continuous zeal and perseverance in prayer, enough to make us seem shameless. I myself can rely on neither. All I can do is to put before you the merits of those I must feed. They deserve what I do not.

3. Brethren, I am asking for these loaves for your benefit; I am asking because of your merits. But do you think we are equal to them? Will I be able to break them? Will you be able to eat them? I fear it may be said to me: "Seek not the things that are too high for you and search not into the things that are above your ability,"[17] and to you: "You have gone back to needing milk instead of solid food."[18] I know well enough that if we presume to ask too much,

11. Cf. note 1 above.   12. Mk 8:3.   13. Lam 4:4.
14. Cf. Mt 25:27.
15. Cf. Mt 14:13ff.; Mk 6:32ff.; Lk 9:10ff.; Jn 6:1ff.
16. Lk 11:10.   17. Sir 3:22.   18. Heb 5:12.

children as we are, our Father has loaves that will break our teeth rather than fill our stomachs, that is, build up our souls.

Who is able to understand? Who can explain? Or who can meditate worthily on the ineffable mystery of the Blessed Trinity? How the Father is of himself alone, the Son is from the Father and the Holy Spirit is from both Father and Son, and how there are three Persons in a unity of substance. That foolish woman, the audacious vanity of heretics, incites itching ears to unravel such mysteries. But we must believe in God, not take him to pieces. "Go on," she says, "try these loaves of mystery."[19] As if you in your ignorance could try what is beyond the power of the angels. And what good would it be to me to try these loaves of mystery which cannot be broken or eaten without danger? Enough for me to know of their existence and that they are three in number. I am not speaking now of the Trinity of Persons but of the trinity of expressions, or rather ideas, that can be held concerning the Persons. There are, then, three loaves of identical size and weight, identical too in shape and taste. Whatever we say about the Father we must also hold about the Son and Holy Spirit—except of course that the difference in the qualities peculiar to each Person, which makes there to be Three Persons in the Blessed Trinity, necessitates a difference in our notions of them.

4. So let us leave those loaves, which may be broken only by such as have the lofty stature of angels, until we have grown and are on an equality with them, worthy to eat at their table. There are any number of other trinities of loaves that the Holy Scriptures can set before us, loaves more suited to our weakness. For example, not to go too far from the Blessed Trinity, of him and by him and in him all things are;[20] we are created by the Father, redeemed by the Son, sanctified in the Holy Spirit. So many things can be spoken of in this fashion that, however hungry your friend may be after his journey, if you were to put before him only half of them he would quite likely be in as great danger from overeating as he was

19. Prov 9:13ff. (Septuagint).
20. Rom 11:36.

of starving. Abundance would bloat him whom before need had straitened.

You could represent in this trinitarian fashion not only him who made us and things which were made for us, but also those things which were written for us. A fine meal can be made of the three loaves of the historical, allegorical and moral senses.[21] The whole content of Scripture divides easily into three and is eaten as if three loaves. It deals, for instance, with righteousness under the natural law, under the written law, under the Spirit; that is, righteousness before the law of Moses, under the law of Moses and, after it, under the law of grace. Nature gave the knowledge, the law, the right action, and grace the will.

Then again the Teacher and Shepherd of the Gentiles in faith and truth teaches that the Church must be nourished on a kind of trinity of loaves: the man who builds up the Church speaks to edify, to encourage, to comfort.[22] To edify, so that you may know what you should do; to encourage, so that you may want to do what you know you should do; to comfort, so that, even in adversity, you may have the strength to do what you know should be done and want to do.

Finally, besides finding trinities of loaves in the natures of things, in the senses and divisions of Scripture, in the ways and manners of preaching, you will find there are a certain three loaves toward which all these are ordered—and full of taste and nourishment they are too. I speak of faith, hope and charity.[23] For the whole purpose of the Sacred Scriptures and of preaching lies in this, that we may believe and hope and love. Charity itself has been defined as the end of the law[24] and is itself of a sort of triple nature, since we

---

21. Guerric, like the rest of the Cistercian Fathers, received from the patristic tradition, and especially Origen (see H. De Lubac, *History and Spirit*, Cistercian Studies Series 27), a deep awareness of and appreciation for the different senses of Sacred Scripture. For an excellent comprehensive study of these senses as they were understood by the Cistercian Fathers and their contemporaries see H. De Lubac, *The Exegesis of the Middle Ages* (Cistercian Studies Series 47).

22. 1 Cor 14:3f.   23. 1 Cor 13:13.   24. 1 Tim 1:5.

must love God with all our heart and all our soul and all our strength.[25]

But it is a mistake to drag out the length of a dinner or to arrange too many courses, so I shall bring my sermon to a close. It will be for you to gather up the broken pieces that are left over,[26] I mean the finer points that have slipped through my fingers. And it will be for both you and me to sing in praise of him who feeds us: blessed be God for his gifts, he who lives and reigns for ever and ever. Amen.

---

25. Mt 12:30.   26. Cf. Jn 6:12.

SERMON 37

THE SERMON FOR THE ASCENSION

"FATHER, as long as I was with them it was for me to keep them true to your name."[1] This was the prayer on the lips of our Lord on the eve of his passion. But it is not unreasonable to accommodate it to the day of his Ascension, when he was about to depart from the children he was then commending to his Father. In heaven he has created a multitude of angels; there he rules over them, teaches them. On earth it was a puny flock of disciples he gathered about him.[2] They were to be taught by his presence in the flesh until their understanding had increased sufficiently for them to be capable of receiving the direction of the Holy Spirit. Thus it was that the Master loved his little ones with a great love, for he had weaned them from the love of the world and saw them, putting all hopes of the world aside, place all their hope in him. For as long as he desired to be with them in the flesh he did not readily manifest his love for them; or if he did, he did not show it to any great extent. Rather than intimacy he had to show that reserve which became a Master and a Father. But when the time was come for him to leave them, he seemed to be overcome by his tender love for them so that he was no longer able to dissimulate the wealth of affection he had hidden till then.[3]

That is why the Apostle writes: "Having loved his own who were in the world, he loved them to the end."[4] On that day he poured out on his friends almost the full power of his love before he

1. Jn 17:11f.   2. Lk 12:32.   3. Ps 30:20.   4. Jn 13:1.

himself was poured out like water for those same friends.⁵ He handed over to them the sacrament of his body and blood; instituted it for them to celebrate in their turn. Was it his marvelous power or his more marvelous love that enabled him to find this new way of remaining with them as consolation for his departure? Although he was to deprive them of his bodily presence, he would nevertheless remain with them; even more, he would remain in them, by virtue of this sacrament. It was then as if completely forgetful of his majesty and as it were doing injury to his own honor, unless it be the glory of charity that one abases oneself before one's friends, with unutterable grace and dignity the Lord, and such a Lord, washed the feet of his servants, leaving them in that one action an example of humility and a sacrament of forgiveness.⁶

2. Finally, after encouraging them at some length, he lifted up his eyes to heaven and commended them to the Father, saying: "Father, as long as I was with them it was for me to keep them true to your name; not one of them has been lost save him whom perdition claims for its own. Now I am coming to you. Keep true to your name those whom you have given to me. I am not asking that you should take them out of the world, but that you should keep them clear of what is evil."⁷ He said much more which I have not the time to quote, let alone explain. But the whole prayer is summed up in the three petitions you have just heard in the text of todays reading. In them is contained the whole of salvation, the whole of perfection: that they be preserved from evil, that they be sanctified in truth, that they be glorified with him. "Father," he prays, "this is my desire, that all those whom you have entrusted to me may be with me so as to see my glory."⁸

How fortunate are those who have their advocate as their judge;

---

5. Ps 21:15.

6. It may be argued here that Guerric is using "sacrament" in a broad sense, but in all likelihood he, as other members of the Cistercian school (e.g. Bernard of Clairvaux, *Sermon for Holy Thursday* [Cistercian Fathers Series 22]; Ernald of Bonval, *De cardinalibus operibus Christi* [PL 189:1650ff.]) believed the washing of the feet to be a true sacrament instituted by Christ.

7. Jn 17:11ff.   8. Jn 17:24.

whose intercessor is to be adored with equal honor as he with whom he pleads. His spoken wish the Father will in no way disregard,[9] since they are one in will and power, because God is one.[10] Whatsoever Christ asks for in prayer must of necessity come about; his word is power, his will fulfillment. For all things that are, he but spoke and they were made, he gave the command and they were created.[11] "This is my desire, that where I am they also shall be."[12] What assurance for them who are faithful, what a pledge for them who believe; only they must not throw away the grace they have received. And this assurance is given not to the Apostles only and to their fellow disciples but to all who through their word are to find faith in the Word of God. "Not for these alone," runs the Scripture, "do I ask, but for all those who are to find faith in me through their word."[13]

3. But the grace that has been granted to you, brethren, the Apostle says, is that of suffering for Christ's sake, not merely believing in him.[14] Faith in the promise of Christ should not lull you into a false security but spur you to eager enthusiasm. It should reward your efforts in the daily struggle against sin with the crown for continual martyrdom. A continual martyrdom, but one that is easy; easy, and yet glorious. It is easy, for nothing is commanded beyond your strength; it is glorious, for your victory is gained only through bringing to bear the full power of the strong man armed for battle.[15] How easy to carry the sweet yoke of Christ;[16] how glorious to find a high place in his kingdom. What is easier than to bear the wings that bear you up? What more glorious than to fly above the highest heavens to where Christ has ascended?[17] It is very true: the saints whose youth will be renewed like that of the eagle[18] will take up wings like an eagle's and fly.[19] Whither? "It is where the body lies," we are told, "that the eagles will gather."[20]

4. But do you think, brethren, that when that day comes a man

9. Ps 20:3.   10. Mk 12:32.   11. Ps 32:9.   12. Jn 17:24.
13. Jn 17:20.   14. St Paul: Phil 1:29.   15. Lk 11:21.   16. Mt 11:30.
17. Eph 4:10.   18. Ps 102:5.   19. Is 40:31.   20. Lk 17:37.

will straight away find himself able to fly heavenward who has not here and now learnt to fly by daily exercises and practice? And if you ask who should teach you, who should show the way, surely Christ does that today. Like an eagle he encourages his little ones to fly, rising above them when he is lifted up from before their eyes, and for a long time is watched by them as he journeys heavenward.[21] He could quite easily have been snatched away from them in a flash and been taken wheresoever he willed. But like the eagle enticing her young to fly and hovering over them[22] he plainly endeavors to raise their hearts to himself through their love of him, while his own body gives assurance that theirs too can be raised up in like manner. So it is that the Apostle, well knowing the eternal mystery, assures us that we will be swept away, borne upon the clouds to meet Christ as he returns.[23] He has mounted above the cherubim and soars high on the wings of the wind,[24] that is to say, he has mounted above all the choirs of angels. Yet he stoops to your weakness, he spreads wide his wings, lifts you up and carries you on his shoulders[25]—provided you do not prove an unnatural offspring—so that you need have no fear at being lifted above the earth to enjoy the purer air on high.

5. Others may fly by contemplation; you at least can do so by love. Paul was carried out of himself and rapt up to the third heaven;[26] John, up to him who in the beginning was the Word.[27] You can at least refuse to drag your tainted spirit in the dust; do not allow your heart, weighed down by sloth, to rot in the mire. Today your High Priest has entered the sanctuary; the ransom he has won lasts forever.[28] There he appears in God's sight on your behalf. To his cry: *Lift up your hearts,* reply in all sincerity: *We lift them up to the Lord.*[29]

And if sometimes you should go after things of earth instead of

---

21. Acts 1:10f.   22. Deut 32:11.   23. 1 Thess 4:16.
24. Ps 17:11.   25. Deut 32:11.   26. 2 Cor 5:13, 12:2.
27. Jn 1:1.   28. Heb 9:12.

29. Guerric here employs part of the dialog which opens the Preface of the great Eucharistic Prayer at the Liturgy: *Sursum corda. Habemus ad Dominum.*

those of heaven,[30] then correct yourself and, turning to God, say with the Prophet: "What else does heaven hold for me, and apart from you what do I desire on earth?"[31] Alas, how I wandered miserably away from the path. Such a treasure laid up for me in heaven and I rejected it continually; and these nothings of earth I have sought so diligently. Christ, your treasure, has ascended into heaven; that is where your heart should be also.[32] It is from there you take your very beginning; there too is your portion and inheritance.[33] It is from there that you may expect the Savior.[34]

---

30. Col 3:1f.   31. Ps 72:25.   32. Mt 6:21.   33. Sir 45:27.

34. Phil 3:20. The Sermon ends rather abruptly here, lacking the doxology which usually concludes Guerric's sermons. Perhaps the text as we have it is incomplete for it is somewhat under the average in length. On the other hand it is possible that Guerric, consciously or unconsciously using an oratorical device, did this so that his hearers would have an experience of expectation which would underline his closing exhortation.

SERMON 38

THE FIRST SERMON FOR PENTECOST

HOW INEFFABLE IS GOD, how unutterable his mercy. Wonderful his name, wonderful all his works. Truly the esteem in which the divine love holds us is completely inexpressible. It was not enough for the Father to have given his Son to redeem his slave, unless he were to give the Holy Spirit also, through whom he adopts the slave as his son. He gave his Son as the price of redemption; he gave the Spirit as the bill of adoption. Finally he reserves himself in all his totality as the inheritance of those he has adopted. O God, if I may be allowed to speak thus, you lavish yourself on man far beyond his dreams. Is he not lavish who brings to bear not only all his resources but even his own person in order to win back mankind, and this not for his own sake but for the sake of man himself? Is he not lavish? Just as he did not spare his own Son but gave him up for us all,[1] so also he has, so to speak, not spared the Holy Spirit, but has poured him out on all flesh[2] with a liberality of a new and astonishing depth. Prodigal indeed was that Son who lavished both his inheritance and himself on harlots. His Father however was much more prodigal in winning back his lost son than the son had been in bringing about his own ruin;[3] if there can be any real comparison between grace and money, spirit and flesh, God and man.

Consider with what liberality the grace of the Holy Spirit is poured out upon the whole world, not only to strengthen the just

---

1. Rom 8:32.   2. Cf. Joel 2:28.   3. Cf. Lk 15:11ff.

but even to justify sinners; how everywhere, among all peoples, the Spirit creates a new race of men and thereby renews the face of the earth.[4] Consider too what a great change is wrought every day by the right hand of the Most High,[5] so that without warning the most profligate of men, tax collectors and harlots, go into the kingdom of God before so many of the righteous;[6] the last become the first.[7] Truly the free gift is not like the trespass,[8] because where sin increased there grace abounds all the more,[9] not only forgiving sin but heaping up the merits of virtue. Redemption has raised the fallen up again, but to a higher position than they possessed through the first creation.

Certainly the more wondrously the grace of God is made manifest in all these actions, so much more is the obstinacy of men condemned, whether it be in refusing the grace that is offered or not preserving it after it has been accepted. For to whom is grace not offered? Upon whom does his light not arise?[10] Who hides himself from his heat?[11] And God does not leave himself without witness in the minds of men. For he enlightens them with the splendor of his truth and warms them with the warmth of his goodness. The true light enlightens every man coming into the world,[12] and God makes his sun to rise on the evil and on the good, and sends rain on the just and on the unjust.[13] But woe to those who rebel against the light,[14] those who resist the Holy Spirit[15] and do not obey the truth[16] they understand only too well. Just as mud is hardened by the heat of the sun, so they grow obdurate under the goodness and beneficence of God, and even outrageously provoke him after he has delivered all things into their hands.[17]

2. But what have we to do with outsiders?[18] This sermon is really addressed to you who have received the Spirit of Sonship.[19] You have this same Spirit as a mark of your adoption and guarantee of your inheritance,[20] the Spirit which as a kind of singular imprint

4. Ps 103:30. 5. Ps 76:11. 6. Mt 21:31. 7. Mt 19:30.
8. Rom 5:15. 9. Rom 5:20. 10. Job 25:3. 11. Ps 18:7.
12. Jn 1:9. 13. Mt 5:45. 14. Job 24:13. 15. Acts 7:51.
16. Rom 2:8. 17. 1 Cor 3:22. 18. 1 Cor 5:12. 19. Rom 8:15.
20. Eph 1:14.

marks off the vessels of mercy from the vessels of wrath.[21] But we should be careful to rejoice with a due modesty about our salvation, or rather our hope of salvation; for what we sorrow over in those others now, we should fear may become our lot owing to our fickle nature. For as it is blasphemous to despair over them, so it is imprudent to be presumptuous about ourselves. Whatever our present state of knowledge may be about ourselves or about them, we can have no foresight of what the future holds in store for either of us. If we were to anticipate his judgment of their case in such a harsh way, and of ours in such an outrageous manner, the affront committed against the Supreme Power, Arbiter of life and death, would be anything but a trifling matter. We have been taken from the common herd,[22] for we were, but a short time ago, like them, children of wrath[23] both by nature and by our way of life, but suddenly we have been transformed into children of grace.

Thus we should be to them an example of hope to lead them to repentance, while they can be a means of exciting our fear lest we fail to persevere. In our case mercy offers itself to be loved, while in theirs judgment is laid open, demanding to be feared. *I will sing of loyalty and of justice to you, O Lord*,[24] giving thanks for the one, making supplications because of the other, joyful and grateful for your mercy, but fearful and diligent owing to your justice. I have been schooled by them both[25] and will rejoice in your

21. Rom 9:22f.   22. Rom 9:21.   23. Eph 2:3.   24. Ps 100:1.

25. Guerric here may be alluding to the training which he had received from Bernard of Clairvaux. In his first sermons on the Song of Songs (see especially 6:9: Cistercian Fathers Series 4, p. 37) Bernard emphasized the importance of meditations on both justice and mercy and of keeping a balance between them: "And if, as happened at times, I should grow forgetful of his mercy, and with a stricken conscience become too deeply involved in the thought of the judgment, sooner or later I was cast down in unbelievable fear, in shameful misery, enveloped in a frightful gloom out of which I cried in dismay: 'Who has yet felt the full force of your fury or learned to fear the violence of your rage?' But if on escaping from this I should cling more than was becoming to the foot of mercy, the opposite happened, I became dissipated, indifferent, and negligent; lukewarm at prayer, languid at work, always on the watch for a laugh, inclined to say the wrong thing. And my interior was no steadier than my behavior. But you know what a teacher experience is:

presence with awe because then I shall walk in your truth if my heart so rejoices that it fears your name.[26]

This fear which love purifies does not make away with joy but guards it; does not destroy it but aids its growth; does not make it bitter to the taste but gives it a wholesome flavor. The more humble it is, the more lasting it is; the more severe it is, the truer it is; the holier it is, the sweeter it is. O pure and sincere joy, how true is the Wise Man's judgment of you: "There are no riches above the riches of the health of the body, and no pleasure beyond the joy of the heart."[27] It is not the nature of this joy to rejoice with the wicked. The Wise Man detests and condemns their stupid buffoonery and worthless joys. "I said of laughter," runs the Scripture, "it is mad; and to pleasure: 'Of what use are you?'[28] Even in laughter the heart is sad, and the end of joy is grief."[29]

3. O blessed Jesus, how different is the joy with which you comfort those who turn their backs on that deceitful and deceiving joy. How much is your steadfast love better than life,[30] for a day in your courts is better than a thousand elsewhere.[31] Your poor are more blessed in your poverty[32] than those who rely on the affluence of the world. There riches come but they quickly go and whoever clings to them is lost with them. With different riches did that poverty-stricken family of Christ abound, that family which was flooded with the surging torrent which makes glad the City of God.[33] For on this day, like a rushing wind the Spirit filled the whole house where the Apostles were sitting.[34] In this way Divine Truth fulfilled the promise made through the Prophet: "Behold I shall bring upon her as it were a river of peace and as an overflowing torrent the glory of the Gentiles."[35] With what riches did they abound who received the outpouring of such a torrent. What

---

no longer of judgment alone or of mercy alone, but of mercy and of judgment I will sing to you, O Lord." This sermon was undoubtedly preached or written by Bernard while Guerric was still a simple monk at Clairvaux.

26. Ps 85:11. 27. Sir 30:16. 28. Eccles 2:2. 29. Prov 14:13.
30. Ps 62:4. 31. Ps 83:11. 32. Mt 5:3. 33. Ps 45:5.
34. Acts 2:2. 35. Is 66:12.

riches streamed forth from them whose innermost being poured forth the waters of life.[36] Not only did the goodness of charity overflow from their hearts, but from their lips poured forth a rushing torrent of eloquence, which their enemies could neither resist nor contradict, as it is said of Stephen: "They were no match for his wisdom and for the Spirit who then gave utterance."[37]

4. It is to joy of this kind, brethren, that your Consoler invites you. It is from this torrent of pleasure[38] that he desires the souls of his lovers thirsting for his delights to drink. "If anyone thirst," he says, "let him come to me and drink."[39] O, the abounding generosity of God. O the unfailing bounty of the divine goodness. He offers the Spirit to all mankind. The Apostles received today the first-fruits of that Spirit. He opens his treasure, the fount of living water, to men as well as to beasts,[40] as if he himself were under an obligation to all, both to the wise and to the foolish.[41] "Everyone who thirsts," he says, "come to the waters."[42] Just that. He is no respecter of persons. He takes no cognizance of their rank, nor does he enquire into their merits; he only wants those who thirst to come to him. Certainly he does not give his grace to the disdainful, but rather he fills the hungry with good things and he sends the rich away empty.[43]

O disdain, which gnaw at the heart, rot the mind, bring a deadly sadness on the soul, you cause the good word of God to be an abomination, the heavenly gift to be despised. You recall your fleshpots and so bring disgust to this manna.[44] What plague is so destructive, what disease so deadly, which thus makes a man unmindful of his own salvation and allures him even as far as the gates of death[45] still cackling in his false sense of security. But why, I ask, has the attack of this plague been so widespread among the sheepfolds of Christ? How has it fallen on the flock, with such devastation that the green pastures where they have been gathered together seem to so many of the Lord's flock a howling waste of the wilderness?[46]

---

36. Jn 7:38. 37. Acts 6:10. 38. Ps 35:9. 39. Jn 7:37.
40. Num 20:6ff. 41. Cf. Rom 1:14. 42. Is 55:1. 43. Lk 1:53.
44. Ex 16:3. 45. Ps 106:18. 46. Deut 32:10.

And in rich pastures where the grass is most lush[47] they miserably wither away through their disdainful sloth.

And have they not, I ask, tasted the heavenly Gift and become partakers of the Holy Spirit, and why have they not tasted the goodness of the word of God and the powers of the world to come?[48] For if they have not tasted the goodness of the word of God, how is it that their hearts have so often overflown with words of goodness?[49] They did so when, recalling his abundant goodness,[50] their lips poured forth a hymn of praise.[51] Now they come to the divine office and doze, they give themselves to idle and pernicious thoughts, they sit down to read but yawn at the book, they listen to the sermon but find it difficult to pay attention. They change from one pasture to another and they loathe the new as much as they did the old, continually trying new dishes of life and yet dying of hunger.[52]

After they have once experienced the delights and pleasing taste of heavenly sweetness, how does such forgetfulness and such unconcern for what is good make its stealthy assault? Whence this languor of spirit? Only the lament of the Psalmist is left, if indeed they have any desire to lament: "My heart is smitten like grass and withered; I forget to eat my bread."[53] They were well on the right track; who has beguiled them into changing their course? They began with the Spirit, how is it they are now ending with the flesh?[54] They feasted on dainties, how is it they now perish in the streets?[55]

5. I beseech such as these to beware lest the enemy who sows his cockle among the good seed of the master of the house[56]

---

47. Ezek 34:14.   48. Heb 6:4f.   49. Ps 44:2.   50. Ps 144:7.
51. Ps 118:171.

52. Guerric is here inveighing against what was undoubtedly not an altogether uncommon occurrence during the first Cistercian decades. Black Monks, perhaps without fully discerning what motivated them, would transfer to the more austere, and for the moment more popular observance of the White Monks, only soon to grow tepid in the new observance and not infrequently begin to think of another change. Bernard of Clairvaux treated this question extensively in his book, *On Precept and Dispensation*, 44ff.; Cistercian Fathers Series 1, pp. 138ff.

53. Ps 101:5.   54. Gal 3:3.   55. Lam 4:5.   56. Mt 13:24ff.

Sermon 38:5

tickle their palate, fresh from that sweet banquet of Christ, with his own poison and thus wipe out not only the desire but even the remembrance of the former sweetness.

Such people are condemned out of hand by the Apostle, who writes: "You cannot drink the cup of the Lord and the cup of demons, you cannot partake of the table of the Lord and the table of demons."[57] But does it not seem to you that the man who is carried away by the vehemence of lust, anger, impatience or similar passions has not so much drunk the cup of demons as become drunk with it? For myself, speaking of those things which are more habits than deliberate sins, I think that even that man is a partaker of the table of demons—he feeding with them, they feeding on him—whose mouth gives free rein to evil and whose tongue frames deceit. "He sits and speaks against his brothers and slanders his own mother's son."[58] Even if he does not actually spread malicious gossip, he freely listens to the detractor who provokes the guffaws of buffoons with his babbling vulgarity. Let him consider whether it is fitting that such a man as this, who has wallowed in the bloody sacrilege and foul doings of the demons, should afterwards be admitted to the table of Christ and his angels.

In speaking like this, my dear brethren, I do not mean to cast any aspersions on your innocence.[59] On the contrary that gives me the greatest pleasure. Your salvation is the sole reason for my words. Through such examples of other men may your caution increase, so that washing your hands in the blood of the wicked,[60] that grace of the Holy Spirit which others lose through their negligence you indeed may take good care to preserve with all due diligence to the praise and glory of the goodness of our Lord Jesus Christ, who lives and reigns through endless ages. Amen.

---

57. 1 Cor 10:21.   58. Ps 49:19f.

59. The harshness of the preceding passage is something unusual for Guerric. Therefore it is not surprising to find him concluding in an almost apologetic way with a note of kindness and encouragement.

60. Ps 57:11.

SERMON 39

THE SECOND SERMON FOR PENTECOST

"THE APOSTLES SPOKE of God's wonders in various tongues."[1] To be sure their tongues spoke from the abundance of their heart.[2] They exalted God with their mouth[3] for the love of God had been poured out in their hearts.[4] O Lord, my God, I would praise you likewise if I had likewise been given to drink. But because my soul is arid,[5] my tongue is inert. However, let my soul be filled as with marrow and fat and my mouth will give praise with lips that exult.[6] My lips will pour forth praise, provided you have taught me your statutes,[7] that is, when you have granted me to taste how sweet you are[8] that I may learn to love you with my whole heart, my whole soul, my whole strength.[9] You are good, and in your goodness teach me your statutes.[10] Your goodness is your anointing, by which you teach those of whom it was foretold that: "They will all be taught by God."[11] Blessed is the man whom you have instructed, Lord, and taught concerning your law.[12] The spotless law of the Lord, converting souls,[13] is charity. A law indeed of fire, which is in his right

---

1. This text, which is based on Acts 2:4, 11, is used as an antiphon at the office of vespers and also at none on the Feast of Pentecost. It is repeated during the great responsory at vespers and is also used as a versicle and response at the morning office of lauds.

2. Lk 6:45.	3. Ps 149:6.	4. Rom 5:5.	5. Num 11:6.
6. Ps 62:6.	7. Ps 118:171.	8. Ps 33:9.	9. Mk 12:30.
10. Ps 118:68.	11. Is 54:13; Jn 6:45.	12. Ps 93:12.	13. Ps 18:8.

Sermon 39:1-2

hand,[14] which is written on the breadth of the heart with God's finger[15] and sets the heart itself on fire with love, makes the mouth fervent with words of fire. From on high, we read, he cast fire into my bones and instructed me.[16]

With what ease and speed, with what abundance and richness that fire which the Lord Jesus cast on to the earth[17] not only instructed men who were ignorant but also freed them from their impediments. Tongues indeed of fire they were that that fire distributed from itself and they so set not only the minds but also the tongues of the Apostles on fire that even now the devout listener is set on fire by their word. A tongue indeed of fire was Peter's! A tongue of fire was Paul's! In their utterances there lives even now a perpetual fire which casts its sparks upon our hearts too if we draw near, if we do not turn our ears or our mind away from their words.

2. If I had been worthy to receive a tongue of this sort I too would say: "The Lord has given me a tongue as my reward and with it I will praise him";[18] as it is written of them: "The Apostles spoke of God's wonders in various tongues."[19] I would say, too, those words: "The Lord has given me a trained tongue, that I may know how to uphold with my word the man who has slipped."[20] The Apostles and those who are like them, with the tongues they have been given, proclaim God's wonders, scourge tyrants, beat devils, irrigate the earth, open the heavens, because their tongues have been made the keys of heaven[21]—for their tongues were sent to them from the very heavens.

As for myself, would that I had been given at least the tongue

---

14. Deut 33:2.

15. Mt 12:28, Lk 11:20. The Holy Spirit is called the finger of God from the juxtaposition of these two texts. *Dextrae Dei tu digitus* as is sung in the Pentecostal hymn *Veni Creator*.

16. Lam 1:13. It can be seen how the first paragraph of this sermon is a veritable mosaic of scriptural texts.

17. Lk 12:49. 18. Sir 51:30. 19. See note 1 above. 20. Is 50:4.

21. Mt 16:19; 18:18. This expression is taken from the antiphon sung with the canticle, *Benedictus,* at lauds on the feasts of two apostles.

of a dog with which I could lick my own sores first and then those of others,[22] if there are any who perhaps will let me do this for them. Blessed indeed are they whose heart is filled with joy and their mouth with jubilation by the love of and attachment to God's praise. But they too are blessed, I would say, who by licking away pus and discharge from the wounds of their soul imbibe that wherewith their soul will wax fat, the Spirit and grace. For they hunger and thirst after justice[23] and they suffer hunger like dogs,[24] they do not feel disgust for anything which they can absorb into their body, they reject no sinner whom they can convert to justice. "What God has made clean do you not call unclean,"[25] it was said to the Prince of the Apostles and, in his person, to the others; and therefore he slaughters and eats every kind of reptile and bird and says: "The things which previously my soul refused to touch are now my food in my straits, so impatient is my desire."[26] Indeed it is surprising how the more bitter a sinner is before his conversion, the sweeter his conversion is afterwards, and the more his salvation was despaired of, the more welcome it is to us. For we admire more the grace of his Savior who brings the lost sheep back on his shoulders and gives greater joy to the angels over one sinner doing penance than over ninety-nine just.[27]

3. Let others then, to whom it has been given, say: "How sweet are your words to my mouth, Lord."[28] But my soul, famished and suffering hunger like a dog,[29] will accept even what is bitter for sweet[30] and what is loathsome for desirable. Let others take pleasure in licking the honey of the Scriptures; I will take pleasure in licking the sores of sinners, my own, that is, and those of people who are like me. The sore of sin is ugly and disgusting to look at, yet what flavor and pleasure there is in licking it is only tasted and understood by one who is hungry for the salvation of those in danger, one who suffers hunger like a dog; of such it was said: "The tongues of your dogs have their portion from the foe."[31]

But woe to the wretches who are so set on their own perdition,

22. Lk 16:21. 23. Mt 5:6. 24. Ps 58:7. 25. Acts 10:15.
26. Cf. Job 6:7. 27. Lk 15:3ff. 28. Ps 118:103. 29. Ps 58:7.
30. Prov 27:7. 31. Ps 67:24.

so eager to inflict death upon themselves, that they cover up their wounds and fly from the ministrations of dogs, regarding the sharpness of the healing tongue as the bite of deadly hatred. They hate him who reproves at the gate and they loathe him who speaks perfectly.[32] When I say "who speaks perfectly" I mean not so much him who discourses of perfection as him who reproves with perfect love. But shall I say with perfect love or with perfect hatred? Both: with perfect love and with perfect hatred, since perfect hatred is nothing other than perfect love, and the perfection of both is one, which the Apostle defines in the words: "Hate evil, cling to good."[33]

4. However, let me return to that which was the starting-point of this digression. I was asking for a tongue with which to praise God, or at least a tongue with which I might care for the sores of those who confess their sins, seeking for myself in the one case the fruit of holy devotion, in the other the gain of my brethren's salvation; as far as you too are concerned, wishing to please in the one case, in the other to be of use. For concerning the art and duty of worldly poets one of them has said: "Poets wish either to be of profit or to give pleasure. He does best who mixes the useful with the pleasing."[34] I was asking, I say, for the grace of utterance with which I might serve God and you dutifully or make up to some extent by my words for the service I do not give by example.[35] Although I look askance at this consolation if I say without doing, if while my tongue makes its contribution my life lacks merit I have perhaps to be afraid rather lest God should say to me in my sins: "Why do you tell of my justice and discourse of my covenant with your mouth?"[36] But what am I to do? If I do not speak my pain will not be appeased, and if I keep silent it will not depart from me.[37] Fear harasses me in either case and I am hemmed in on both sides.[38] My position and my duty demand that I should speak,

32. Amos 5:10. 33. Rom 12:9.
34. Horace, *Ars poetica*, 333, 343; trans. E. Blakeney, *Horace on the Art of Poetry* (London: Scholastic Press, 1928), p. 54.
35. See above, Sermon 36:1. 36. Ps 49:16. 37. Job 16:7.
38. Phil 1:23.

my life contradicts what I say. But I remember the words which I found on the Wise Man's lips: "Let the soul of him who toils toil for himself, since his mouth has compelled him."³⁹ I will speak then, not as my position requires but as my understanding allows, or rather as the Lord grants, in whose hand are we and our utterances. I will speak, I say, and oblige myself by my own tongue, so that I am compelled eventually to toil for very shame. And if my body excuses me from manual labor, at least let the soul of him who toils toil for himself, that it may say with David: "I have toiled in my groaning."⁴⁰ Would that I were given those unspeakable groanings with which the Spirit intercedes for the saints that I might toil in them.⁴¹ Without any doubt the toil of such groanings would be ample compensation for my daily manual work.

5. But do you also, brethren, if you have learned to desire the better spiritual gifts,⁴² ask for such groanings to be given you by the Spirit. I do not know if there be in the gifts of the Spirit any other more fitting or more helpful to men who are encompassed with weakness and wretchedness. I do not know if to the Holy Spirit, who appeared as a dove,⁴³ any other accents are better known or more pleasing⁴⁴ than moaning. But this I do know, that in nothing we do are we so well provided with apt material as in our moaning and lament, unless our pride covers up our wretchedness or our feelings are hardened by senselessness or madness. Now this is the first effect of the Holy Spirit's healing operation in the weak souls whose care he takes upon himself, he who is our enlightening and our salvation,⁴⁵ that the madman comes to his senses and knows himself, and turned inwards upon himself tells the Lord with the Prophet: "After you converted me I did penance, and after you showed me I struck my hip."⁴⁶ For unless a man acquires knowledge he will not acquire sorrow,⁴⁷ unless he feels sorrow he does not deserve consolation. "Blessed are they who mourn, for they shall be comforted."⁴⁸

---

39. Prov 16:26.   40. Ps 6:7.   41. Rom 8:26.   42. 1 Cor 12.
43. Mt 3:16.   44. Is 59:11.   45. Ps 26:1.   46. Jer 31:19.
47. Eccles 1:18 (Septuagint).   48. Mt 5:5.

Not even in the Apostles, I think, would the Paraclete's consolation have found a place today, if they had not been mourning for themselves as abandoned; for it could not be that the sons of the Bridegroom would not mourn when the Bridegroom was taken away from them.[49] Hence it was that he told them: "Unless I go away the Paraclete will not come to you."[50] Unless you are abandoned by my bodily presence my spiritual visitation will not console you. "Give strong drink," we read, "to them that mourn and wine to them that are bitter in spirit,"[51] not, that is, to those who are drunk with the world's joy and luxury. For what has justice in common with iniquity?[52] Can they drink the cup of the Lord and the cup of devils?[53] Rather we read, "let them (the Apostles in their poverty) drink and forget their want;"[54] as if to say: "As in want, yet enriching many."[55] Let them drink in their grief at the Bridegroom's absence and be mindful of their sorrows no longer,[56] but say: "Although we have known Christ according to the flesh, now we know him so no longer."[57] You yourself also, if you can say with the Psalmist's devout affection: "I am poor and sorrowing,"[58] you will be so enriched, so gladdened by the sober inebriation of this excellent cup[59] that, although you are poor, poverty will not scorch your spirit. Although you grieved because you had sinned, the guilt of sin will no longer bite into your conscience.

6. Consider however if the Holy Spirit himself did not come into this world for judgment,[60] so that those who grieve should not grieve and those who laugh should deliver themselves over to eternal and inconsolable mourning. It is better then to go to a house of mourning than to a house of feasting.[61] And in fact, although the wise man sometimes deserves consolation so as to be mindful no longer of his sorrows, those, that is, for which he receives consolation, yet in order to make room for fresh consolations he is

49. Mt 9:15.   50. Jn 16:7.   51. Prov 31:6.   52. 2 Cor 6:14.
53. 1 Cor 10:20.   54. Prov 31:7.   55. 2 Cor 6:10.   56. Prov 31:7.
57. 2 Cor 5:16.   58. Ps 68:30.   59. Ps 22:5.   60. Jn 9:39.
61. Eccles 7:3.

always looking for fresh causes of sorrow in himself. He does not immediately flatter himself that he is just in all respects. But he more searchingly accuses and judges himself the more he has begun to be enlightened; the more strictly, the more he has begun to be justified.[62] To such a man, if I am not mistaken, the Spirit of consolation comes often, for he already anticipates his own coming; that is, he comes to accord consolation but he anticipates by teaching to mourn.

Devout and religious mourning occupies the first place and is outstanding in usefulness in the Spirit's teaching.[63] It is the highest wisdom of the saints, the safeguard of the just, the sobriety of the moderate, the first virtue of beginners, the spur of the proficient, the crown of the perfect, the salvation of those who are perishing, the harbor of those in danger: in a word it promises consolations in the present and joys in the future. To these may we be led by him who lives and reigns for ever and ever. Amen.

---

62. Prov 18:17.

63. "The monk's duty is not to teach but to mourn." St Jerome, *Against Vigilantius*, no. 15; PL 23, 351 B. St Bernard, *On the Song of Songs* 64:3. Cistercian Fathers Series, vol. 31.

SERMON 40

THE FIRST SERMON FOR ST JOHN BAPTIST

"AH, LORD GOD, behold I know not how to speak, for I am only a youth."[1] Brethren, if Jeremiah, as you heard from yesterday's lesson, in order to avoid the office of preaching, more modestly than rightly put forward his youth as an excuse, how much more would I not be entitled to put forward my lack of understanding? If one who was holy from the womb and clearly sent by God's own choice[2] was deterred by his lack of years, how can I dare to speak when my conscience does not assure me of any holiness and I have no knowledge to make speech flow? He was afraid of his youth; shall I not fear my puerility? Yet, you, Child, Prophet of the Most High,[3] in honor of whom our position makes it a duty to deliver a sermon today,[4] do not allow our puerility to be excused from making the attempt at least, after the fashion of children, to lisp out something or other, we who even when the matter is of less moment have not learned yet to form complete words. It will be for you, Voice of the Word, Voice of Wisdom, to loose the bonds of the tongue which is dedicated to you. Before

---

1. Jer 1:6. As Guerric indicates, this quotation is taken from the reading at the mass on the vigil of the Feast of St John the Baptist. It is also repeated during the readings of the night office for the Feast itself.

2. Jer 1:5.   3. Lk 1:76.

4. The Feast of St John the Baptist was one of those feasts which the early Cistercians called a Feast of Sermon, on which the abbot was expected to address the whole community. See below, Sermon 49, note 2, p. 179.

you could speak you were able to restore the power of speech to your father.[5]

Neither was it without great profit that the suspended ability to speak came back; for it brought with it the grace of prophecy, so that both parents rejoiced that they had been granted some share in their son's privilege.

2. For he who was to be a prophet and more than a prophet,[6] indeed had begun to prophesy before he could speak, to be conscious of God before he was conscious of himself. He also made his parents prophets and imbued them with the abundance of his spirit and his grace, those who had transmitted to him the substance of his flesh. Elizabeth, after the child exulted with joy in her womb,[7] then prophesied herself, filled as she was with the Holy Spirit,[8] for her son, who could not yet speak, revealed to his mother by his manifest exultation the hidden presence of the Lord. He greeted the Savior with what movement he could and, eager Forerunner as he was, strove to break out to meet the Lord.

Truly an incomparable grace, inestimable power of God's might. As Mary's voice sounds in Elizabeth's ears[9] it penetrates to John's heart where he lies hidden within his mother's womb, gives life to his spirit and feeds him with salutary joy. Although the power of nature had as yet scarcely finished imparting his soul, the power of Mary's voice imparts the gift of prophecy in all its fullness, so that it seems to be communicated abundantly to the mother from the son's fullness. In truth Mary was full of grace.[10] The God of all grace was clearly in her, when from his liberality grace's generous gift flowed both abundantly and magnificently into his mother in the first place, from his mother into John, from John into his parents. Rivers indeed of living water flowed from Mary's bosom.[11]

---

5. Zachary, John the Baptist's father, had been deprived of his speech as a punishment for his lack of faith when the angel Gabriel announced to him the forthcoming conception and birth of his son. His speech was restored after the birth of his son (Lk 1:64). Here Guerric attributes that restoration to John himself.

6. Mt 11:9. 7. Lk 1:44. 8. Lk 1:41.
9. Lk 1:44. 10. Lk 1:28. 11. Jn 7:38.

A fountain of life and grace rose from the midst of Paradise to water the trees of Paradise.[12]

3. Near to the fountain was this noble cedar, John, the Bridegroom's cousin and friend,[13] the Lord's Forerunner, Baptist and Martyr; and thus watered more copiously he grew to such a height that no one among those born of women could be found more lofty than he.[14] Indeed he was near to the Savior, not only by ties of blood and intimate friendship, but also more than others by the glory of his annunciation, the novelty of his birth, his holiness even before birth, his preaching so similar, his authority to baptize, his strength in suffering. If all else were lacking, if all the oracles of the prophets were silent concerning him, the grace of his name alone, which was given by the angel before he was conceived in the womb,[15] would be enough to bear ample witness to the grace of God which would be in him.

It was fitting, to be sure, that the Grace of God, brought forth by a woman who was full of grace, should be proclaimed by a man full of grace; that he should be distinguished by outstanding grace who marked off like a boundary the time of grace from the time of the Law. For up to John the Law and the prophets prophesied;[16] he was the first to manifest the presence of the one whom the Law and prophecy had promised would come.

4. Rightly then did the birth of this child make many rejoice then[17] and does make many rejoice today: born in the old age of his parents[18] he was to preach the grace of rebirth to an aging world. Rightly does the Church solemnly venerate this birth which is wonderfully brought about by grace and at which nature wonders—especially since it sees that through this birth it has been given trustworthy pledges of that unique birth whose grace restored nature. The Church proves itself not ungrateful, not unmindful; faithfully it acknowledges with what devotion, what thanksgiving it ought to welcome the Forerunner through whom it recognized the Savior himself.

12. Gen 2:6, 10.   13. Jn 3:29.   14. Mt 11:11.   15. Lk 1:13; 2:21.
16. Mt 11:13; Lk 16:16.   17. Lk 1:14.   18. Lk 1:18.

To me certainly the birth of the world's Lamp[19] brings fresh joy, for it enabled me to recognize the true Light shining in the darkness but not mastered by the darkness.[20] His birth brings me a joy utterly unspeakable, for so many outstanding benefits accrue to the world through it. He is the first to give the Church instruction, to initiate it by penance, to prepare it by baptism. When it is prepared he delivers it to Christ and unites it with him. He both trains it to live temperately and, by his own death, gives it the strength to die with fortitude. In all these ways he prepares for the Lord a perfect people.[21]

5. O brethren, you whose profession it is, and indeed whose desire it is also, to hasten to perfection, how quickly Christian perfection is attained by the man who has followed this master with a docile mind. The first elements of his justice surpassed the measure of human perfection, his first steps in earliest childhood outshone the gravity of old age's wisdom. Since he was holy before he was born, is it surprising that as his life progressed in its course he became more than holy?

We can wonder at your holiness, most holy among the saints, but we cannot imitate it. It is altogether necessary that, as you hasten to prepare for the Lord a perfect people out of publicans and sinners,[22] you should speak to them more accommodatingly than you live and define the measure of perfection not in accordance with your own rule of life but in accordance with the possibilities of the common run of men. "Bring forth worthy fruits of repenance,"[23] he says.

Our boast, brethren, is that we speak more perfectly than we live; whereas John, though living on a higher level than men can even understand, speaks to them in accordance with what they can take in. "Bring forth worthy fruits of repentance,"[24] he says. "I speak to you humanely because of the weakness of your nature.[25] If there is no room in you as yet for the plenitude of all good things, at least be truly sorry for all your evils. If you are unable as yet to

---

19. Jn 5:35.   20. Jn 1:5.   21. Lk 1:27.   22. Lk 1:17.
23. Lk 3:8.   24. *Ibid.*   25. Rom 6:19.

Sermon 40 : 5-6

bring forth the fruits of perfect justice, let this be your perfection for the moment, to bring forth worthy fruits of repentance."

6. If we wish to recall yesterday's lesson, brethren, what was said to Jeremiah, or rather to John under the figure of Jeremiah, applies to the worthy fruits of repentance: ". . . that you may pluck out and break down and destroy and overthrow;" and to the fruits of justice: ". . . that you may build up and plant."[26] Blessed is he who helps the hand of this extirpator, for he is God's helper: he cooperates with God's word and grace and devotes all his attention and energy to the task of plucking out and destroying from his affections and his behavior every plant that his heavenly Father has not planted,[27] breaking down and overthrowing every building of Babylonian pride and confusion, so that afterwards he may the better build up and plant and there may come about what was written: "The bricks have fallen, but we will build with dressed stones. The sycamores have been cut down, but we will put cedars in their place.[28] Instead of the thorn shall come up the cypress, and instead of the brier the myrtle."[29] All the beauty and grace of virtues shall replace the uncultivated squalor of vices.

Who, do you think, among us is so perfect as to have at least this beginning of perfection? Who is so worthily and perfectly repentant, condemning with the utmost rigor the evil deeds which he has done, renouncing his former vices of whatever description? Who plucks out by the roots and destroys from the field of his heart every weed of malediction, so that no poisonous root is allowed to bear its bitter fruit?[30] Who once and for all breaks down and overthrows every height that raises itself up against Christ's humility,[31] so as not to build up again what he has broken down?

How happy the church of the saints would be today, with what peace and graciousness the congregations of the blessed poor would flourish, if the repentance of the uncultivated or the justice of those who wish to seem perfect and holy were to yield the fruits which they ought. However, let us who have neither the justice of the holy

26. Jer 1:10.   27. Mt 15:13.   28. Is 9:10.   29. Is 55:13.
30. Deut 29:18; Heb 12:15.   31. 2 Cor 10:5.

nor the repentance which is shown by sinners, compensate at least partially for our lukewarmness by devout veneration of the saints, especially blessed John, whose holiness flowered so magnificently above the measure of others that he might be considered the saint of saints. Let us speak of and meditate on the glorious splendor of his holiness,[32] my brethren, that he may render propitious to our sins[33] him whose friend he especially merited to be, the Son of God, who lives and reigns with the Father and the Holy Spirit for ever and ever. Amen.

---

32. Ps 144:5. 33. Ps 78:9.

SERMON 41

THE SECOND SERMON FOR ST JOHN BAPTIST

"SINCE THE DAYS OF JOHN THE BAPTIST the kingdom of heaven suffers violence and the violent are even now seizing it."[1] Rightly therefore are we glad at his birth whose advent is so auspicious that the kingdom of God is henceforward open to be seized by us whose justice did not suffice to merit it. Rightly so many rejoice in his birth, as the angel promised;[2] he brought with him so happy a change in the condition of the times that the kingdom of God, previously not to be won by all the justice of the innocent, is now invaded and possessed by the violence of the repentant. For what else ought the repentance of sinners to be called but violence done to the kingdom of heaven? Is it not violence to seize by virtue what had not been granted to nature, so that men who were by nature sons of wrath[3] and hell should by dint of unremitting toil, which is all-conquering, make an entry for themselves into the inheritance of the saints and the fellowship of glory?

Did not the untiring wrestler, the patriarch Jacob, do violence to God? As it is written, he was strong against God and prevailed, wrestled with him until morning perseveringly and with all his might held fast to him when he asked to be let go. "I will not let you go," he said, "unless you bless me."[4] I say that he wrestled with God, for God was in the angel with whom he wrestled. Otherwise the angel would not say: "Why do you ask for my

---

1. Mt 11:12.   2. Lk 1:14.   3. Eph 2:3.   4. Gen 32:23ff.

name? It is wonderful;"⁵ and Jacob would not say: "I have seen the Lord face to face."⁶ Nor again would the Lord say of Jacob, through the prophet Hosea: "At Bethel he spoke with us."⁷ It was a good sort of violence then that extorted a blessing; happy the wrestling in which God yielded to man and the vanquished rewarded the victor with the grace of a blessing and the honor of a holier name. What if he touched the sinew of his thigh and it withered, and so he went limping?⁸ A man will readily sacrifice his body and soon be comforted for the harm done when it is compensated for by such a gift, especially the man who could say: "I have loved wisdom more than health and all beauty."⁹ Would that not only the sinew of my thigh but the strength of my whole body would wither, provided I might win but one blessing from an angel. Would that I might not only limp with Jacob but also die with Paul¹⁰ so as to obtain the grace and name of Israel¹¹ as an everlasting gift. Jacob bears a withered hip, but Paul a dead body, because the mortification of the body's members¹² begun by the first practices of the Prophets was brought to completion by the Gospel. Jacob goes limping, because in part his thoughts dwell on the things of the world while his other foot he bears raised up from the earth. Paul's thoughts dwell only on the things of God¹³ whether in the body or out of the body I know not, God knows; he is wholly free in spirit and flies up to heaven.¹⁴

2. So to you, brethren, we say, you whose set purpose it is to win heaven by force, you who have come together to wrestle with the angel who guards the way to the tree of life,¹⁵ to you we say: it is wholly necessary that you should wrestle perseveringly and without remission, not only until the thigh from which the flesh propagates itself is deprived of its vigor but also until the body is mortified. But your toil will be able to achieve this only by the touch of God's strength and through his bounty, that is, when

5. Gen 32:29.
6. Gen 32:30.
7. Hos 12:4.
8. Gen 32:25, 31.
9. Wis 7:10.
10. Phil 1:21.
11. Gen 32:28.
12. 2 Cor 4:10.
13. 1 Cor 7:34.
14. 2 Cor 12:3f.
15. Gen 3:24.

he has proved that he cannot overcome your perseverance. For so it is written: "When he saw that he could not overcome him he touched the sinew of his thigh and at once it withered."[16] Do you not seem to yourself to be wrestling with an angel, or rather with God himself, when day by day he resists your impatient prayers? You wash as if with snow water to be clean in heart and in body and he plunges you in filth.[17] You say: "I will be made wise," and Wisdom withdraws further from you.[18] You cry to him and he does not listen to you;[19] you wish to approach him and he repels you. You make a decision and the opposite happens; and so in every way he sets himself against you with unrelenting hand.

O Mercy, you conceal yourself and pretend to be unrelenting. With what loving kindness you fight against those for whom you fight. For although you hide these things in your heart, I know that you love those who love you[20] and that the abundance of your sweetness which you hide away for those who fear you is immense.[21] Do not despair then, persevere, happy soul, that have begun to wrestle with God; he loves to suffer violence from you, he desires to be overcome by you. For when he is angry and stretches forth his hand to strike, he seeks, as he himself confesses, a man like Moses to resist him;[22] and if he does not find one he complains and says: "There is no one to rise up and hold me."[23] For if his anger is implacable and his sentence unbending, Jeremiah, who had attempted to resist, will weep and say: "You were the stronger and did prevail."[24]

3. But God forbid, brethren, God forbid that he who willed to become weak, and even to die for you, will be strong against you who ask for what is pleasing to him. He has been pierced with so many wounds, his whole body has suffered crucifixion; from where can he draw strength to resist that charity which led him, as if conquered and a prisoner, through every kind of weakness even to death, death on a cross?[25] No longer is love as strong as death,[26]

16. Gen 32:25.   17. Job 9:30f.   18. Eccles 7:24.   19. Job 30:20.
20. Job 10:13; Prov 8:17.   21. Ps 30:20.   22. Ezek 22:30.
23. Is 64:7.   24. Jer 20:7.   25. Phil 2:28.   26. Song 8:6.

but stronger than death, since God's strength through the power of his love has been made weak unto death. Yet his weakness has been found stronger than all the strongest, his death has been proved to be your death, O death.[27]

Be armed then with the power of love, whoever you are who in your devotion would force an entry into the kingdom of heaven and make it your prize; and be assured that you will easily conquer the King of heaven himself. If he seems to oppose you with difficulties or hardness, do not be fainthearted but understand what his purpose is in so acting. By the very contradiction he seeks to give a finer edge to your spirit, as the nature of the magnanimous and the strong is wont to be; he seeks to exercise your forces, to prove your constancy, to multiply your victories and increase your crowns.

4. Wherefore gird yourselves, sons of Israel, and show how strong you are.[28] All you need is magnanimity and constancy, which cannot be frightened by any opposition. Let the weak say: "I am strong;" and for the joy of his hope let him not know himself to be weak when he can immediately make heaven his own with such ease. Truly that man takes heaven by violence who does violence to his own infirmity or age. Or rather, to speak more precisely, he does violence to his own perdition who cannot spare himself when the trumpet sounds the order. For, as Scripture says: "In his toil a man toils for himself and does violence to his own perdition."[29]

Gird yourselves, I say, men of strength; and follow the leader and master of this happy warfare—I mean John the Baptist—from whose days heaven begins to be open to force. He it is who, like another David, has become a prince of robbers[30] and a leader of devout bandits, and using that laudable and holy violence he has led that victorious army of publicans and sinners after himself into the kingdom of heaven. For who is the criminal or the man of the world who heard his trumpet: "Do penance, for the kingdom of

---

27. Hos 13:14.   28. 1 Mac 3:58.   29. Prov 16:26 (Septuagint).
30. 1 Kings 11:24.

heaven is at hand,"[31] and did not at once prepare himself for war? Follow, I say, this leader, whose standards are red with his own blood, whose feats and triumphs you have sung today with due veneration. He, if I am not mistaken, will help by his merits and commend by his intercession those whom he has drawn after himself by his example, since among those born of women[32] no one is more pleasing to the King on high, Jesus Christ our Lord, who lives and reigns for ever and ever. Amen.

31. Mt 3:2.   32. Mt 11:11.

SERMON 42

THE THIRD SERMON FOR ST JOHN BAPTIST

"AMONG THOSE BORN OF WOMEN there has not arisen one greater than John the Baptist."[1] Solomon says: "Let it be your neighbor's lips that praise you."[2] But how much happier and more glorious when a man is praised by the lips of his God. For God can neither be deceived nor can he flatter. God does not easily praise anyone whom he sees may be puffed up by praise or whom from his end he foresees will have to be damned. Man is rightly told not to praise a man during his life[3] since he can neither know what is within him nor foreknow his end and he must confess on his own account: "My conscience does not reproach me, but that is not where my justification lies."[4] For there are men just and wise and their works are in the hand of God; and yet no one knows whether he deserves love or hatred, all things are kept in uncertainty for the future.[5] Happy then is he who merits to know by the witness of the Judge himself that he is worthy of love, except that the witness of present justice does not take away from human changeableness suspicion and fear in regard to the future. Yet it is an indubitable token of outstanding virtue and great perfection when that judgment of God which no one

---

1. Mt 11:11. These words of our Lord are quite naturally employed with some frequency in the Office for this Feast: the great responsory at the first vespers, the twelfth responsory at the night office, the antiphon at sext, as well as a versicle and response at that hour and also at the second nocturn of the night office.
2. Prov 27:2.   3. Sir 11:30.   4. 1 Cor 4:4.   5. Eccles 9:1f.

can withstand finds a man, still subject to corruption, worthy to receive his praise.

Truly those words of Supreme Justice to Noah are no mean commendation of justice: "I have seen that you are just in my presence."[6] It is a mark of great merit that God declares to Abraham that on his account the promises that were made to him are to be fulfilled.[7] But what a proud boast is that which the Lord makes of blessed Job against the Enemy: "Have you considered my servant Job, how there is not his like upon the earth; a man simple and upright, fearing God and avoiding evil?"[8] What a favor it was also that on Moses' account he strove with and confounded his rivals: "If there be a prophet of the Lord among you," he says, "I will appear to him in a vision or speak to him in a dream. But not such is my servant Moses, who is most faithful in all my house. For I speak to him face to face and he sees God openly, not in riddles. Why therefore did you not fear to speak against my servant Moses?"[9] But who among them all is like David, of whom the Lord rejoices that he has found a man according to his own heart.[10]

2. Yet however great these or any others may have been, neither among these nor among other men born of women, as he declares who was born of a virgin, has there arisen one greater than John the Baptist.[11] For although star differs from star in brightness,[12] and in the choir of the holy constellations which enlightened the night of this world before the rising of the true Sun some shone forth with a wonderful brightness, none was greater or more splendid than this Morning Star, the burning and shining Lamp[13] which the Father prepared for his Christ.[14] He is the Morning Star that anticipates the light, the Forerunner of the Sun, proclaiming to mortals that the day is at hand, crying out to those who sleep in darkness and the shadow of death:[15] "Do penance; for the kingdom of heaven is near."[16] As if to say: "The night has passed away, day is

---

6. Gen 7:1.   7. Gen 17; 22:17f.   8. Job 1:18.   9. Num 12:6ff.
10. 1 Kings 13:14; Acts 15:22.   11. Mt 11:11.   12. 1 Cor 15:41.
13. Jn 5:35.   14. Ps 131:17.   15. Ps 106:10; Lk 1:79.
16. Mt 3:3.

at hand; cast away the works of darkness.[17] Rise up, you who sleep, and arise from the dead, and Christ will enlighten you."[18]

3. It is not to be lightly passed over, but to be pondered again and again, how lofty in merit, how excelling in grace and virtue that eye, which nothing deceives, discerned him to be. After such commendation of those who went before, this was the judgment he gave on him, that among those born of women no one had arisen greater than he, and that no one was to take precedence over him who did not belong to the order of angels or had not reached equality with the angels. Neither was it on a single occasion or perfunctorily or briefly that he praised him, but as often as he had occasion to speak of him he took pleasure in dwelling on his praises, as the Gospel narrative demonstrates clearly enough.

Therefore Mark also and Luke and John dedicated the beginning of their books to his praises, in order that the authority of so great a name occurring at the outset might make the whole Gospel which follows the more acceptable. The Lamp burning and shining[19] at the very entrance and in the porch might lead to the Light which was shining in the darkness but could not be mastered by the darkness.[20] Matthew, preoccupied with the Lord's birth in the beginning of his Gospel, as soon as he had brought the Child of Nazareth to be reared, turns his pen to his Forerunner and Baptist,[21] regarding as incomplete whatever he might say of the Bridegroom if he kept silence concerning the Bridegroom's inseparable friend.[22]

This concern ranked high not only for the evangelists in their narrative but also for the prophets and angels in their predictions. The Lamp of Christ, the Witness of the Lord, should be presented in such a light as easily to confound his enemies by his splendor and authority and clearly to demonstrate the incomparable greatness of the Most High by his own greatness. For when the greatest among those born of women declared that he who was born of a virgin so far surpassed him (he confessed himself unworthy to carry his shoes[23]), what was to be deduced? That he was the great

17. Rom 13:12.   18. Eph 4:15.   19. Jn 5:35.   20. Jn 1:5.
21. Mt 3.   22. Jn 3:29.   23. Mt 3:11.

Sermon 42:3-4

Lord whose greatness is not to end,[24] the one of whom it is said: "Who in the clouds shall be compared to the Lord? Who will be like him among the sons of God?"[25]

And this was John's greatness, in virtue of which he reached such heights of greatness among the great that he crowned his great and countless virtues, in which he was second to no mortal man, with the greatest of all the virtues, humility. Reckoned as he was the highest of all, he freely and with the greatest devotion preferred to himself the Most Lowly One—and he put him before himself to such an extent as to declare himself unworthy to take off his shoes.

4. Let others wonder that he was foretold by prophets,[26] that he was promised by an angel and the same angel as Christ (although Christ was promised only in an inner room, John in an oracle in the Temple[27]), that he came of so holy and noble parents,[28] that he was given to aged and sterile parents against the laws of nature by a gift of grace,[29] that he was holy before he was born, a prophet before he prophesied,[30] that he was more than a prophet because he was an angel, with an angel's function[31] and living an angelic life on earth, in the flesh and yet transcending the flesh, and although wholly innocent yet exhibiting a pattern of penance more by his example than by his word,[32] that he preceded the coming of the Redeemer in the spirit and power of Elijah[33] and prepared his way in the desert,[34] that he converted the hearts of fathers to their sons and of sons to their fathers,[35] that he merited to baptize the Son, to hear the Father and to see the Holy Spirit,[36] finally that he strove for the truth even to death and, so that he might go before Christ also to the lower regions, was Christ's martyr before Christ's passion.[37]

Let others, I say, wonder at these things, provided there is anyone worthy to wonder; what is set before us, brethren, not only to be wondered at but also to be imitated, is the virtue of his humility,

---

24. Ps 144:3.
25. Ps 88:7.
26. Is 40:3; Mal 3:1.
27. Lk 1:13ff.; 31ff.
28. Lk 1:5f.
29. Lk 1:7, 18.
30. Lk 1:44.
31. Mal 3:1; Mt 11:9f.
32. Mt 3:1ff.
33. Mal 4:5; Lk 1:17.
34. Mal 3:1; Is 40:3; Mt 3:3.
35. Mal 4:6; Lk 1:17.
36. Lk 3:21f.
37. Mt 14:3ff.

by which he refused to be regarded as greater than he was, although he could have been, but rather to the best of his ability corrected those who did so regard him lest they should be mistaken.[38] For as a faithful friend of the Bridegroom,[39] a lover more of the Lord than of himself, he wished that he himself might diminish in order that Christ might grow[40] and made it his business to increase Christ's glory by means of his own diminution. Before St Paul he made his own in act and in truth those words of the Apostle: "We do not preach ourselves but the Lord Jesus Christ."[41]

Therefore great is his glory in your salvation,[42] in your Jesus, Lord, to whose justice and goodness it belongs to love those who love him[43] and to glorify those who glorify him. Great indeed is his glory in Jesus, great is it from Jesus, who glorified him with himself by giving him a share in his own glory and with men by the witness of his voice. John was convinced of the Wise Man's trustworthy advice: "Let him who boasts boast in the Lord; for it is not the man who commends himself who is approved but the man whom God commends."[44] So he preferred to boast in the Lord rather than vainly in himself; because he preferred also to be commended truthfully by the Lord rather than deceitfully by himself. Therefore he has been approved by God and by men[45] and his glory is truth with men, happiness with God. If he had glorified himself his glory would be nil.

5. "O sons of men, how long will you be dull of heart? Why do you love vanity and seek after falsehood?"[46] Why do you love vain and deceitful glory and receive or seek glory from one another, while you will have none of the glory which comes from God alone?[47] But how do you seek? Would that it were by doughty actions, not by lofty words; would that it were by speaking the truth, although in vain, and not by lying; would that it were by lying only about yourselves and not also by detracting from others. This is no longer to receive or accept glory but rather to steal and

38. Jn 3:28ff.   39. Jn 3:29.   40. Jn 3:30.   41. 2 Cor 4:5.
42. Ps 20:6.   43. Prov 8:17.   44. 2 Cor 10:17f.
45. Rom 12:17; 2 Cor 8:21.   46. Ps 4:3.   47. Jn 5:44.

rob it. For to seek glory not in the way proper to it but by a way opposed to it, that is, by the way to which not glory but ignominy is due, not staking a lawful claim by virtue but stealing by falsehood and detraction, what else is this but criminally to rob that which you covet evilly? To be sure if you did not seek glory from man[48] but accepted it when it was offered, on this account you would already not be walking according to the truth. But now what shall we say, when you not only accept it if it is offered to you but seek it when it is not offered? What shall we say when you cut someone else to pieces, so to speak, with your poisonous and insidious tongue in order to seize on his glory for yourself, so that you may appear the better through the evil spoken of him, the more honored through the contempt in which he is held? Let us then regard the former pattern of behavior, the accepting or seeking of glory from man, as the vanity of fools; as for the latter, what is it but the cruelty of savages? If the one, to put it mildly, is a temptation such as befalls mankind, what is the other but imitation of the devil? Truly those who are on the side of the devil, that is, all the proud, imitate him. For he is king over all the sons of pride.[49]

6. How do they imitate him, you ask? The devil, because he waxed proud, envied one better than himself, that is, God; because he envied him he detracted from him. So as soon as the sons of pride are infected with his vice, that is, with the love of their own excellence, they envy the excellence of others. When they begin to envy they will begin to detract, if they can, so that what they take away from others may accrue to themselves. How much more wholesome it would be if they imitated John's humility, who detracted from himself to add to another, who strove to be regarded as less important than he was regarded in order that another might begin to appear what he was not judged to be.[50]

Finally, if humility does not attract by virtue of its own worth and justice, let it attract at least by its usefulness, for there is no straighter or easier way to the glory which is of God nor any finer or more just way to favor with men, and often there is none which

---

48. 1 Thess 2:6.   49. Job 41:25.   50. Lk 3:14f.

leads more quickly to the desired result. "The greater you are," we read, "humble yourself in all things, and you will find favor before God and men."[51] This it was that glorified John with God and men, just as this day made glorious by his birth affords consolation to the world, joy to heaven, and glory to God, to whom be honor and glory for ever and ever. Amen.

---

51. Sir 3:20.

SERMON 43

THE FOURTH SERMON FOR ST JOHN BAPTIST

"JESUS BEGAN TO ASK THE CROWDS concerning John: 'What did you go out to see in the desert?'"[1] Behold what the Bride boasts of concerning the Bridegroom in the Canticle of their love: "I to my beloved and my beloved to me,"[2] so John to Jesus and Jesus to John. John proclaims Jesus; Jesus commends John. Like is returned for like and in an interchange as friendly as it is just, charity for one another is stimulated or rewarded. "For," Jesus says, "I love those who love me[3] and I will glorify those who glorify me."[4] Holiness promises well both for this life and for the next.[5] The Lord even now begins to glorify his beloved by giving him praise, and he will glorify him in the future by giving him his reward, raising his witness to high honor among men by his own witness to him.

"What did you go out into the desert to see?" he asks. You wonder at a man dwelling in the desert; but through him the beautiful places of the desert will grow fertile and the solitude will bloom when everywhere, following John's example, a new race of men will grow up who make the desert their home. Then the desert will be like Paradise in its delights and solitude like the garden of the Lord.[6] Then the glory of Lebanon will be given to it, the beauty of Carmel and Saron.[7]

But what, I say, did you go out to see in the desert? A reed

---

1. Mt 11:7.   2. Song 6:2.   3. Prov 8:17.   4. 1 Sam 2:30.
5. 1 Tim 4:8.   6. Is 51:3.   7. Is 35:2.

trembling in the wind?[8] Although he dwells in the desert he is not a reed of the desert but a cedar of Paradise, a column of heaven, the glory of the human race, the wonder of the world, by virtue and merit surpassing the measure of men, only by his mortal condition falling short of the nature of angels.

2. He is not a reed trembling in the wind but a palm stronger than every storm, which no tempestuous wind can shake, or rather a cypress planted eternally on Mount Sion,[9] too high to fear the raging of winds. He is not affected by the storms of our atmosphere because he rises above all the desires of the world. He has fixed his root in heaven, where not a breath of any gale blows, from where free from fear he can laugh at the threats and the battling of the winds and all the world's adversities.

Let Herod be angry, Herodias lay traps. From within them let the tempest seethe and let the evil storm wind[10] which lurks in the depths of their hearts bring into play all its forces and all the resources of malice; nothing will frighten him, nothing will move him from his judgment or prevent him from condemning their incestuous marriage.[11] For how should adversity bend the man whom prosperity could not soften? There was a time when soft and caressing winds, the breezes of popularity, did blow;[12] but not even by these could he be turned aside from his rectitude.

"You sent to John, and he bore witness to the truth."[13] For the Jews sent priests and Levites to question him: "Who are you?" And he acknowledged, without concealment: "I am not the Christ"[14]—even though popularity was enticing him and the general opinion coaxing him not to declare himself the Christ, but only not to contradict those who believed him so to be.

On another occasion too, when his disciples told him: "Master, behold he to whom you bore witness is baptizing and everyone is coming to him,"[15] could he be shaken by this wind or moved to grief or envy because he was abandoned while another was being sought by the crowds and receiving honor? Rather driving back

---

8. Mt 11:7. 9. Sir 24:17. 10. Ps 10:7. 11. Mt 14:3f.
12. Lk 3:15. 13. Jn 5:33. 14. Jn 1:19f. 15. Jn 3:25f.

the wind and breaking it with immovable constancy he answered: "You yourselves bear witness to me that I said: 'I am not the Christ.' I have been sent to go before him."[16]

3. "But what did you go out to see? A man clad in soft garments?"[17] He had praised him for his constancy of spirit; now he praises him for his contempt of the body; and last of all for the supreme excellence of the grace which made him a prophet[18] and the dignity of his angelic office and name.[19] For these are the two stages by which man's lowliness climbs to things spiritual and divine: immovable perseverance in the face of the temptations which assail him like winds, and mortification of the body out of desire for the good things of the spirit. As the body is to be chastised[20] at the beginning so that sin may not reign in it[21] and we may overcome temptations, so too when the temptations have been overcome we must persevere in the same practices not only for fear of falling back but also out of desire for progress. Thus through the mortification of the flesh the spirit may thrive the better and, the lighter and more slender the fetters which attach it, the more freely it may rise to spiritual things. John, who had been sanctified before he came forth from the womb,[22] who could apply to himself the words: "Holiness grew up with me from my infancy, it came forth from my mother's womb with me,"[23] whom no wind of temptation could shake, was for all that not clad in soft garments nor did he feed on delicacies, well aware that just as sinners need a rather strict rule of life to become holy so the holy need it to become more holy.

But now thanks be to God who has given us—if in fact he has—victory without a battle, pardon without repentance, justification without good works, holiness without toil, an abundance of the delights of the flesh and of the spirit at the same time. Our clothes, if not of purple and lawn, are certainly softer and warmer than purple and lawn; we feast splendidly every day; and shall we none-

---

16. Jn 3:28.
17. Mt 11:8.
18. Mt 11:9.
19. Mt 11:10; Mal 3:1.
20. 1 Cor 9:27.
21. Rom 6:12.
22. Jer 1:5.
23. Job 31:18.

theless, replete as we are and belching for surfeit, sleep with the once poor Lazarus in Abraham's bosom,[24] or rather in Christ's bosom together with John?[25]

Truly, if it is so, we have been treated better than they were who bought at the price of such labors what we in our luxury possess gratis. Truly if it is so John's life should be laughed at rather than preached; and it would be more fitting to reject than to imitate the whole race of God's sons[26] who have followed the Only-begotten of the Father by the hard and narrow way.

4. It seems more probable however that it is not so, but that rather, as Truth says, it behooves us to enter the kingdom of God through many tribulations,[27] and, as the Disciple of Truth tells us, that a widow who lives in luxury is dead.[28] Therefore when the Lord had praised the friend who was most faithful in all his house for the roughness of his garments he said: "Behold, they who are clad in soft garments are in the houses of kings."[29] By this he meant that those who make the pleasures of the flesh their quest are enrolled in the kingdom of this world, not the kingdom of God. Alas, what a terrible sentence I have heard from heaven against the softness of that great purple-clad harlot: "Requite her with anguish and sorrow for all her pride and luxury."[30]

Would that the tenderness of delicate souls were content with only these pleasures of soft garments and tasty food, and that the thornbush of voluptuousness did not produce other thorny vices. Would that their sin were only indulgence in pleasure and not a wallowing in luxury. It is for them to consider whether that pestiferous fire which is native to us has been so far put out in them that it cannot be kindled again for all the tinder which is applied to it, especially when winds blow in such a way as to fan it, the winds of wanton words and laughter with their temptations. Yet I usually hear that it is often alive even in a dying man, flourishes in an old man, comes to life and blazes up even without any tinder, rages without any provocation.

---

24. Lk 16:19ff. 25. Jn 13:23. 26. Ps 72:15. 27. Acts 14:21.
28. St Paul: 1 Tim 5:6.   29. Mt 11:8.   30. Rev 18:7.

It is for themselves to consider then; it is no business of mine to pass judgment on other people's consciences.[31] I know that many people have lived temperately and modestly in the midst of an abundance of worldly possessions and glory, while many too have behaved evilly whose garments were rougher and whose food more sparing. But I know also that a king of Israel wore a hair-shirt next to his skin under his purple robes,[32] and that kings have sometimes been given bread and nothing else to eat; whereas today the garb of penitents, or rather of those who make a show of penance, is a cloak for the finest and softest of clothes, while their dainty appetites cannot be satisfied with all the resources of the world, all the arts and concoctions of their cooks.[33]

However, since in cases of this sort everyone easily finds an advocate to plead for him: one man his weakness, another the company to which he has to accommodate himself, another the position of honor which he seeks or is already his—let it be so. Let them dress as they will, eat as they will, provided that the evil does not go to further excesses and reach the point where people refuse to admit what they want to do because they cannot defend it. Here there applies the proverb of the bad woman who eats and, wiping her mouth, says: "I have done no evil."[34] As for the great Babylon from the midst of which these delicate penitents seemed to have gone forth, I would make bold to say of it: "Let it be clad in purple as much as it likes, let it be as delicate as it likes, only let it not be a harlot and spread its feet wide to every passer-by."[35]

5. You then, brother, if you cannot imitate John in the roughness of his garments or in his sparing diet, strive at least to imitate him in this: not to be a reed trembling in the wind, and, as the Wise Man says: "Turn not with every wind, nor walk in every way."[36] For sinners do that in their hypocrisy. But be firm in the way of the Lord, lest the wind blow you off the face of the earth,[37]

---

31. 1 Cor 5:12.   32. 2 Kings 6:30.

33. These passages of Guerric are reminiscent of some of the polemic satire of Bernard of Clairvaux in his famous *Apologia*, 20ff.; *The Works of Bernard of Clairvaux*, vol. 1 (Cistercian Fathers Series 1), pp. 55ff.

34. Prov 13:20.   35. Ezek 16:25.   36. Sir 5:11.   37. Sir 5:12; Ps 1:4.

whether that be the place to which you are bound by profession or the kingdom for which you must be prepared. A strong wind is wont to come rushing suddenly from the desert region and strike the four corners of the house which shelters Job's children.[38] The ruin is great if it was founded on sand and not upon the rock,[39] if it is built of reeds instead of stones, or rather if its builder, who dwells in it, is a reed, shiny on the outside through hypocrisy, making fine sounds with his boasting or empty promises, but on the inside empty of truth.

In the covert of this reed Behemoth likes to sleep, for it grows and luxuriates more often and more plentifully in damp places,[40] where there is no lack of transitory things but everything luxury could desire abounds. If a man leans on this reed it will run into his hand;[41] for if anyone takes such a man on as a help in any work, or entrusts him with the performance of some duty, he will inflict a grave wound on the man who was hoping in him by the scandal he gives.

Yet the Lord in his patience does not break a reed of this sort even when it is already crushed.[42] He takes care of it in order that it be changed for the better. Sometimes he even rebukes the wild beasts of the reeds[43] that, together with their leader, sleep in the covert of the reeds. And sometimes the just run hither and thither in the reed-bed like sparks of blazing air,[44] setting on fire, like coals that spread desolation,[45] all its sterile brushwood and preparing a clean place for a new fruit.

This is what John did as the voice of one crying in the desert.[46] He was not a reed but a spark in the reed-bed, for his words were as it is written, words of fire to move the lazy and unfeeling heart,[47] to prepare a way for the Lord. May the same Voice do this in us now too, with the cooperation of the Word himself whose voice he was, Jesus Christ our Lord, who lives and reigns for ever and ever. Amen.[48]

38. Job 1:19.   39. Mt 7:24ff.   40. Job 40:10, 16.   41. Is 36:6.
42. Is 42:3; Mt 12:20.   43. Ps 67:31.   44. Wis 3:7.
45. Ps 119:4.   46. Is 40:3; Mt 3:3.   47. Wis 2:2.
48. See above, Sermon 11, note 65; vol. 1, p. 75.

SERMON 44

THE FIRST SERMON FOR SAINTS PETER AND PAUL

ZECHARIAH SAID: "I answered and said to the angel who talked with me: 'What are these two olive trees on the right and the left of the lampstand?' 'These,' he said, 'are two sons of the Shining Oil who stand before the Lord of the whole earth.' "[1] The Prophet had understood the meaning of the lampstand which he had seen, all of gold, with its seven lamps upon it,[2] and we cannot be in doubt who walk in its light[3] and in its light see the light.[4] While this light shows up other things it does not allow itself to be unknown but bears witness to itself[5] in the words: "I am the Light of the world."[6] The light comes from the godhead, the lampstand from humanity. And it is wholly of gold, not merely gilt; for whether by gold we understand divinity or wisdom or charity Christ is all these things not through participation but substantially. As for us, by nature lead or rather earthenware, we by his grace and by participation in him are not gold nor decked with gold but at the most gilt. The seven lamps upon it are the seven spirits, the seven eyes of the Lord which roam through the whole earth.[7]

---

1. Zech 4:4ff. This text is found in the twelfth responsory sung at the night office on the octave day of this feast. Part of it is also used as the antiphon sung with the canticle, *Benedictus,* on the same day. In the old Cistercian Antiphonary, at least in the Bernardine recension of ca. 1147, this same part was used as the fourth antiphon for the first vespers of the feast itself.
2. Zech 4:2.   3. Is 2:5.   4. Ps 35:10.   5. Jn 8:14, 18.
6. Jn 8:12.   7. Zech 4:10.

In no doubt then as to these, the Prophet inquires what the two olive trees are and is told by the angel who is talking with him: "These are the two sons of the Shining Oil who stand before the Lord of the whole earth."[8] Others may give what interpretation they will or can: Enoch and Elijah who live hidden with God,[9] or Moses and Elijah who were seen with him on the mountain,[10] or the two orders of preachers, that is, of the Old and New Testaments, those of the Old at the left on account of the temporal nature of what they promised, those of the New at the right on account of the eternal nature of what they promised. For myself I accept, venerate and embrace whatever is in accord with the rule of faith and does not stray too far from the liturgical context.

2. Yet, with all allowance made for a better understanding, it is not absurd, I think, to understand Peter and Paul. Indeed it seems absurd to put forward any other interpretation today, since throughout the world the Church sings and preaches of nothing else today than the praises of its Fathers and Teachers. For although it can be applied to others, it is, I think, more particularly appropriate to these that the Prophet sees them as two olive trees by the lampstand or that the angel calls them two sons of the Shining Oil. And the one explains the other, the angel's interpretation explains the Prophet's vision. We understand that they are olive trees because they are sons of the Shining Oil, they are by the lampstand because they stand before the Lord. For since they have been reborn from the oil of the Holy Spirit, they bloom and bear fruit today also like a fruitful olive tree in the house of the Lord,[11] imparting the sap of their fatness and sweetness even to the wild olive of the Gentiles which has been grafted upon them.[12] Long unfertile and bearing bitter fruit, the Gentile stock should give them thanks; although it is not from them, it is through them that it is enriched with such abundant and such precious fruit throughout the world.

3. But you, brethren, who share the same property and the same house, who share also the same heart and soul,[13] you ought especially,

---

8. Zech 4:11.   9. Gen 5:24; 2 Kings 2:11.   10. Mt 17:3.
11. Ps 51:10.   12. Rom 11:7.   13. Acts 4:32.

I think, to glory in them, since like olive branches you have imbibed from their root not only the sap of faith but also a pattern of life and the model of your Order.[14] If you are olive branches, you are also anointed, belonging to that Anointed who is the Christ of God; and of you it will be said when you approach the altar today: "Your sons are as olive branches around your table."[15] O noble olive branches, high-born scions of trees so rich and so fertile, I beg you to remember always from what stock you have sprouted, from what root you have grown up, lest sterility in works or bitterness of behavior should ever prove you to be degenerate or—what I pray may not happen—consign you, useless as you are, to the flames. Beware of the mark of unhappy times, concerning which you remember it was prophesied: "The fruit of the olive tree will fail and the fields will produce no food."[16]

There are two things of which I think you should beware especially: either through lukewarmness becoming like the olive tree which sheds its flower, as you read in the Prophet,[17] that is, not bearing the fruit of which you gave promise in your fervent beginnings as a novice; or losing it through pride when you have borne it, so that Jeremiah would say to you: "An olive tree, sturdy and fair and fruitful, so it was the Lord loved to think of you; but alas, at the sound of his majestic voice fire has broken out and all those shoots are burned away."[18] But we have a better confidence in you, beloved, although we speak thus.[19] Our confidence is that the Shining Oil, or rather the Oil which is brilliance, of which you are sons as were our fathers the apostles, will by its anointing teach you everything; and that it will not only banish sluggishness because it is oil but also dispel error because it is brilliance.

4. I know that the phrase "of the Shining Oil" can be under-

---

14. Here and below in n. 5 Guerric may be alluding to the theory of John Cassian who traced the origins of the monastic orders to the apostles themselves. See *Institutes,* Preface, 8. For a thorough discussion of this matter and further bibliography see Jean Leclercq, *La Vie parfaite* (Paris, 1948), pp. 82–105.

15. Ps 127:3.   16. Hab 3:17.   17. Job 15:33.
18. Jer 11:16.   19. Heb 6:9.

stood in the sense of what proceeds from that brilliance which is the Son or what spreads abroad the illumination of that brilliance, but it is not inappropriate, I think, so to construe as to understand that the oil is the brilliance. For the Spirit is of its nature both: a spiritual anointing and an invisible brilliance. He produces both these effects in us by the gift of himself. He anoints the affections inasmuch as he is brilliance. Yet it is not from two distinct sources but from one and the same that he is both oil and brilliance, because he is one and the same. He anoints the affections because he is charity; he enlightens the understanding because he is truth. He anoints the affections when he gives devotion; he enlightens the understanding when he reveals mysteries. When he teaches goodness, that we may be innocent as doves, he anoints the affections; when he teaches knowledge, that we may be wary as serpents, he enlightens the understanding.[20] He enlightens that we may have salt in ourselves; he anoints that we may have peace between us.[21] You will then prove yourself to us as a son of the Shining Oil if you let us see that you are pleasing and abounding in your kindness, discreet and mature in your wisdom; so that pleasing manners are seasoned with truth and charity is well ordered by equity.

The Holy Spirit, I think, gave us to understand this twofold power of his or effect of his gift, on account of which he wished to be called Shining Oil, in that fire also in which, invisible as he is, he appeared visibly to the apostles.[22] For as he was brilliant to the gaze of their eyes, so, if I am not mistaken, he was oil to their bodily senses; so that they seemed to themselves to be immersed in a bath as it were of oil when that heavenly fire was poured out upon them. But whatever bodily perception they had of that fire (for what matters is not how it is felt but how it works) it may be more probably asserted, I think, and more devoutly believed that the same fire which inflamed and enlightened their hearts cooled their bodies, so that through charity their minds were set afire and through chastity their members were cooled. There can be applied to them respectively what Jeremiah says: "From on high he sent

20. Mt 10:16.   21. Mk 9:50.   22. Acts 2:3f.

fire into my bones,"²³ and the Psalmist's words: "My flesh has been changed by oil."²⁴ Unless perhaps it was the Spirit's will to leave something of the law of sin in their members to contend with the law of the mind,²⁵ so that power might be brought to perfection in weakness.²⁶

5. But let us continue with our original text: "These are two sons of the Shining Oil who stand before the Lord of the whole earth." You have goodness in the oil, knowledge in the brilliance. Understand discipline in the words "they stand before the Lord of the whole earth." Thus you may recognize that they were truly disciples of him to whom we sing: "Teach me goodness and discipline and knowledge."²⁷ For this is the perfection of discipline both in mind and in body, always to keep the Lord before our gaze.²⁸ Always and everywhere, with fear and reverence, in watchful faith and devotion, we stand before the eternal majesty which looks upon us and judges us unceasingly. "As the eyes of slaves are upon the hands of their masters, so are our eyes directed to the Lord our God,"²⁹ with the utmost attention and without admitting any distraction, watching for any indication of his will, of his behest, so that our devotion may render obedience as quickly as possible. Thus did Moses wait upon him who is invisible as if he saw him,³⁰ nor could he ever disguise his fear of the judge who was always at hand. Thus did Elijah and the other prophets, who said: "As the Lord lives, in whose sight I stand."³¹ Hence it was they obtained the grace and the name of seers, because what they always looked upon in unfeigned faith³² they deserved often to look upon in an outward appearance, created though it was.

This watchful faith, unfeigned, making no pretence, is, in my opinion, what alone or with the greatest saving in time and energy, leads to perfection. It bestows gravity on our orderliness and sobriety on our moderation both interior and exterior, and as if with the well-ordered service of domestics makes us stand always

23. Lam 1:13.   24. Ps 108:24.   25. Rom 7:23.   26. 2 Cor 12:9.
27. Ps 118:66. 28. Ps 85:14.   29. Ps 122:2.   30. Heb 11:27.
31. 2 Kings 5:16.   32. 1 Tim 1:5.

before the Lord. By this virtue the apostles deserved to be spoken of as sons of the Shining Oil, so that as on earth they stood before the Lord by contemplating him in faith, so now they may stand before him in heaven contemplating him in visible appearance, and their eyes may see the king in his beauty[33] on whom their hearts meditated here in fear. In this path, brethren, follow the Fathers of your faith and the Founders of your Order,[34] so that led on by their example and helped by their intercession you may be able to reach the point at which they arrived today before you, through the assistance of our Lord Jesus Christ, who lives and reigns for ever and ever. Amen.

---

33. Is 33:17f.   34. See above, note 14.

SERMON 45

THE SECOND SERMON FOR SAINTS PETER AND PAUL

"YOUR TWO BREASTS ARE LIKE TWO FAWNS, twins of a gazelle, that feed among the lilies, until the day breathes and the shadows are lengthened."[1] Take care, brethren, not to be unworthy of your parentage. To say nothing of your father's nobility, the mother who bore you is high-born, noble are the breasts at which you were suckled. Your mother is the Bride to whom these words are spoken, whose breasts are praised by the Bridegroom's voice. That these two breasts of the Church are Peter and Paul is not only the interpretation suggested to us by the present day on which we are given to drink with all pleasure and abundance from the breasts of their consolation, but also proved by the manifest witness of their work and the records of their teaching. For at what other breasts have the sons of the Church, whether Gentiles or Jews, been fostered?

These are they, I hold, whom God's consolation promised of old to the Church when it was small and poor: "Kings will be your nurses,"[2] and "You shall suck the breasts of kings."[3] For unless it had been nourished with such noble milk it would never have reached this summit of virtue and glory. It was to his breasts Peter

---

1. Song 4:5f.   2. Is 49:23.
3. Is 60:16. For this idea of the Church as mother, cf. the second Sermon for Christmas, no. 2; the third for Epiphany, no. 1 (vol. 1, pp. 44, 83). This is based on Scripture (Gal 4:26; Rev 12) and is common in the earliest of the Fathers, e.g. St Hippolytus, *On Christ and Antichrist*, ch. 61; St Cyprian, Letter 8, *To the Martyrs and Confessors*, PG 10: 780–781; PL 4:254c.

invited those whom he told: "Like new-born babes desire milk."[4] It was his breasts Paul had offered to those whom he told: "I gave you milk to drink."[5] And again: "I became in your midst like a nursing mother who sits and feeds her children."[6]

With what plenitude of spiritual milk he overflowed is aptly borne out by that flow of visible milk which is said to have issued from his body instead of blood when he was beheaded today and gave his life too for those to whom he had given his breast.[7] Truly there was no element of blood but the whole was of milk in him whose thoughts were concerned with nothing carnal, nothing of his own but only what was useful to others. It was not so much that he possessed breasts as that he was all of him a breast: he abounded with such a wealth of loving kindness that he yearned not only to impart the milk of his spirit in its totality to his children but also to give them his body.

2. Before the primitive Church received these two breasts, Peter and Paul, on earth, the Church of the holy and blessed spirits complained in heaven: "Our sister is small and has no breasts."[8] For when Christ went back to heaven, leaving the little flock of his disciples, and had not yet sent his Spirit with which the wombs and the breasts of the saints were to be impregnated, that Church in heaven was, I think, anxious over the Bridegroom's children, whether already born or still to be born. Who would be entrusted with the feeding of them? They saw that this Church was small in numbers, virtue and authority and without the breasts of doctrine.

The Bridegroom himself in the days of his earthly life had begotten some children by the word of truth[9] and as long as he was with them he had suckled them at the breasts of edification and consolation.[10] The Bridegroom himself has breasts better than

---

4. 1 Pet 2:2.   5. 1 Cor 3:2.   6. 1 Thess 2:7.

7. This legend of the Apostle's blood appearing as milk is found in a work attributed to St John Chrysostom: "How your blood was ennobled, when it appeared as milk on the dress of your executioner."—*On the Princes of the Apostles*, no. 2; PG 59: 494. The story appears again in the *Annals* of Baronius, year 69, no. 12.

8. Song 8:8.   9. Heb 5:7; Jas 1:18.   10. Is 66:11.

wine,¹¹ that is, than the teaching of the Law or than worldly joy. The Bridegroom, I say, has breasts, lest he should be lacking any one of all the duties and titles of loving kindness. He is a father in virtue of natural creation or of the new birth which comes through grace, and also in virtue of the authority with which he instructs. He is a mother, too, in the mildness of his affections, and a nurse because he is so attentive to the care such a duty imposes. So those whom he fed were little ones, some beginning of his creation,¹² but only a beginning, and there remained a great deal of careful work to be done before they would be brought to perfection¹³ and Christ formed in them.¹⁴

But when he had left them, the celestial spirits, although glad at the return of the Only-begotten, were anxious over the newly adopted offspring and seemed in some way by their concern to complain to him: "Who will foster them? You suckled them with milk, but you weaned them prematurely. You did not make them grow to be young men, you did not bring maidens to their full growth. Who will foster them? Our sister is small and has no breasts.¹⁵ You told Peter: 'Feed my lambs,'¹⁶ but not even he has enough milk in his breasts yet. His loving care would soon dry up since he still fears more for his own skin than for the souls of his little ones. He would easily abandon his lambs in temptation when he denied his shepherd and theirs under interrogation."

But behold all at once the Holy Spirit was sent from heaven, like milk poured out from Christ's own breasts, and Peter was filled with an abundance of milk. Not long afterwards Saul became Paul, the persecutor became the preacher, the torturer became the mother, the executioner became the nurse, so that you might truly understand that the whole of his blood was changed into the sweetness of milk, his cruelty into loving kindness.

3. With these two breasts attached to her body the Church glories in being not only a fertile mother but also a fortified city.¹⁷ "I am a wall," she says, "and my breasts are a tower."¹⁸ A thousand

11. Song 1:1. 12. Jas 1:18. 13. Heb 7:19. 14. Gal 4:19.
15. Song 8:8. 16. Jn 21:15. 17. Jer 1:18. 18. Song 8:10.

shields now hang from these towers, all the armor of the strong.[19] The Bridegroom himself also speaks in mysterious terms of the same breasts to the praise of his Bride, when he says in the Canticle of Love: "Your two breasts are like two fawns, twins of a gazelle."[20]

The gazelle in this place we understand to be the Church: keen of sight to penetrate Christ's mysteries, nimble in her leaping to bound over the thorny places of this world, well able to vanquish the poisons of the ancient serpent. Her two twins are not inappropriately, I think, understood to be these two Apostles, brothers in faith, alike in devotion, equal in merit and virtue, of one mind in charity, joined also in their very passion and death. As they loved one another in their life, so in death too they were not separated.[21]

Now since desires of greater things are fed by progress among lesser things until grace breathes upon them and they rise to contemplate the highest, it is well added of these fawns: "That feed among the lilies until the day breathes and the shadows are lengthened."[22] When animals shun the heat of the day they take to the shady pastures of the valleys,[23] where there is usually a richer crop of lilies, until the cool evening breeze blows and they go forth to the open plains or the slopes of the mountains. So our fawns, as long as the gentle breeze of the eternal day does not blow upon them so that they can contemplate, feed among the lilies of the valleys, that is, they take pleasure in the virtues of humble folk or even occupy themselves with their actions.[24] But when that day breathes upon their minds they go forth, bounding up to the richer and happier pastures of the eternal mountains. "If a man," says the Shepherd and the Door, "enters through me he will be saved;"[25] he will come into the Church and go forth

---

19. Song 4:4.   20. Song 4:5.   21. 2 Sam 1:23.
22. Song 4:5f.   23. Song 4:5; 2:1.

24. Guerric here presents what is common doctrine among the Cistercian Fathers, namely, that when the graces and consolations of contemplation are not present the monk does well to turn to charitable activities. See e.g. Bernard of Clairvaux, *On the Song of Songs*, Sermon 51:2 (Cistercian Fathers Series 31); William of St Thierry, *Exposition on the Song of Songs*, 59, 198 (Cistercian Fathers Series 6), pp. 47, 160.

25. Jn 10:9.

again, often in contemplation, ultimately departing for the heavenly fatherland. "He will find pasture,"[26] both here and there. Here among the lilies of the field; there among the trees of Paradise. Here amid flowers, there amid fruit. Here in the virtues of the saints, there in the joys of the angels.

4. Indeed it is in a place of pasture the Lord settled me,[27] when he joined me to the company of the Church of the saints, whose belly is like a heap of corn encircled with lilies,[28] so that I may feed at one and the same time on the flavor of the corn and the sight of the lilies. For what is the heap of corn but the abundance of God's word in so many books gathered together from all sides? What are the lilies but the just who grow like lilies and bloom forever before the Lord? Their whiteness is so bright in holiness of body and purity of heart, their fragrance is so sweet in their reputation, their healing virtue is so potent in word and deed. No mean repast this for the faithful soul, to see around itself so many lilies blooming in such loveliness and grace, where it can take from them examples of all the virtues, one from one, another from another. This one is more solidly grounded in humility, that one has a more all-embracing charity. Another is more stalwart in patience, another quicker to obey. This one is more sparing and frugal, that one does more service by his work. This one is more devout in prayer, that one applies himself to reading more studiously. This one is more prudent in administration, that one is holier in repose. And even while you admire some outstanding bloom of grace in each, each possesses not one but many virtues, as lilies possess many flowers. For there are as many lilies as there are just souls; lilies have as many flowers as the just have virtues. When a man then sees these things and rejoices in them, or even advances through them, what is he doing but feeding among lilies?

5. Paul fed others; but nonetheless he himself was fed among those whom he fed. He fed them with his words; he was fed by their works. His own stomach, and indeed those of others, he fed with his own hands; but his mind he fed not so much with his own

26. *Ibid.*   27. Ps 22:2.   28. Song 7:2.

good things as with those of others, since he sought what was useful not to himself but to others. "Now we live," he said, "if you stand firm in the Lord. For what is my glory or my joy or my crown?"[29] Is it not yourselves before God?"[30] Therefore the day of eternal light often breathed for him and the gentle breeze of the Holy Spirit blew upon him, by the force of which he was taken up to the interior pastures, sometimes of Paradise, sometimes of the third heaven, "... whether in the body or outside the body I know not," he says, "God knows."[31] It was fitting indeed that he who faithfully fed should be fed happily, and who outside rejoiced in the good things of the Lord's family should be bidden to enter into the joy of his Lord[32] and be filled with the good things of God's house,[33] not only of this visible house for which he toiled but also of that invisible house after which he sighed and from which the day breathed upon him.

6. Nothing less is to be thought of blessed Peter, in my opinion; since it is Paul's greatest glory to be ranked on a par with the merits of him whom the judgment of Truth placed over all in power and primacy. For when the Father who is in heaven[34] revealed the truth about the Only-begotten to Peter, what else was it but the eternal day breathing upon him and day pouring forth speech to day?[35] To whom is it to be believed that heaven was more accessible than to the doorkeeper himself, whose tongue was made the key of heaven?[36] Having power "to close heaven with clouds and to open its gates,"[37] how would he not be believed often to have entered himself? Once Peter was hungry and heaven was opened to him, while he was still on earth. And such a plentiful supply of food was sent him that much still remained over although he slaughtered and ate a great deal, changing unclean and poisonous animals into holy and blooming lilies.[38] Thus he might feed with delight among lilies

---

29. 1 Thess 3:8.   30. 1 Thess 2:19.   31. 2 Cor 12:3.   32. Mt 25:21.
33. Ps 64:5.   34. Mt 16:17.   35. Ps 18:3.
36. Cf. the antiphon sung with the *Benedictus* in the common office for two Apostles as it is found on the Feast of Sts Philip and James (May 1st) and Sts Simon and Jude (October 28th).
37. Rev 11:8.   38. Acts 10.

until the day breathed and he might feed with glory in the heavens themselves.

But behold while we have been commending to you these two breasts of the Bride the time has run out during which we desired to give you milk from these breasts. However, we can do this and are wont to do it on other days. For we draw milk for you from the Apostles' breasts as often as we use their words to treat of your spiritual growth. Now then let it be sufficient for the time being to exhort you, if indeed you need to be exhorted, that as you love these breasts so always may you desire their milk[39] in order that through it you may grow unto salvation until you show your Savior formed in you,[40] Jesus Christ our Lord, who lives and reigns for ever and ever. Amen.

---

39. 1 Pet 2:2.   40. Gal 4:19.

SERMON 46

THE THIRD SERMON FOR SAINTS PETER AND PAUL

AGAIN ON WHAT IS WRITTEN: "Until the day breathes and the shadows are lengthened."[1] You are mistaken in me, brethren, but through love, I think, or humility rather than inconsiderateness. You think I have some knowledge of the Scriptures, I who have scarcely crossed the threshold of knowledge. For you are displeased, it seems to me, that I did not continue to the end with the passage of Scripture about which I spoke to you yesterday;[2] as if I had the ability to explain the Scriptures or even to recall to memory worthily and aptly the explanations of others. It is not even my customary intention to expound the Scripture from which I take the text for my sermon, but only to begin with it and draw inspiration from it in delivering the sermon for which the day calls.[3]

Moreover there is the fact that our Master,[4] that exegete of the

1. Song 4:6.
2. We have an indication here that these sermons for Sts Peter and Paul were not preached on the Feast itself over the course of successive years but were rather preached on successive days during the octave of the Feast.
3. Guerric here gives us a very candid insight into his use of Sacred Scripture. He was not in his preaching primarily concerned with the literal sense of Sacred Scripture but rather with the allegorical, tropological or anagogical senses. For a very complete study of the various senses of Scripture as they were used by Guerric and his contemporaries, see H. De Lubac, *The Exegesis of the Middle Ages,* Part I (Cistercian Studies Series 46).
4. The Master to whom Guerric refers is Bernard of Clairvaux. Guerric was a disciple of Bernard's, having been a monk of Clairvaux for thirteen years or so, and as Abbot of Igny both he and his community continued to

Holy Spirit, has planned to speak on the whole of that nuptial canticle and from what he has already published has given us the hope that, if he reaches the place about which you enquire: "Until the day breathes and the shadows are lengthened," he will bring the shadows themselves into the light of understanding, telling us in the light what has been or will be told him in darkness.[5] You say, and rightly say, that when new things arrive you will throw away the old,[6] and the more these old things of ours are unseasoned or rancid, the more savory and pleasing will be those new things of his. For Jesus himself keeps the good wine to the end,[7] knowing well how our ailing appetites should be healed.

2. Since then you compel me, for I see you are impatient of delay, and an uncertain hope for the future does not satisfy present desire, I accommodate myself to you and will join the end of the verse about which we were speaking yesterday to its beginning as well as I can. What you seem to be asking is what is meant by the lengthening of the shadows when the spiritual day breathes, since it would seem more in keeping for them to be said not to grow but to diminish and fade away. For if we keep to the precise meaning of the word, to grow for shadows is to be lengthened, since it is of the nature of shadows that the more they are lengthened the greater they are, and the more they are shortened the less they are. Hence it is that when the poet wishes to speak of evening he says: "Longer shadows fall from the high mountains."[8] But you must know that although this is the nature of bodily shadows, that of spiritual shadows is quite different, and it is of these doubtless that the Holy

---

look to Bernard as a superior since Igny was a foundation of Clairvaux. Guerric seems to express some uncertainty as to whether Bernard would ever get to this particular verse of the Song of Songs. And with good reason, for in the course of the almost twenty years during which Bernard did comment on the Song of Songs he actually only covered the first two chapters and began the third. Gilbert of Swineshead took up the commentary where Bernard left off, but his reflections on this particular verse are very brief indeed. See Sermon 27:7 (Cistercian Fathers Series 14).

5. Mt 10:27.   6. Lev 26:10.   7. Jn 2:10.
8. Virgil, *Bucolics*, 1:83; trans. Davidson, *The Works of Virgil* (New York: Harper, 1859), p. 4.

Spirit is speaking here. For just as for bodily shadows to be lengthened is to grow, so for spiritual shadows to be lengthened is to move off, diminish or fade away.

Spiritual shadows are the shady and foul spirits of men or of devils, shadows are the darkness of error; shadows are the obscure meanings of ancient mysteries.[9] And while the shadows of such meanings have already lengthened to their sunset and come to an end, and the shadows of error are from day to day lengthened so as to diminish, the shadows of dark spirits will in the end be lengthened to come to hell and death. The first happened when the eternal Day breathed, appearing in the flesh; the second is happening daily as he breathes more and more, shedding abroad the rays of truth; the third will happen at the end of time when he breathes in the full glow of his majesty.

3. However, I seem to see other shadows too within us, which are born in our minds from other things as if in a mirror. They overshadow us or shade us. Those overshadow us which leave us in the cold and the dark; those shade us which bring us coolness and enlightenment. The former are harmful and a nuisance; the latter are pleasant and wholesome. The former are from the things below, the things of this world; the latter are from the things above, the things of God.

For the human soul was created and established in the middle, with the world underneath it and God above it. Above it there is he by whom and to whom and for whom it was made; under it there is what was made for it. As the body is for the soul, so for the body is its house, that is, the world. So when it stoops to corporeal or worldly things shadows from the lower regions mount up into it; when it is raised to the things of God shadows from the higher regions fall upon it. For the soul forms for itself a shadow of the thing of which it thinks.

---

9. Gilbert also sees two of the shadows mentioned here. The shadow of error and the shadow of mysteries or types (Sermon 27:6) and for him, too, the eternal Day, "the Day of days, Christ Jesus," will overcome all the shadows (n. 7). He also sees a third kind of shadow which Guerric will speak of later, namely, the refreshing shadow of the Spouse.

Yet a shadow cast by the things of God is very nebulous, however keenly our mental vision be sharpened to perceive it; or rather it is not a shadow of the thing itself, but something else takes its place, except when that day breathes. Then also, in my opinion, all that is seen is a shadow. Although it is luminous and glorious it is still a shadow, as when on the surface of a mirror that has been wiped clean and is in the light there appears the brilliant likeness of a most brilliant object.

But to see the face of Truth himself, or the truth of his face, will never be accorded to us while we are in this body, and does not belong to the present time. Neither will it ever come about until the body is broken by mortality and set free by immortality and time is swallowed up by eternity, and immortal and unchangeable divinity raises up to itself and strengthens in itself the spirit which is now weighed down by the body and changed by time.

4. The beginning of this grace and the perfection of that glory were quite precisely distinguished by Paul when he said: "At present we are looking at a confused reflection in a mirror; then we shall see face to face."[10]

But in order for even this to come about, that is, to see in a mirror, it is necessary not only that the surface of our mirror be wiped clean of every phantasm and shadow of bodily things, but also that he who dwells on high in light unapproachable[11] deign to stoop to us and be made manifest if only through a shadow of his likeness. For however much we strive to reach invisible things with visible things as our starting-point, our lowliness will not grasp anything unless that majesty comes down to meet us. Moses went up into the mountain[12] and the Lord bowed the heavens and came down.[13] And someone else says: "Rise up, come to meet me and see."[14] Therefore not even a shadow is seen unless it is lengthened, and it is only said to be lengthened when the day breathes; for not even as a confused reflection in a mirror can we see God unless majesty stoops and the favor of grace breathes.

10. I Cor 13:12.   11. I Tim 6:16.   12. Ex 24:18.
13. Ps 17:10.   14. Ps 58:6.

To be sure, what is called a shadow in comparison with manifest truth is for the most part something of unspeakable glory and splendor, that is, in those in whom the mirror of the mind is wholly clear. In his knowledge of this happy experience Paul was speaking of himself and those like him when he said: "It is given to us, all alike, to catch the glory of the Lord as in a mirror, and so we become transfigured into the same likeness, borrowing glory from that glory, as the Spirit of the Lord enables us."[15] So we were told in the promise: "He will fill your soul with splendors."[16] If you would know that these glories are shadows, listen to David saying: "My days have stretched out like a shadow."[17] David himself, you see, passed from glory to glory as if from day to day.

But alas this winter has such short and dark days, such long and toilsome nights, that the prophet too, toiling in his lament and flooding his bed with tears every night,[18] rightly moaned: "My days have stretched out like a shadow.[19] Truly one day in your courts is better than a thousand of my days;[20] for my days are as a shadow,[21] however bright, while that one day is true and unmixed light, without any shadow and so without any evening, and my days are multiplied and shortened by the regular interruption of long nights."

5. Now if the question be raised why shadows are spoken of in the plural, while the object of which they are shadows is single, the reason is that the power of the Most High overshadows us[22] now more, now less; the Truth that reveals itself to us is delineated now more clearly, now more obscurely. As it does not always breathe with equal force, so it does not always form likenesses for us in like manner. The Apostle too indicates this when he confesses that he passes on from glory to glory,[23] that is, from the lesser to the greater; and the prophet indicates it when he promises that the soul will be filled not with splendor but with splendors.[24] Thus James refers to God as the Father of lights,[25] although the Light of which he is the Father is one and single; yet he may be understood

15. 2 Cor 3:18. 16. Is 58:11. 17. Ps 101:12. 18. Ps 6:7.
19. Ps 101:12. 20. Ps 83:11. 21. Ps 101:12. 22. Lk 1:35.
23. 2 Cor 3:18. 24. Is. 58:11. 25. Jas 1:17.

to be the Father of lights in the same sense that he is Father of mercies.[26]

6. As for you, brethren, who toil in your spirit as you bear the burden of the day and its heat,[27] or, according to Isaiah, as you meditate in the straits of your spirit through the day's heat,[28] it is a pleasure to invite you to these shadows which that fair Day, breathing the dew of loving kindness, desires to cast on those who are afflicted with the heat. Listen to the Day itself graciously inviting you to the refreshment of the shadows: "Come to me all you who toil and are burdened, and I will refresh you."[29]

For, as Job says, the slave toiling in the sun longs for the shade,[30] to be refreshed from his work, if only for the half an hour while there is silence in heaven,[31] and so be restored to his work. When he has obtained this through the indulgence of his foreman he declares his happiness in the words: "Beneath the shadow of him for whom I yearned I have sat."[32] And because this shade affords not only a chance to sit and rest but also refreshment to satiety, he aptly goes on to say: ". . . and his fruit was sweet to my mouth."[33] For so did the Prophet say: "Let them return and sit in his shade; they shall live on grain and blossom as the vine."[34]

The slave or the hireling who is often refreshed by this shade will look forward patiently to the end of his work. For so we read: "The slave longs for the shade and the hireling looks forward to the end of his work."[35] The shade brings not the end but a rest; the end of the work and its recompense will come when all shadows are banished and we see him as he is[36] to whom we say at present: "In your shadow we shall live among the nations."[37] Among the angels we shall live not in any shadow but in clear light.

7. But this is to be noted, that while the shadows cast by the things of above fall over us, the shadows cast by the things of below fall beneath us. For as we draw near to the things of God we overcome the things of the world; and insofar as we approach even the shadow of light, to that extent we emerge from the shadow of

26. 2 Cor 1:3.   27. Mt 20:12.   28. Is 27:8.   29. Mt 11:28.
30. Job 7:2.   31. Rev 8:1.   32. Song 2:3. 33. *Ibid.*
34. Hos 14:8.   35. Job 7:2.   36. 1 Jn 3:2. 37. Lam 4:20.

death. For light and life are in heaven, death is in hell, while the shadow of death is in this dark and earthly place.

So when the Spirit raises us up high between heaven and earth we are not touched by the shadow of earthly things; and although we do not yet enjoy to the full the light of heaven, we are illumined by the shadows of the eternal mountains,[38] or rather of that shaded and wooded mountain from which the Holy of holies comes.[39] Shortly however our own weight drags us back into the region of the shadow of death[40] and there we are forced to sit for a very long time until we are consoled by the visitation of him who rises from on high.[41]

We are forced, I say, and would that we were forced and did not take pleasure in it; would that what we suffer were a matter only of necessity and not of will or pleasure. But alas, we cast ourselves down so easily, so gladly, and go to sleep in the oppressive shade of a thorny and unfruitful broom.[42] So negligent and free from concern are we that we become sluggish and perish amid the cares and desires of this world. Therefore Leviathan, who sleeps in the shade,[43] makes his bed in us unless we take precautions, because he finds in our feelings and affections the shadows of this world of which he is so fond. As Job declares, these shadows protect his own shadow,[44] since the cares and desires of the world which are in us hide from us the shadow of impending damnation so that we have no foresight of it until we come up against it.

Breathe, O Day of days, overshadow our head in the day of battle.[45] Cast over us shadows of salvation and refreshment and let the shadows of sluggishness and weariness, and indeed of blindness and death, fall under us. And although shadows may fall upon us from thinking of earthly things let not darkness overwhelm us, that is, the denser shadows cast by love of them, but may we always aspire to your luminous love, O Father of lights,[46] who live and reign for ever and ever. Amen.

38. Ps 75:5. 39. Hab 3:3. 40. Is 9:2. 41. Lk 1:78.
42. 1 Kings 19:5. 43. Job 40:16. 44. Job 40:17. 45. Ps 139:8.
46. Jas 1:17.

SERMON 47

THE FIRST SERMON FOR THE ASSUMPTION

"COME MY CHOSEN ONE, and I will set up my throne in you."[1] Many are called but few indeed are chosen.[2] Blessed are those whom you have chosen, Lord; they shall dwell in your courts. More than that, you will live in them, you will reign in them, and you will set up the throne of your kingdom in them. Of them all, Mary is the most blessed. She of all the elect was in a unique way chosen and singled out, for the Lord has chosen her; he has chosen her to be his dwelling, saying: "She shall be my rest for ever and ever; here will I dwell, for I have chosen her."[3] He lived in her for nine months; he lived with her and was subject to her for so many more years. While living in her, he poured into her graces of a unique kind; while living with her, he nourished her with his salutary words of divine wisdom and with the ineffable sweetness of his example. But now, through his dwelling in her and with her for all eternity and in a manner incomprehensible, her cup of joy overflows with the glory of the beatific vision. Outwardly he shows her the form of his glorified flesh, while within he imprints the form of the glorifying Word.

"O Mary," the Lord says, "you will no longer be called *Forsaken*, and your land will no longer be called *Desolate* for although a

---

1. This text is found in a responsory sung at the vigils in honor of a virgin: the tenth responsory for the common office of virgins and also other holy women. It is also used as an antiphon at tierce on the feast days of some holy women.
2. Mt 22:14.   3. Ps 131:13f.

virgin you will not be unfruitful. No. You will be called *My Pleasure* (that is, my beloved Son) *is in her,* because the Lord has been well pleased with you and your land will be inhabited. For the young man shall dwell with the virgin, and your son shall dwell in you."[4]

But let us keep more strictly to the words of Scripture: "and your children shall dwell in you."

2. What? Does heresy raise up its head? Does it make the mystery of God's loving kindness an occasion for spite and rancor? She bore only one Son. In heaven, he is the Only-begotten of the Father; on earth, likewise, he is the Only-begotten of his Mother. She bore no other children despite the heretic's blasphemy. But rather the seal of perpetual virginity in the mother, like the mystery of Catholic unity in the offspring, remains inviolate. She who is the only Virgin-Mother, she who glories in having borne the Only-begotten of the Father, embraces that same Only-begotten of hers in all his members and so can be truly called Mother of all in whom she recognizes her Christ to have been formed, or in whom she knows he is being formed.

The first Eve[5] is not so much a mother as a stepmother since she handed on to her children an inheritance of certain death rather than the beginning of light. She is indeed called the mother of all the living,[6] but she turned out to be more precisely the murderer of the living, or mother of the dead, since the only fruit of her child-bearing was death. And as Eve was incapable of fulfilling the vocation of her title, Mary consummated the mystery. She herself, like the Church of which she is the type, is a mother of all who are reborn to life.

4. Is 62:4ff.

5. Guerric touches here on a common patristic theme, the contrast between Mary, the new Eve, and the original Eve of Eden. It is common also among the Cistercian Fathers. It is found, for example, in two of St Bernard's more famous sermons on the Blessed Virgin Mary: the sermon on the twelve prerogatives of Mary preached on the Sunday within the octave of the Assumption and the sermon, *De Aquaeductu,* for the Feast of Mary's Nativity. See above, ser. 18, n. 1 and below, ser. 51, n. 1.

6. Gen 3:20.

She is in fact the mother of the Life by which everyone lives, and when she brought it forth from herself she in some way brought to rebirth all those who were to live by that Life. One was born, but we were all reborn, since in that seed which holds the power of rebirth we were all already then in him.[7] Just as from the beginning we were in Adam by the seed of carnal generation, so even before the beginning we were there present in Christ much more by the seed of spiritual regeneration.[8]

3. Thus the blessed Mother of Christ, knowing that she is the mother of all Christians by reason of this mystery, shows herself a mother by her care and loving attention. For her heart is not hardened against these children as if they were not her own; her womb carried a child once only, yet it remains ever fruitful, never ceasing to bring forth the fruits of her motherly compassion. The blessed Fruit of your womb,[9] O holy Mother, left you pregnant with inexhaustible tenderness. He was born of you once and for all, yet he remains in you always, making you ever fruitful. Within the locked garden of your chastity he makes the sealed well-spring[10] of charity always abundant in its supply: that well-spring though sealed is yet channeled to the outer world and its waters are at our disposal in courtyard and street.

For although this fountain of charity belongs exclusively to the Church and cannot be shared with those outside, yet still it delights to bestow its gifts on her enemies as well. In short, if the Servant of Christ by his care and heartfelt tenderness bears his little children again and again until Christ be formed in them,[11] how much more is this true of the very Mother of Christ? Paul begot his children by preaching the word of truth[12] through which they were born again; but Mary in a manner far more holy and like to God, by giving birth to the Word himself. I do indeed praise the ministry of preaching in Paul, but far more do I admire and venerate that mystery of generation in Mary.

4. Then again, is it not true that her children seem to recognize

7. Heb 7:10. 8. 1 Cor 15:22. 9. Lk 1:42. 10. Song 4:12.
11. Gal 4:19. 12. Jas 1:18.

her as their Mother by a kind of instinctive devotion which faith gives them as second nature, so that first and foremost in all their needs and dangers they run to call upon her name just as children run to their mother's breast? So I think it is quite reasonable to understand of these children that promise of the Prophet to her: "Your children shall live in you;"[13] provided that the prophecy is always understood to refer principally to the Church. Already we really dwell in the help of the Mother of the Most High; we do live in her protection,[14] as if under the shadow of her wing.[15] And afterwards in participating in her glory we shall be cherished as if in her bosom. Then a single cry of rejoicing and thanksgiving will be heard addressed to this Mother: "The dwelling place of all of us who rejoice and are glad is in you, holy Mother of God."[16]

You will not think it a greater happiness and glory to dwell in the bosom of Abraham[17] than in the bosom of Mary, when the King of Glory has erected his throne in her.

5. "Come, my chosen one," he says, "and I will set up my throne in you."[18] There is no more expressive or more fitting description of her glorious privilege than to say that she is the throne of the God who reigns supreme. The Divine Majesty has never been seen to lavish his abundance on any soul so completely and so intimately as on her in whom he has especially chosen to reside before all others.

The Lord told his disciples, who became poor to follow him in his poverty: "In the new world, when the Son of Man shall sit on his glorious throne, you also will sit on thrones."[19] And in another place our Champion, who keeps close watch from heaven, and encourages the contenders, has promised the same thing: "He who conquers," he says, "I will grant him to sit with me on my throne, as I myself conquered and sat down with my Father on his throne."[20]

To the Mother whose merits are so much greater than theirs he has promised a reward so much the greater. "Come," he says, "my chosen one, and I will set up my throne in you." "To sit with the

---

13. Is 62:5.   14. Ps 90:1, 4.   15. Ps 16:8.   16. Ps 86:7.
17. Lk 16:23. 18. See note 1.   19. Mt 19:28. 20. Rev 3:21.

judges," he says, "is nothing compared with becoming my throne. Then you will possess within you my sovereign majesty, so joyfully and so intimately, and you will grasp so much more fully than they the incomprehensible. You have sheltered the Child in your womb; you will embrace the Infinite in the depths of your soul. You were the resting place for the Pilgrim; you will be the palace of the Sovereign. You were the tent of the Warrior as he prepared for battle in the world; you will be the throne of the Victor in heaven. You were the bridal chamber of the Bridegroom in the flesh, you will be the throne of the King in all his majesty."

6. Nothing, O Son of God, nothing at all gave you displeasure in that guest-chamber which your loving kindness so gladly accepted as your own and so lavishly decked out in recompense. No stain did you find in it, because no lust was there, but only the purest chastity. No hint of downfall did you perceive, because no pride was there, only the deep foundation of humility; no dark corners there, because faithlessness had been shut out; nothing cramped, because the breadth of charity was there. The virgin most prudent had adorned her bridal chamber both to receive you, Christ, her King, as Guest, and to hold you as Bridegroom. She had adorned herself, I repeat, with the manifold beauty and glory of virtue and perhaps more lavishly because of her greater poverty, and it was all safer and surer because more interior. The Psalmist stood in wonder at that adornment: "All the glory of the king's daughter," he said, "is within, within golden borders clothed about with varieties, much variety."[21] So also the Wise Man who wrote: "O how beautiful is the chaste generation with charity."[22] Such beauty and holiness befit your house, O Lord. That beauty invited you to come; it allured you to return. By entering you increased the grace of blessing, by returning you multiplied it beyond all measure. When you entered you were born as man in her;[23] when you returned you were glorified as God in her. Then you made in her a shrine of grace for yourself; but now you have set her up as a throne of glory.

21. Ps 44:14f.   22. Wis 4:1.   23. Ps 86:5.

There are said to be, and in fact are, other Thrones, certain holy spirits,[24] as far as we know, filled more with the majesty of God enthroned on high than are the other orders subject to them.[25] The Scriptures do not tell us what privilege these spirits have, although their title suggests that they have one. Then again the soul of the just man is called a seat of wisdom. And what is a seat of wisdom now will one day be a seat of glory. So the place of heaven will be full of seats and thrones and on each of them God will take his rest, giving himself to all as and how their merits deserve.

But there is a belief that neither implies an insult to these other seats nor provokes them to jealousy. It claims that, quite fittingly, there is another special throne of the King, exalted and elevated[26] above the glory of all the rest. Mary, I say, has been exalted above the choirs of the angels. The Mother therefore can contemplate nothing above herself but her Son alone; the Queen can gaze in wonder at nothing above herself but the King; the Mediatrix can venerate nothing above herself but the Mediator. May she, by her prayers, represent, reconcile and commend us to her Only-begotten Son, Jesus Christ, to whom are honor and glory for endless ages. Amen.[27]

---

24. See Col 1:16.

25. St Bernard, who might be called the Doctor of the Angels so often does he treat of them and their role in the economy of salvation, develops this prerogative of the Thrones more at length when he treats of the nine choirs of angels in his Nineteenth Sermon on the Song of Songs (no. 4). Guerric may have been in the chapter at Cîteaux when and if Bernard preached this sermon; see J. Leclercq's introductory essay, "Were the Sermons on the Song of Songs actually preached?" in Volume Three of the *Works of Bernard of Clairvaux*, Cistercian Fathers Series 7.

26. Is 6:1.   27. Rom 16:27.

SERMON 48

THE SECOND SERMON FOR THE ASSUMPTION

"DAUGHTERS OF JERUSALEM, tell the Beloved that I languish with love."[1] If it please you in your charity we wish to consider how these words which we sang at the night office today are appropriate to the Assumption of Blessed Mary. It would seem that this is to be done with that kind of language which the authors not only of secular but also of ecclesiastical literature sometimes have used, especially in treating of the Song of Songs from which these words are taken. This kind of language, while preserving the truth of the matter, allows itself a greater freedom in developing its theme. As St Jerome says, it does not so much speak of what was in fact done or said as show that the matter was such that, although what is related was not done or said, it could without absurdity be believed to have been done or said, or even have been in the affections of the one doing or saying it.

So when Mary was about to depart from the body she took to her bed, as is the way with human weakness. Then the daughters

1. Song 5:8. This text is sung as the fourth responsory at the vigils or matins on the Feast of the Assumption. In the Cistercian office (which was essentially in form that which St Benedict prescribed in the Rule for Monasteries, RB chs. 8ff.) the singing of this responsory would have been followed by the chanting of six psalms. We might then have here an example of the type of meditation that might have occupied Guerric during the chanting of these psalms.

of the Jerusalem which is above,[2] that is, the angelic powers, well aware that the Son's favor is to be won by attention shown to the Mother, were visiting their Lady, the mother of their Lord,[3] with dutifulness and devotion. And perhaps, after duly greeting her, the angels first spoke to her in some such way, adapting their language to human affections as they adapted their appearance to a human form.

2. "Why is it, Lady, I beg, that you seem so ill and faint? Why is it that, unlike your wont, you are sad and inactive, that for some time now you do not revisit the holy places as you were accustomed to do, feeding your love by contemplating them? For some days now we have not seen you climbing the rock of Calvary to flood the place of the Cross with tears or at the tomb of your Son worshipping the glory of his resurrection, or on Mount Olivet kissing the last traces he left as he ascended."

For this very reason she is believed to have dwelt in the valley of Josaphat (where her tomb also is pointed out, as St Jerome says, in a church built with an extraordinary stone floor), in order not to go far from the holy places but to visit them often. In this way, although she kept everything in her memory, she too embraced more tenderly those events as it were bodily portrayed in the very places in which they had occurred, and by this means at least consoled her love to some extent.

3. When therefore the angels enquire the reason why she no longer does this and has taken to her bed, she says: "I languish."

"Why do you languish? For what place can languor claim in your body in which the Health of the world dwelt for so long? From the body of that Son of yours power went forth and healed everyone,[4] so much so that even the hem of his garment healed the woman with the issue of blood;[5] and you held him for so long in

---

2. Gal 4:26. The dialog in this sermon is not unlike that found in St Bernard's Ninth Sermon on the Song of Songs, and might well depend on it. Scholars have also noted a likeness to the *Liber Amoris* which has been attributed to Guerric, but the truth of the matter might be that both this sermon and the *Liber* were influenced by the same Bernardine source.

3. Lk 1:43.   4. Lk 6:19.   5. Mt 9:22ff.

your womb, in your bosom, on your lap, how could you be liable after that to any weakness or languor?"

"There is no reason why you should be surprised at that," she says, "if you remember how it was once with that body of my Son. I know how weak it was and subject to how many needs, although of his own free will. I know, who fed him in the womb, suckled him at my breasts, cherished him in my bosom, and saw the needs not only of his infancy but also of subsequent periods in his life, tending them as far as I could. At the end it was not without suffering that I beheld the mockery and the torments of his Passion and Cross,[6] learning through them one by one how truly Isaiah spoke of him when he said: 'Indeed he bore our ills and himself carried our pains.'[7] Why should I grieve then that he has not given to my body what he did not give to his own? I am not so softly nurtured or so proud that I cannot or will not suffer to some slight extent what he saw fit to suffer. For him it was a question of free will and compassion: for me, of nature and necessity. To be sure, health is one thing, holiness another. Holiness he gave to my body by the mystery of his body in its conception; health he promised to give after the pattern of his risen body. In a word, that you may wonder less at my languor, I languish with love. I languish more from the impatience of love than from suffering pain. I am more wounded with charity than weighed down by infirmity."

4. "Alas," they say, "how frequent, indeed continual, are the causes of your languor. Good Jesus, how this Mother of yours was practically always languishing after she gave birth to you. At first she languished with fear, afterwards with sorrow, now with love. With fear from your birth until your passion, since she saw that the life of her Son was always the object of scheming and attempts at murder; with sorrow throughout the time of the passion until she recovered you restored to life; now she is tormented more happily but more pitifully with love and desire, because she does not possess you as you sit in heaven. How, good Jesus, have you who are the fruit of supreme joy become for her the cause of so long a

---

6. Jn 19:25.   7. Is 53:4.

martyrdom, that so many and so sharp swords pierce unceasingly the soul dearest of all to you?[8] But we beg of you, Lady, what would you have us to do for you? Do you wish at least that Gabriel, that partner in your initiation into the mystery, should stay here, sit by you and wait on you, he who from the beginning was aware of your secret and ministered to it, deserving also to be appointed guardian of your chamber?"

"There is no need for that," she says. "My virgin suffices for me, the new angel in the flesh, the disciple whom Jesus loved.[9] Of that love he left me the heir when on the Cross he commended him to me and me to him,[10] and nothing pleases me better than his attentions, since nothing could be more chaste than his way of life and his affections, nothing more delightful than his behavior, nothing more pure than his faith, nothing more holy than his speech."

"As for ourselves then," they say, "in what can we be of service to you?"

"Daughters of Jerusalem," she says, "tell the Beloved that I am languishing with love. He knows how my languor is to be healed."

5. "But you know," they say, "that although he knows everything he asks questions about many things as if he did not know. If he should ask what it is that you wish to be applied to your wound, what answer shall we give him?"

"You are the Bridegroom's companions," she says, "this Gabriel of mine is his chosen attendant; I hardly think the mystery of my love is to be hidden from you. I will tell you of it simply in order not to be judged rash, seeming to seek what is beyond me. 'Let him kiss me with the kiss of his mouth.'[11] If my conscience had anything on it I would be content with Mary Magdalen to kiss his feet,[12] where forgiveness of sins is obtained.[13] But my heart had

8. Lk 2:35. 9. Jn 21:20. 10. Jn 19:26ff.
11. Song 1:1. 12. Lk 7:38, 45.

13. In his Third Sermon on the Song of Songs, St Bernard makes this same comparison where he traces out the stages of spiritual growth using the analogy of the kiss: the kiss of the feet, of the hands and of the mouth. See M. B. Pennington, "Three Stages of Spiritual Growth According to St Bernard" in *Studia Monastica*, 11 (1969), pp. 315-326.

nothing to reproach me with in the whole of my life. I do not think it overweening of me to implore the joyful grace of the kiss of the mouth. Why should I seem overweening if I ask for that mouth again which he, the Created and the Creator, formed for himself from me? When I held him as a little child in my arms, I was able to kiss him, more beautiful than the sons of men,[14] as often as I wished; he never turned his face away, never repelled his Mother. And if perhaps the impatience of my desire was excessive, he, as is his wont, bore with his Mother. He was glad to fill her with the grace that was poured out on his lips[15] and with the sweetness with which he was wholly full, he who is the whole object of chaste souls' yearning and desire. Therefore as he confesses of himself: 'They who eat me will still hunger and they who drink me will still thirst.'[16] The more sweetly I tasted the grace of that mouth, the more ardently I seek it again now. He has grown in glory and majesty; but he has not changed at all as far as his natural mildness and goodness are concerned. That maxim of worldly pride has nothing to do with him: 'Honors change behavior.' He is more lofty but not more proud. He is more glorious but not more contemptuous. He will not disdain the Mother whom he chose; he will not reverse her eternal election by a new judgment."

6. "Do not be afraid, Mary," says Gabriel, as on a former occasion, "you have found favor with God.[17] Even in others who are by far inferior to you he is wont to approve the impatience of this affection and prayer; for he does not regard as excessive or harmful to himself any advance which true charity makes toward him."

And turning to the multitude accompanying him he says: "Let us go, let us go; lest we seem to wrong the Son himself if we delay his Mother's glory."

So when they went back and told their Lord these things, what shall we think Jesus said if not something such as this: "It is I who bade sons honor father and mother;[18] I who, in order to do what I

---

14. Ps 44:3.   15. *Ibid.*   16. Sir 24:29.   17. Lk 1:30.
18. Mt 19:19; Ex 20:12.

taught and be an example to others, went down on to earth to honor my Father; nonetheless, to honor my Mother, I came back up to heaven. I came up and prepared a place for her, a throne of glory, so that the Queen might sit with the King at his right hand, crowned and decked with gold-woven robes of many colors.[19] And I do not say this in order that a throne be placed for her apart; rather she will be my throne. Come then, my Chosen One, and I will place my throne in you. In you I will set up for myself a seat over my kingdom, from you I will make judgments, through you I will listen to prayers. No one ministered to me more in my lowliness: there is no one I want to minister to more plentifully in my glory. You imparted to me, besides other things, what makes me a man; I will impart to you what makes me God. You implored the kiss of my mouth; rather the whole of you will be kissed by the whole of me. I will not press my lips to your lips, but my spirit to your spirit in an everlasting and indissoluble kiss. Because I have desired your beauty[20] with greater longing even than you have desired mine, I shall not regard myself as sufficiently glorified until you are glorified with me."

"Glory be to, you Lord Jesus," the choir of angels answered. Glory be to you, Lord Jesus, let the company of the faithful echo. May the glorification of your Mother make for your glory, for our pardon; do grant this, you to whom honor and glory belong for ever and ever. Amen.

---

19. Ps 44:10.   20. Ps 44:12.

SERMON 49

THE THIRD SERMON FOR THE ASSUMPTION

"IN ALL I SOUGHT REST."[1] Rest is welcome to the weary. It is welcome, then, and it comes as a most opportune interlude to you who are weary, this day of rest and leisure. Therefore while we celebrate the rest of God's holy Mother not only may our bodies be refreshed by this rest of a day from the work of the harvest but also our hearts may draw breath in remembrance and love of that eternal rest.[2] Yet there too, brethren, there too you will reap, but it is rest you will reap, you who are now sowing the work of this harvest. The fruit of this work will be that rest; rest from work, recompense for work, of which even the remembrance in faith restores a man's strength at his work. It is shade for those who are hot, food for the hungry. For so says she who overflows with the memory of its abounding sweetness:[3] "In the shade of him for whom I longed I sat and his fruit was pleasant to my mouth."[4]

O you who toil, O you who bear the day's burden and its heat;[5]

---

1. Sir 24:11. These are the opening words of the reading (chapter—*capitulum*) at the first vespers for the Feast of the Assumption. It is repeated at the office of tierce.

2. The Feast of the Assumption was for the Cistercians what they called a Feast of Sermon, a day on which there was no labor and on which the community, including the lay brothers, gathered after prime and the early mass to hear a sermon on the theme of the feast. See *Consuetudines Ordinis Cisterciensis*, Part One, *Officia Ecclesiastica*, ch. 67, in *Nomasticon Cistercienses*, ed. nova (Solesmes, 1892), p. 141.

3. Ps 144:7.   4. Song 2:3.   5. Cf. Mt 20:12.

in the shade of Jesus' wings[6] you will find rest for your souls,[7] firm support, shelter when the hot wind blows, shade at noonday.[8] Thus the mouth's confession will be truly heartfelt: "Lord God, strength of my salvation, you have cast your shadow over my head on the day of battle,"[9] on the day of heat and toil, struggle and temptation. For when meditation on eternal rest casts its shadow on the heads of those who toil it brings not only refreshment from the heat of temptation but also fresh strength and spirit for work, according to what is written of the strong ass Issachar: he saw that rest was good and the land very good, and he bowed his shoulder to bear,[10] that is, for desire of that rest and inheritance he freely brought himself down to toiling. So he also could say: "In all I sought rest and in the inheritance of the Lord I will dwell."[11]

2. Happy is he who in all his labors and in all his ways seeks blessed rest, always hastening, as the Apostle exhorts, to enter into that rest.[12] For desire of it he afflicts his body, but already prepares and disposes his spirit for that rest, being at peace with all men[13] as far as it lies with him. Giving the preference, where his will is concerned, to the rest and the leisure of Mary, to the extent that necessity demands he accepts the toil and the business of Martha, yet does this with as much peace and quiet of spirit as he can, and always brings himself back from that manifold distraction to the one thing necessary.[14]

A man of this sort is at rest even when he is working, just as on the contrary the godless man has to work even when he is resting. For how should they rest upon whom God sends the lot of evil men, to whom he has sworn in his anger: "They shall not enter into my rest."?[15] Outside it there is only affliction and wretchedness, and all around it is a mighty storm.[16] Just as happens in nature, whatever is outside the simplicity and unity of a point is in movement and agitation; any circle whirls around all the faster the further it is from the immobility of its principle, from its axle, its center. Truly the godless walk around in circles, upon them God sends a

6. Ps 16:8.   7. Mt 11:29.   8. Sir 34:19.   9. Ps 139:8.
10. Gen 49:14f.   11. Sir 24:11.   12. Heb 4:11.   13. Rom 12:18.
14. Lk 10:42.   15. Ps 94:11.   16. Ps 49:3.

wheel of evils; and therefore they cannot enter into that interior and eternal rest. Therefore there are havoc and unhappiness in their ways, because they have not known the way of peace,[17] because they have not even sought for it, so as to be able to say: "In all I sought rest," that is, in the midst of their manifold activity by which they are harassed and harass others to have in mind and to seek after the one thing necessary.[18]

Those words belong rather to the just, who can say: "One thing have I asked the Lord, this will I seek.[19] Your face, Lord, I have sought; your face will I seek again."[20] They belong to those who toil only for love of that rest, who prefer with all their heart to have rottenness enter into their bones in order that they may rest on the day of tribulation,[21] rather than live out their days in pleasure and go down to hell in a moment.[22]

3. If, however, anyone should wish to enquire more carefully, who it is principally who says: "In all I sought rest," it is the voice to be sure of Wisdom, it is the Church's voice, it is Mary's voice, it is the voice of any wise soul. Wisdom sought rest in all, but found it in the humble alone. The Church sought rest among all the nations of the world, but found it in believers alone. Mary, too, like any faithful soul, sought rest in all her actions; but today at last she has found it, when after Herod's persecution and the flight into Egypt, after so many plots and outrages on the part of the impious Jews, after so much suffering in her Son's passion and death, after so many and such sharp swords piercing her soul, at length today she can say: "Turn, my soul, into your rest, for the Lord has done well to you.[23] He who created me, was created from me and found rest in the tent[24] of my body; he will not be able to refuse me the rest of his heaven. He heaps up grace for other?", free gift: how should he not return like for like to his Mothers as a

Continue, Mary, continue free from anxiety in the good things of your Son; act with all confidence[25] as Queen, the King's Mother

17. Ps 13:3. 18. Lk 19:42. 19. Ps 26:4. 20. Ps 26:8.
21. Hab 3:16. 22. Job 21:13. 23. Ps 114:7. 24. Sir 24:12.
25. Ps 44:6.

and Bride. You sought rest but what is owed to you is of greater glory: queenship and power. He wishes to share his empire with you, he who shared with you in one flesh and one spirit the mystery of love and unity (that is, when, with due honor shown to nature and through a twofold gift of grace, his Mother was united with him in matrimony). Rest then, happy that you are, in the arms of the Bridegroom. He will recall to you amid embraces and kisses, if I am not mistaken, how pleasantly he rested in the tent of your body, how with greater delight he dwelt in the inner chamber of your heart. God is not unjust, brethren, so as to forget a good work: the memory of a boon once received is always alive with him. Blessed is he with whom God has found rest if but once, in whose tent he has rested if only for one hour.

4. Behold now Wisdom too cries in the streets:[26] "In all I sought rest; I knocked and there was no one who would open,[27] I called and there was no one who would answer."[28] Having become the Son of Man, he is, as the prophet said, like a stranger in the land and a traveler turning aside to seek refuge;[29] he has nowhere to lay his head.[30] He stands outside, his head drenched with dew and his locks with the drops of the night.[31] Who is there among us so kind and hospitable as to rise and open to him,[32] leading him into his chamber; or rather showing him a large upper room, furnished and prepared, in which he may eat the new pasch with his disciples?[33] For I say this, brethren: unless he finds with us the rest he is seeking, we shall not find in him the rest we desire.

The Lord tells me through his prophet: "This is my rest, that you should restore the weary; and this is my refreshment."[34] Blessed is he who attends to the needy and the poor: on an evil day the Lord[35] will do the same for him and prepare for him rest and refreshment.

If then God reckons as done to himself the kindness shown to his members, how much more will he recall with thanksgiving

---

26. Prov 1:20.   27. Rev 3:20.   28. Is 66:4.   29. Jer 14:9, 8.
30. Mt 8:20.   31. Song 5:2.   32. Song 5:5. 33. Mk 14:14f.
34. Is 28:12.   35. Ps 40:2.

what is done to his Spirit, saying: "I was a stranger and you received me."³⁶ Shall the poverty of many holy people, because it is unable to bring in wanderers and feed the hungry, be unkind and inhospitable to the Lord, who is accustomed to find his lodging with the poor by preference? "Upon whom will I rest," he says, "if not with the humble and the quiet and him who fears my words?"³⁷ O humility, straitened yourself but with ample room for the godhead; poor and inadequate for yourself but adequate for him whom the world cannot contain, you give him to eat plentifully and delightfully who feeds even the angels.

"Upon whom," he says, "shall I rest if not with the humble? In all I sought rest, but I found it with a humble handmaid." No one was found like her³⁸ in the grace of humility, therefore all the fullness of the godhead³⁹ rested even in bodily form in this fullness of humility. Yet it rested in another way in the Son, for although the Mother was very humble, the Son was far more humble. Therefore the sevenfold Spirit not only rested upon him⁴⁰ but also prepared various dwelling-places of happiest rest in him for all who have learned from him to be meek and humble.⁴¹ Or rather it made him to be wholly a golden couch⁴² for rest. A foretaste of the most blessed rest which this couch affords would seem to have been given in some way to him who merited to lie upon his breast at the Supper.⁴³

5. But I would like to consider further how reasonable and appropriate are the words: "Upon whom shall I rest if not upon the humble and the quiet?"⁴⁴ For how should anything rest upon the restless; how should a column stand immovable upon a base that shifts or totters? However, who but the humble man can be quiet? Who but he can possess himself in the peace of a quiet and modest spirit? As for the godless man, the wind sweeps him off the face of the earth;⁴⁵ he is tossed about by every wind of doctrine.⁴⁶

36. Mt 25:35.   37. Is 66:2.   38. Sir 44:20.   39. Col 2:9.
40. Is 11:2.   41. Mt 11:29.   42. Song 3:10.

43. "One of the disciples, whom Jesus loved, was reclining on the breast of Jesus."—Jn 13:23. This is believed to be St John.

44. Is 66:2.   45. Ps 1:4.   46. Eph 4:14.

"The godless man," says the Prophet, "is like a stormy sea that cannot rest."[47] He seethes with anger, he is inflamed with avarice, he swells with pride, he is continually harassing himself with interior conflict and cast down by sedition in his own house.

In order then, my brethren, that he who loves quiet and bestows it may rest in you, make a point, as the Apostle advises, of being quiet. How will this come about? "I tell you," he says, "to attend to your own business and to work with your hands."[48] Work is a load by which, as ships are given weight so hearts are given quiet and gravity, and in it the outward man finds a firm foundation and a settled condition.

As you have read, a wayward woman is the beginning of great evils: she is impatient of quiet, her feet are unable to stay at home, she lurks now in the street, now in the market, now at the corners.[49] Nor is it without reason that the Teacher of the Nations is so suspicious of this evil of restlessness that he judges it should be visited not only with a rebuke but with ostracism. "We beg you, brethren," he says, "to rebuke the restless."[50] And again in the second epistle to the Thessalonians, among other things he thunders as it were from heaven upon the restless: "We are told that there are those among you who are restless and live in idleness, neglecting their own business to mind other people's. We charge all such to earn their bread by going on calmly with their work. If anybody refuses to listen to what we have said in our letter, take note of that man and have nothing to do with him, that he may be ashamed of himself."[51]

6. If perhaps somebody like this, which God forbid, is found among you, it were better and more seemly that before he is branded so seriously and publicly he should be ashamed by his own impulse—ashamed because although he should be corrected a blind eye is turned to him, although he is blameworthy he is tolerated. But let him be ashamed in such a way that shame corrects him, rebuke gladdens him, and he makes not only us but also the Spirit of God glad, who says: "In all I sought rest," but only finds

---

47. Is 57:20.   48. 1 Thess 4:11.   49. Prov 7:10ff.
50. 1 Thess 5:14.   51. 2 Thess 3:11ff.

it in the quiet and only bestows it on the quiet. Through the Prophet he recalls and curbs the restless: "If you turn back and become quiet, you will be saved."[52]

Let us all then together so make a point of being quiet[53] that in our quiet we may always be occupied with meditation on eternal quiet, and for desire of it be found ready for every work. May the blessed Mother of God, whose rest we are celebrating, obtain this for us by her prayers from him who rested in the tabernacle[54] of her body and her heart. He is eternal rest, Christ Jesus, to whom be honor and glory for ever and ever. Amen.

52. Is 30:15.   53. 1 Thess 4:11.   54. Sir 24:12.

SERMON 50

THE FOURTH SERMON FOR THE ASSUMPTION

MARY HAS CHOSEN THE BEST PART.[1] This was said of Mary, the sister of Martha, but it was realized today with greater fullness and holiness in Mary, Mother of the Lord. For today the blessed Virgin Mary chose the best part; or rather she entered today into unending possession of what she had chosen long before: to keep close to the Lord, to be inseparable from him, and to enjoy God's Word for all eternity. Neither is it strange or inappropriate if what was said of the one Mary is transferred to the other; since the aptness of the application is borne out by similarity not only in name but also in deed. The one welcomed the Lord to the shelter of her roof, the other to the bridal chamber of her womb. "And he who created me," we read, "rested in my tent."[2] The one sat at the Lord's feet and listened to his word;[3] the other, carefully tending his humanity, kept all the words which concerned him, pondering them in her heart.[4]

But also when Jesus was going round towns and villages preaching the Gospel[5] Mary was his inseparable companion, clinging to his footsteps and hanging upon his words as he taught, so much so

---

1. Lk 10:42. This is sung during the communion service at the mass on the Feast of the Assumption. It is taken from the Gospel passage which is used in the Cistercian rite for this Feast.

2. Sir 24:12. This text occurs in the reading at the first vespers of the Assumption.

3. Lk 10:39. We are again drawing from the Gospel of the day.

4. Lk 2:19, 51.   5. Mt 9:35.

that neither the storm of persecution nor dread of punishment could deter her from following her Son and Master. By the Lord's cross there stood Mary, his Mother.[6] Truly a Mother, who did not abandon her Son even in the face of death. How could she be frightened of death, when her love was as strong as death,[7] or rather stronger than death? Truly she stood by Jesus' cross, when at the same time the pain of the cross crucified her mind and as manifold a sword pierced her own soul[8] as she beheld the body of her Son pierced with wounds. Rightly therefore was she recognized as his Mother there and by his care entrusted to a suitable protector, in which both the mother's unalloyed love for her Son and the Son's kindness toward his Mother were proved to the utmost.

On other occasions he seemed as it were to ignore his Mother, whether at the wedding feast when she asked for a miracle and he answered: "Nay, woman, why dost thou trouble me with that?"[9] or in the midst of his preaching the Gospel when someone told him: "Behold your Mother and your brethren are standing outside, asking for you," and he answered: "Who is my mother?"[10] But he had to give such an answer to his Mother when she asked for a miracle in order to show that miracles came to him not from his Mother but from another source. And he could give no better answer to the man who interrupted the words of the Gospel by announcing his relatives than to demonstrate that spiritual things must come before those of the flesh. It was as if, in the same way as before, he were to say to his relatives seeking him while he was busy with the work of the Gospel: "Why do you seek me? Do you not know that I must concern myself with my Father's business?"[11]

2. It could not be that he spurned his Mother, he who was so careful to lay down the law that parents should be honored.[12] It could not be that on earth he showed disgust for his Mother when he had desired her beauty from heaven. Rather he was setting charity in order in us[13] both by his words and by his example

---

6. Jn 19:25.   7. Song 8:6.   8. Lk 2:35.   9. Jn 2:4.
10. Mt 12:47f.   11. Lk 2:49.   12. Ex 20:12; Mt 15:4ff.
13. Song 2:4.

teaching us to put before our affection for carnal attachments not only the love of God but also the love of those who do God's will.

For the affection which is demanded from the hearts of all of us whom the supreme Father has deigned to adopt[14] is one which will make us say in faith together with his Only-begotten: "Whoever does the will of my Father who is in heaven, he is my brother and sister and mother."[15] Indeed those words belong to God's sons; neither does the Spirit himself bear any more faithful witness to our spirit that we are God's sons[16] than that this utterance of God's Only-begotten should sound from our hearts.

So Jesus demonstrates that Mary, who was his mother according to the flesh, is his mother in another way also, since she too so valued the Father's will that the Father could foretell to her: "You shall be called 'My will is in her.'"[17] Therefore where the Son seemed to ignore her, there he is found to have honored her the more; since the honor of the name of mother is doubled for her; she now bears in spirit also through inspiration the same Son whom she bore in her womb through incarnation.

3. Further, loving her as he did Jesus loved her to the end,[18] so as not only to bring his life to an end for her but also to speak almost his last words for her benefit. As his last will and testament he committed to his beloved heir the care of his mother, whose debtor he knew himself to be. So did Christ divide his inheritance between Peter who loved the most and John who was loved the most: the Church fell to Peter, Mary to John.[19] This bequest belonged to John not only by right of kinship but also because of the privilege love had bestowed and the witness his chastity bore.

For it was fitting that only a virgin should minister to the Virgin, so that the blessed Virgin, languishing for love of God, should be stayed up with the flowers of chastity;[20] and the young man's virginity should receive that much recompense in the meantime:

14. Rom 8:15.
15. Mt 12:50.
16. Cf. Rom 8:16.
17. Is 62:4.
18. Jn 13:1.
19. Jn 21:15ff.; 19:26f.
20. Song 2:5.

to make progress by living with such great holiness. But he also merited, because he was proved faithful in his service of the inviolate Mother, to have confided to him the mysteries of the Godhead and hidden truths concerning the inviolate Word. It was fitting, I say, that none other than the beloved of her Son should minister to the Mother of the Lord, so that the Mother, always sighing for her Son, might be refreshed the more sweetly by her Son's beloved. And the disciple complaining that his Master had been taken away from him too soon, might rejoice in having found the Mistress of all truth. Providence also arranged very conveniently that he who was to write a Gospel should have intimate conferences on each matter with her who knew about them all, for she had taken note from the beginning of everything that happened to her Son and treasured up all the words that concerned him, pondering them in her heart.[21] She showed herself to be a Martha in her care for the Child's rearing in such a way that nonetheless she fulfilled the part of Mary in her application to knowledge of the Word.

Especially, however, after her Son ascended to where he was before,[22] the mother, released from all temporal anxiety and more fully enlightened by the Holy Spirit (besides the special first graces she received at the incarnation, she received him in common with the Apostles), rejoiced to be still and see that Jesus is God.[23] A vision of wholly ineffable joy and supreme delight for all who love Jesus,[24] but before all others for her who gave birth to Jesus. As the grace of giving birth to God was conferred on her apart from all others, so was the privilege of glorying in him to whom she gave birth. Altogether her own and without comparison was the glory of the Virgin Mother, to see God the King of all in the diadem of the flesh with which she crowned him,[25] so as to recognize God and adore him in her own body and see her own body glorified in God. These are the truths which in the meantime Mary rejoiced to contemplate, this is the best part which she had chosen, which today

---

21. Lk 2:19, 51. 22. Jn 6:63. 23. Ps 45:11.
24. 1 Cor 2:9. 25. Song 3:11.

has not been taken away from her but brought to perfection in her.[26] For since she was not careless or remiss in Martha's work she has not been left without Mary's fruit. Toil is in action, fruit or reward in contemplation. "Inasmuch," we read, "as her soul toiled, he shall see and be filled."[27]

4. We say these things to you, brethren, so that if anyone feels a desire for that best part which is praised in Mary, he may know that it is the reward of the man who cannot be reproached for failing to do Martha's part: it is not right that reward should be sought before merit. It behooves Jacob first to be united with Lia before enjoying Rachel's embraces;[28] and he himself has to be called and to be Jacob before becoming Israel.[29] "If they will make you master of the feast," says the Wise Man, "make good provision for the guests, and so take your place among them; your duty done, recline at ease and rejoice on their account and receive the crown that marks their favor."[30] The toil involved in work or the anxieties of administration are seeds of justice, through which joys are to be reaped from the fruit of consoling mercy. For so the Prophet says: "Sow for yourselves in justice, reap from the fruit of mercy."[31] But he who sows sparingly will also reap sparingly; and he who sows with a blessing will also reap with a blessing.[32]

No one to be sure sowed with so generous a blessing as she who was blessed among women[33] and brought forth blessed seed from her womb. But shall I say seed or fruit? Better to say both. For he who is seed to those who are working out justice is fruit to those who are reaping glory. He is seed in his passion, fruit in his resurrection. "Powerful on earth is that seed"[34] which, falling upon the earth, speedily stirred up its power to bring forth much fruit,[35] so

---

26. Lk 10:42. 27. Is 53:11.
28. Gen 29:24ff. Lia and Rachel, like Martha and Mary, are commonly used to typify and contrast the active and contemplative lives. Cf. e.g., St Bernard's *Sermons on the Song of Songs* (Cistercian Fathers Series 4, 7, 31) 9:7; 41:5; 46:5; 51:3.
29. Gen 32:28. 30. Sir 31:1ff. 31. Hos 10:12.
32. 2 Cor 9:6. 33. Lk 1:42. 34. Ps 111:2.
35. Jn 12:24f.

that in that seed all nations should be blessed.[36] Hence the psalm continues: "the race of the upright shall be blessed."[37]

5. So let Mary reap her blessings; let her who sowed the blessing of all nations[38] receive in a way all her own the blessing of all nations. "All generations," she says, "will call me blessed."[39] This is too little. All the orders of blessed spirits will call you blessed. The daughters of the heavenly Sion saw her today as she went up and called her happy, and queens praised her.[40] Mary does indeed reap her blessings today, because that all-embracing blessing which she brought forth from herself has been given back to her spiritually. Give her, says the Holy Spirit, of the Fruit of her womb and let her be filled with him to whom she gave birth.

O Mother of Mercy, be filled with your Son's glory and leave what you have over to your little ones.[41] You are now at the table, we are dogs under the table.[42] Like a maid with her eyes on the hands of her mistress[43] this hungry family looks to you for the food of life. Through you we have shared in the fruit of life at the table of these present sacraments; through you may we share at the table of everlasting joys in the same fruit of life, Jesus, the blessed Fruit of your womb,[44] to whom be honor and glory for ever and ever. Amen.

---

36. Gen 22:18; 26:4.   37. Ps 111:2.   38. Sir 44:25.
39. Lk 1:48.   40. Song 6:8.   41. Ps 16:4.
42. Mt 15:27.   43. Ps 122:2.
44. The Latin words are quoted exactly from the *Salve Regina*. In Guerric's time this antiphon was sung at vespers in the office of the Assumption.

SERMON 51

THE FIRST SERMON FOR OUR LADY'S BIRTHDAY

"AS THE VINE I HAVE BROUGHT FORTH a pleasant odor."[1] Today we celebrate the birthday of the blessed Virgin Mother from whom the Life of all things took his birth. Today is the birthday of that Virgin from whom the Savior of all men willed to be born in order that he might give to all who were born to death the power to be reborn to life. Today is the birthday of that new Mother who has destroyed the curse brought by the first mother[2] so that all those who through the fault of the first had been born under the yoke of eternal condemnation might instead, through her, inherit a blessing. She is indeed the new Mother, for she has brought new life to her children already hardening with age and has healed the defect of both inborn and acquired senility. Yes indeed. She is the new Mother, who by an unheard of miracle has given birth in such a way that, becoming a mother, she has not ceased to be a Virgin. And she has given birth to the Child who created all things, even the Mother herself.

It is indeed a wonderful new thing, this fruitful virginity, but far more wonderful is the novelty of the Child born of it. No one who admits that the Child was God, finds any difficulty in believing

---

1. Sir 24:23. This text from Sirach is read as the short reading at both vespers on this feast of Our Lady's birthday. It is also part of the first reading at Mass.

2. See above, Sermon 47:2, note 5.

his Mother remained a Virgin. His birth in no wise could injure the physical integrity of his Mother, this Child who went about making even the diseased whole. Nor could the reality of the body he assumed be thought to limit the power of the Creator as if he could not retain for himself what he gives to many of his creatures. For you find not a few creatures that are born without any harm to the integrity of the parents. In their own way all these bear witness to their Creator's own immaculate birth.

2. But the Mother herself, who was quite aware of the mystery surrounding her, has spoken and taught us how and what she brought forth. She speaks however not in contemporary or recent arguments[3] but in the ancient oracles of prophecy, because, as the Apostle Peter tells us, the word of prophecy is a stronger witness than miracles.[4] Indeed what is less open to deceit or suspect of falsity than the testimony from heaven about one not yet born? Long before her birth therefore the Spirit, who would later make his abode in her, borrowed Mary's voice to defend both the divinity of the Child and the integrity of the Mother—all his own handiwork—against the blasphemies of unbelievers. In her person, if we are to follow a common opinion, he uttered the words you have just heard: "As the vine, I have brought forth a pleasant odor."

In their context, these words must be applied to the Person of Wisdom himself, that is, the Son. But you know quite well from the rules of Sacred Scripture that this does not mean they cannot be applied also to the Mother, like so many other passages. You know too that there is other evidence, enough and more than enough, bearing on this question, which is more familiar to you and much clearer than this. But you must not be cheated in your expectations of what today's lesson can teach us.

3. Let Mary therefore reply to the blasphemies, both on her

---

3. Guerric here gives some indication of his sharing the common feelings of the early Cistercians, "the last of the Fathers," in regard to the new scholasticism. See for example Bernard of Clairvaux, *On the Song of Songs*, 22:10 (Cistercian Fathers Series 7).

4. 2 Pet 1:19.

own behalf and on that of her Son; let her put an end to all heresies with a single word. "As the vine, I have brought forth a pleasant odor." It is as if she were to say: "My childbearing is unique among woman-kind, but it has its like among things of nature. Do you want to know how virginity gave birth to the Savior? In the same way as the flower of the vine produces its fragrance. If ever you find the flower corrupted through giving off its sweet odor, then you may hold that my virginity was violated in giving birth to my Savior."

Can you find fault with the aptness of the simile? What else is virginity than the flower of an undefiled body? What else is the Child of virginity than its sweet odor?[5] But take care that you do not die of this good odor. To some it is truly a good perfume of life, bringing life; it is so to them who have been saved. But to others it is the fume of death, bringing death to those who perish;[6] just as the scent of the flowering vine is death to animals that have been poisoned.

The spirit of the old Patriarch was refreshed by the sweetness of this odor. Touching his son and breathing the fragrance of Christ, he was filled with the memory of the abundance of that fragrance and exclaimed: "Behold the smell of my son is as the smell of a plentiful field which the Lord has blessed."[7] God the Father smelled that same sweet odor and, well pleased with it, had mercy on the human race when his Son offered himself as an oblation and victim to God in the odor of sweetness.[8] By that same sweet odor we are drawn when by conversion we run toward him; the young maidens too are drawn by it when in their love they run after him.[9] There is a fragrance to be perceived in his wonderful preaching, but this is not the same as the fragrance which comes from his vestments and ointments and which is, in a manner of speaking, given off even more abundantly by his body itself. That is none other than the virtue which goes out from him[10] to rouse the luke-

---

5. As Guerric goes on here, we have a good example of how a particular word brings to his mind passages from all parts of the Sacred Scriptures.
6. 2 Cor 2:15f.   7. Gen 27:27.   8. Eph 5:2.
9. Song 1:2f.   10. Lk 6:19.

warm and infuse in them the fervor of love, so as to make them rejoice to run the way of his commandments.[11]

4. Mary is overjoyed because she has brought forth so fragrant a fruit. "As the vine," she says, "I have brought forth a pleasant odor." Well does she say, "as a vine," for a cluster of cypress is her love to her.[12] From him not only has the winepress of the passion pressed out the red must of precious Blood with which the goodly chalice inebriates us[13] in the sacrifice of the mass, but day after day holy piety presses out for itself a wine which delights the heart of man[14] and inebriates him with joy and love. True, the flavor of the vintage does not inebriate before the sweetness of the fragrance has drawn, nor does the joy of full vision fill the soul with gladness if loving reverence for his renown has not allured it first, because unless we have believed we will not understand nor will we taste that the Lord is sweet.[15] It is faith that smells, experiential knowledge that tastes and enjoys.[16] Thus Mary, describing her Jesus by his powers and influence, first of all calls him a pleasant odor because he has to implant this in us at the beginning if the fragrance of his holy renown is to draw us to him.

What the fruit is from which that odor emanates and by which we are drawn, she makes abundantly clear when she adds: "My flowers are the fruit of honor and integrity."[17] No doubt about it, the fruit, Jesus, is the pleasant odor that attracts, the integrity that sanctifies, the honor that glorifies; the pleasant odor by which we are, as it were, brought to the road, the integrity by means of which we are led along it, the honor to which we are brought at the end of it. Right well is it called integrity, the condition as it were of honor. For the honor of supreme dignity and glory can have no place in us in heaven unless integrity of life and conduct prepares

11. Ps 18:6; 118:32.   12. Song 1:13.   13. Ps 22:5.
14. Ps 103:15.   15. Ps 33:9.
16. This is the goal of the monastic life as it was understood by the Cistercians: the experience of God. Much of their writings, especially their commentaries and sermons on the Song of Songs, is dedicated to describing this experience and the means by which the soul can hope to attain to it or at least, under the impulse of grace, prepare for it.
17. Sir 24:23.

a throne for it in this life. No one in that life, any more than in this, will be seen everywhere honored unless he has integrity of conduct, just as no one is found with integrity of manners who has not at least some honor. Jesus therefore is first of all a pleasant odor to them whom he calls, then integrity of conduct to them whom he justifies, finally honor to them whom he glorifies. For whom he predestined, them also he called; and whom he called them also he justified; and whom he justified them also he glorified.[18]

5. "Such is my beloved," says Mary, "and he is my Son, O daughters of Jerusalem.[19] He is the blessed fruit of my womb,[20] the fruit my flowers produced." She does not say "my flower," but "my flowers," for though she is a holy virgin, the flower of virginity in her is multiform. In her, by a singular privilege, it grows in greater profusion than in anyone else. She who was wholly beautiful within and without, was bedecked with the perfect fullness of the blossoms and loveliness of virginity. In you too, if chastity reaches perfection, not only will the bloom of it show in your body, but a certain divine holiness[21] will take possession of your whole being. There will be no petulant or wandering gaze, but a demeanor radiant with modesty; no suggestive or improper talk, but speech pleasantly diffident or seasoned with wisdom; there will be no itching ears eager to listen to new ideas or filthy stories, nor will the palate be ever desirous of tasty morsels; the gait will not be hurried but reserved; dress will not be—I will not say immodest—it will not be unbecoming; instead it will be in perfect accord with the religious life; the whole man will be so alive with the grace of your holy way of living that you will be able to say, when you invite the Bridegroom into your chamber: "Our bed is strewn with flowers."[22] In fact you will be wholly a most beautiful flower of the kind with which he desires his spouse to support him and refresh him as he faints with love. "Stay me up with flowers," he says to her, "compass me about with apples because I languish with love."[23]

18. Rom 8:30.
21. Ps 131:18.
19. Song 5:16.
22. Song 1:15.
20. Lk 1:42.
23. Song 2:5.

A just man like this, even when his roots in the earth have grown old and his trunk has turned into dust, at the fragrance of the living water in the resurrection, that is, in the renewal of the just, will grow like the lily and will blossom for ever in the presence of the Lord, who is himself the Flower of the flower, virgin-born Son of the Virgin, the Crown, too, and the Spouse of virgins. He is the Flower, I make bold to say, which will crown not only the integrity of virgins but the chastity of those who, having lost their virginity, have dedicated their virtue again. To him be glory for endless ages. Amen.

SERMON 52

THE SECOND SERMON FOR OUR LADY'S BIRTHDAY

"I AM THE MOTHER of fair love, of fear, of knowledge and of holy hope."[1] You will remember that when we spoke last year on the beginning of today's lesson we attributed the text, not unsuitably, I think, to the blessed Mother of God while retaining the interpretation which holds that the whole lesson strictly speaking refers to her Son, who is the Wisdom of God. The voice and the person of the Virgin are much more obvious in the passage we have just quoted from the same book; but we should realize how beautifully and aptly this list of virtues describes her Son.

Now the Mother knew her Son just as well as he did who said: "Even if we used to think of Christ in a human fashion, we do so no longer."[2] The Mother knew him from the first according to the form of flesh in which she gave him birth; but this is far from knowing that form in which the Father generated him.[3] In the first he was seen for a short space of time and there was no beauty or comeliness in him;[4] in the other he is the splendor of glory[5] and the glow that radiates from eternal light,[6] with whom there is no change nor swerving from his course.[7] The sight of him in the first form increased the sin of disbelievers; the sight of him in the other is reserved for the reward of the just.

1. Sir 24:24. See above, Sermon 51, note 1.   2. 2 Cor 5:16.
3. Phil 2:7.   4. Is 53:2.   5. Heb 1:3.   6. Wis 7:26.
7. Jas 1:17.

And so we are right in saying that between the form of the flesh and the form of the Word, like a bridge between the two, another form can be distinguished in Christ, spiritual in its nature yet showing itself clearly in the flesh: the form, that is to say, of the life he lived in his body in order to convey his message to those who were to believe in him.[8] And when Christ has been formed in us[9] according to this form, according to the pattern of virtuous life he manifested in his own person, then we shall be capable of seeing not only the form which has been formed for us but even that which formed us.

2. Yes. Christ has taken one form in the flesh; shows another in his conduct; is begotten from eternity in a third by way of knowledge. He is our brother according to the flesh, our teacher by his conduct, our God by his generation as the Word. He accepted his fleshly form to accomplish the mystery of our salvation; he manifests himself in his life as our example; he will reveal himself as the eternally begotten as our reward. Then even to look upon his bodily form upon which the angels desire to gaze[10] will not be the least part of our glory. And the man who will be so blessed is he who in this present life has become a lover of the form which is proposed as our example, for the man who seeks to pry into that other form which is stored up for us as our reward will be dazzled by the brightness.[11]

He was such a lover and an admirer of this form who said: "Yours is more than mortal beauty."[12] Do you want to be certain that he was speaking of the moral stature of Christ, not of his bodily appearance? Of the beauty of his virtues, not of his limbs? Then listen to what follows: "Gird yourself with all your majesty and beauty; ride on triumphant and reign." Perhaps it would still be doubtful had he not continued: "on account of truth and meekness

---

8. 1 Tim 1:16.   9. Gal 4:19.   10. 1 Pet 1:12.

11 Prov. 25:27. The threefold form of Christ—the middle form for his formation in us—this is Guerric's outstanding contribution to spiritual theology. It is discussed at greater length in vol. 1, Introduction, pp. xxxi–xxxiv.

12. Ps 44:3.

and justice."[13] This certainly is your comeliness and your beauty by which you have acquired the kingdom, O Most Beautiful of kings: truth of speech, meekness of behavior, rightness of judgment. With this beauty you have easily allured and subjected to yourself even the hearts of enemies, indeed you are the fulfillment of every yearning and desire. How wonderful the triumph of grace, a new and perfect type of victory: the enemy is not hounded to death by strength but converted to love by beauty. Behold the whole world goes out after him,[14] desiring the fairness of his beauty, not because it has seen his face but because it has heard so much that is lovable about his meekness, truth and justice. The fairness of his beauty is from Sion,[15] because the Lord's command came out from Sion, his word from Jerusalem.[16] That is to say, the Gospel is sent to us from there, in which a more beautiful portrait of Christ has been revealed; the form, that is, of life and doctrine which he has passed on by his teaching and shown in his own person by his example.

3. To know Christ now in this form is loving service for Christians; to know him in the form of flesh was scandal to the Jews;[17] to know the divine form is the complete happiness and joy of the angels. This is the reason why Paul, knowing the flesh profits nothing without the spirit which gives life,[18] repudiates any knowledge of Christ according to the flesh.[19] He does so in order to give all his attention to the life-giving spirit.

Mary seems to have understood this too. Wishing to introduce the Beloved of her womb, the Beloved of her desires, into the affections of all her children, she describes him not according to the flesh but according to the spirit as if she too would say: "Even if I knew Christ according to the flesh, now I know him so no longer."[20] For she desires to form her Only-begotten in all her sons by adoption. Although they have been brought to birth by the word of truth,[21] nevertheless she brings them forth every day

---

13. Ps 44:5.   14. Jn 12:19.   15. Ps 49:2.   16. Is 2:3.
17. 1 Cor 1:23.   18. Jn 6:63.   19. 2 Cor 5:16.   20. *Ibid.*
21. Jas 1:18.

by desire and loyal care until they reach the stature of the perfect man, the maturity of her Son,[22] whom she bore and brought forth once and for all. We can go further and say with Isaiah: before she was in labor she brought forth,[23] because she brought forth without sorrow; nor did she experience the difficulty and trouble of childbirth when she brought forth the fruit of eternal gladness.

4. Commending therefore this fruit she says to us: "I am the mother of fair love, of fear, of knowledge and of holy hope."[24]

Is he then your Son, O Virgin of virgins? Is your beloved such a one as this, O most beautiful of women? "Clearly so, my beloved is such a one and he is my Son, O daughters of Jerusalem.[25] My beloved is fair love in himself, fear, hope and knowledge in whoever is born of him."[26] For he is not only the one whom we love, fear and acknowledge and in whom we hope, but it is he who brings about all those things in us; and as these virtues grow in strength like the limbs and members of our body they bring him to maturity and perfection in us. Then Christ will have been perfectly formed in you,[27] as far as is possible in this life; then his own truth will have been made manifest in you if you have acknowledged the truth which is himself, and having acknowledged it you have glorified it in fear as well as in hope. And lest this hope should be in vain, charity has also been poured into your heart.[28] But you may think that this interpretation is not apt because the sequence of these virtues or stages of spiritual progress is different from the order in which they are mentioned. The text does not say: "It is I that gave birth to all true knowledge and fear, hope and love," but on the contrary: "It is I that gave birth to all noble loving, all fear, all true knowledge and the holy gift of hope." And yet some fitness and logical sequence can perhaps be found in this order.

We have seen that fear is born of knowledge, that hope comes to sweeten this fear lest it fall into despair, and that love bears hope

---

22 Eph. 4:13. Mary does her part in the formation of Christ in us. Here is the final development of Guerric's teaching concerning Mary's work for our redemption and sanctification. See Introduction, vol. 1 pp. xxxiv–xxxvi.

23. Is 66:7.   24. Sir 24:24.   25. Song 5:9, 16.   26. Jn 1:13.

27. Gal 4:19.   28. Rom 5:5.

company lest it be in vain. Similarly, in inverse order, love brings forth chaste fear and fear with love enlightens knowledge, as the Wise Man says: "You who fear the Lord, love him and your hearts will be enlightened."[29] The more truly God is acknowledged by a heart which has been enlightened the more trustingly that heart hopes in him. That is why it is written: "Those who acknowledge your name, O Lord, can trust you."[30] Hope indeed is holy, as John says speaking of the hope of seeing God: "Now a man who rests these hopes in him lives a life of holiness; he too is holy."[31]

5. It is called fair love, beautifully and fittingly, because God is love[32] and for this reason highest beauty. And this virtue, love, is almost the whole beauty of the Church, which the Bridegroom himself is found to extol and marvel at in her so greatly and so often in the Canticle of Love. Certainly that love is fair which is from a pure heart, good conscience and unfeigned faith.[33] For where the heart is pure there is no wrinkle; where the conscience good, nothing unclean;[34] where faith is unfeigned there is nothing that can be displeasing in the eyes of the Bridegroom and so deprive him of the joy he finds in the Church, at present the object of his mercy but destined to share his glory in heaven. Then too by this adjective the love of the saints should be distinguished from natural love, whether that love be unclean, which sort should not even be mentioned among the faithful, or natural, by which parents are loved, or worldly, by which men love each other on account of worldly necessities or desires. Sinful love should be driven far, far away; rather it should never fall under God's gaze. It is time to have done with all natural love. The love of the inward and eternal beauty should alone reign supreme, by which those who are truly beautiful love God alone or others for his sake.

And now do you, good Jesus, you who give the saints their charm and who excel in beauty not only the sons of men[35] but the heavenly hosts as well, do you gird yourself with all your majesty and beauty, ride on triumphant and reign;[36] and may the

---

29. Sir 2:10. 30. Ps 9:11. 31. 1 Jn 3:3. 32. 1 Jn 4:8.
33. 1 Tim 1:5. 34. Eph 5:27. 35. Ps 44:3. 36. Ps 44:5.

reign of your fair love be extended so far and wide that it may disenthrone and abolish all manner of foulness from the furthest boundaries of its kingdom. May it draw to its own likeness all worldly love and subdue to itself and set in order natural love so that the world may come to love you with that beautiful and true love, the same love wherewith you have loved the world,[37] you its Savior,[38] who live and reign, God, world without end. Amen

---

37. Jn 3:16. 38. Jn 4:42; 1 Jn 4:14.

SERMON 53

SERMON FOR THE FEAST OF ALL SAINTS

"BLESSED ARE THE POOR IN SPIRIT."[1] This saying immediately calls to mind the famous and inspired words which the Son of God uttered as witness to himself through the mouth of his Prophet even before his birth in the flesh. Then later, after his birth but before his fame had spread, he himself uttered the self-same words declaring that they referred to him: "The Spirit of the Lord is upon me, he has sent me to preach the good news to the poor."[2] And here he is preaching the good news to the poor; here he is bringing the good news of the kingdom. "Blessed are the poor in spirit," we hear him say, "for theirs is the kingdom of heaven."[3] This is, indeed, a happy beginning, full of the new grace of the new dispensation. No matter how lacking in faith a man may be, or how reluctant to respond, he will be almost compelled to give his attention and even more to act when he hears blessedness being promised to the wretched and the kingdom of heaven to those in exile or in want.

This, I say, is a happy beginning of the new law, full of promise. From the very first, the Lawgiver confers the manifold blessings of these beatitudes on mankind which is thereby attracted to progress from virtue to virtue[4] by climbing these eight steps which the structure of this Gospel chapter has set in our hearts according to the model of the heavenly image,[5] the model which was shown to

---

1. Mt 5:3.   2. Lk 4:18; Is 61:1.   3. Mt 5:3.   4. Ps 83:8.
5. Heb 8:5.

Ezechiel on the mountain of the visions of God. In this arrangement of the virtues in a series of eight steps there can clearly be seen a certain stairway for the heart and a progression in merits. Man is led step by step from the lowest states of evangelical perfection to the very highest until he enters the temple on Sion and beholds the God of Gods. It was in reference to this temple that the Prophet speaks: "And the ascent to it was by eight steps."[6]

2. The first virtue in this ascent, proper to beginners, is renunciation of the world, which makes us poor in spirit. The second is meekness, which enables us to submit ourselves in obedience and to accustom ourselves to such submission. Next comes mourning to make us weep for our sins and to beg God for virtue. It is here that we first taste justice,[7] and so learn to hunger and thirst more keenly after justice in ourselves as well as in others, and we begin to be roused to zeal against sinful men. Then, lest this zeal should grow immoderate and lead to vice, mercy follows to temper it.[8] When a man has learned to become merciful and just by diligent practice of these virtues he will then perhaps be

---

6. Ezek 40:31ff. It was common among the Cistercian Fathers to see traced out in the beatitudes the Cistercian way to holiness. As Aelred explicitly expresses it: "This is the way, my dearest ones, by which you must return to the fatherland, by which we enter into the society of those whose feast we celebrate today."—Third Sermon for the Feast of All Saints (PL 195:352B; Cistercian Fathers Series 35). In their sermons for this Feast the Fathers traced out this way, and while there is a very common tone and flavor to be found among these sermons, each has his own particular way of doing it and his own particular mode of expression. Cf. Bernard of Clairvaux, First Sermon for the Feast of All Saints (Cistercian Fathers Series 34); Isaac of Stella, Sermons for the Feast of All Saints, 1–5 (Cistercian Fathers Series 11); Aelred of Rievaulx, *op. cit.* Aelred (nn. 3f.) and Isaac (Sermon 5:6) also employed the idea of steps without however using it as the basic form of their development as has Guerric.

7. Bernard, too, has developed this idea that it is the first taste of justice, the consolation that comes after mourning one's sins, that creates the hunger and thirst for more—*loc. cit.,* n. 10.

8. Here Guerric differs from all the other Cistercian Fathers in his interpretation. They see the fourth and fifth beatitudes totally in relation to God, and because no man no matter how just can stand before the most just God, he must then resort to mercy in order to obtain mercy. Cf. Bernard of Clairvaux, *loc. cit.,* n. 11; Aelred of Rievaulx, *loc. cit.,* n. 4; Isaac of Stella, Sermon 3:10ff.

fit to enter upon the way of contemplation and to give himself to the task of obtaining that purity of heart which will enable him to see God.[9] Tested and proved in this way in both the active and the contemplative life, he who bears the name and office of a son of God through his having become the father[10] and servant of other men will then and only then be worthy to be a peacemaker between them and God.[11] Thus he will fulfill the office of mediator and advocate, and be worthy to make peace among the brethren themselves and even between the brethren and those who are outside the community. For thus it is written in praise of our holy Fathers: "They were men bringing peace in their houses."[12] If a man is faithful and constant in this office, he will often attain that virtue and merit which belongs to the martyr, for he suffers persecution for justice's sake,[13] and this even on occasion at the hands of those for whom he is fighting, so that he can say: "The sons of my mother have fought against me,"[14] and: "With them that hated peace I was peaceful; when I spoke to them they fought against me without cause."[15]

3. How much glory, and how rich a reward, will finally crown such perfection in heaven—if indeed it is something we can measure like this—since even to those who are taking their first steps in renouncing the world our Lord promises so much happiness when he says: "Blessed are the poor in spirit, for theirs is the kingdom of heaven."[16] Clearly the men who are truly blessed are those who throw off the cheap but heavy burdens of this world, and renounce

---

9. Here Guerric is in harmony with the other Cistercian Fathers in seeing in the first five beatitudes the exercises of the active life (as it was understood in those times and in the patristic tradition, namely, the development of the virtues) and with the sixth the transition into the contemplative life. Bernard, *loc. cit.,* n. 14; Aelred, *loc. cit.,* n. 5; Isaac, Sermon 4:1.

10. Guerric links spiritual fullness and plenitude with spiritual paternity. Whether he has in mind here the abbatial office is not absolutely clear. However it is clear that he links the paternal dignity with service.

11. Deut. 5:5.   12. Sir 44:6.   13. Mt 5:10f.
14. Song 1:5.   15. Ps 119:7.   16. Mt 5:3.

all desires for any wealth save the richness of the Creator of the world alone. For his sake they are as men having nothing, yet in him possessing all things.[17] Do not they truly possess all things if they have God for their portion[18] and inheritance,[19] and possess him who contains all things and disposes of them all? This is the God who, lest there be anything lacking to those who fear him,[20] gives to them for their use all things outside himself, in the measure that he knows is good for them, and keeps himself for their ultimate enjoyment.

When the heir of God and the coheir with Christ[21] comes of age and is set free from all restrictions, and so enters into the full possession of the longed-for inheritance, he will then be given an absolute rule and a free sway over all creatures; but for the moment, as long as he is a child, he is no better than a slave, even if he is, in fact, the lord of all, for he is placed under the authority of tutors and agents until the time fixed by his Father.[22] It is only then that the world will recognize the just and legitimate heir as the lord for whom it was created, and it will recognize too that he is no longer conformed to itself, but that he has been transformed by the renewal of his mind[23] into that image of God in which he was made.[24]

Even now, however, the world is full of riches for the man of faith. He makes use of them to help him to know and love their Creator, treating them as if they had been given him for this precise purpose. He also sees that creation points to the Creator in the same way as do the Scriptures, and so he delights in the way of the testimonies of God as much as in all riches.[25] But most of all he has

---

17. 2 Cor 6:10.
18. Ps 118:57; 141:6. For Isaac in his development of the beatitudes a similar psalm text holds its place: "The God of my heart is my portion."—Ps 72:26 (Sermon 5:13, 18). He develops, too, the growth of the soul from being an enemy to becoming first a servant, then a friend, then a brother of Christ, a son and heir, who finds complete union with the Inheritance who is God himself. (*Ibid.*)
19. Num 18:20.   20. Ps 33:10.   21. Rom 8:17.   22. Gal 4:1f.
23. Rom 12:2.   24. Col 3:10; Gen 1:27.   25. Ps 118:14.

learned to be so content and full of gratitude that he reckons the next to nothing that he possesses or the very fact that he possesses nothing at all as the equal of the riches of the whole world.

For this reason Solomon was right to declare the blessedness of the Church of the saints in these words: "Many daughters have gathered together riches; you have surpassed them all."[26] For though it is poor for Christ it is still rich in him. Some men take by force the possessions of another, yet they are always in want; the saints distribute to others their own possessions, yet by that very fact they become all the richer.[27] For the rich suffer want and hunger; but those who seek the Lord lack no good thing.[28]

4. With the covetous much wants more, even though what he thinks he has he does not in fact possess at all, since he is in fact the possessed not the possessor, the slave of money and the bondsman of avarice, a cultivator of money-bags and a detestable idolater whose God is money. Most appropriately even now, here on earth, divine justice avenges itself on such sinners by turning the things they love into a source of torment to them, making their own vices become their own punishment. For whereas money serves to justify the just man still further and only makes him more truly rich once he has distributed it or given it all away, it becomes a source of torment for the miser who hoards it, and degrades the spendthrift who wastes it. Blessed indeed are the poor of Christ, for their faith which makes such a mockery of the wisdom of the world remains alone in recognizing the best way to make use of wealth. It is obvious that when riches are loved they do no more than make men poor and wretched, and only when they are despised for the sake of Christ do they make men truly rich and happy.

I thank you, Father, Lord of heaven and earth, that you have hidden these things from the wise and knowledgeable and have revealed them to little ones,[29] that is, to the humble: for indeed it is the humble who are the poor in spirit and here they are pronounced blessed.

26. Prov 31:29.   27. Prov 11:24.   28. Prov 33:11.   29. Mt 11:25.

5. What I have said is not new to you, my brethren, but I still want to impress upon you that truly blessed poverty of spirit is to be found more in humility of heart than in a mere privation of everyday possessions, and it consists more in the renunciation of pride than in a mere contempt for property. Sometimes it may be useful to own things, but it is never anything but mortally dangerous to hold on to pride. The devil owns nothing in this world, nor does he desire to own anything; it is pride and pride alone that damns him.

For this reason it is of little use to renounce the possessions of the world unless we renounce the ways of the world at the same time. Indeed it would be ridiculous and stupid to strip ourselves of riches and then become entangled in the vices of the rich; to become poor in material possessions and not become rich in virtue; to leave all things and then to refuse to follow Christ,[30] or rather perhaps to further the cause of Antichrist in the very camp of Christ. We are quite clearly furthering the cause of Antichrist if we give ourselves to the service of pride, and so while professing Christ's holy name with our lips or our habit we make war on that name by our manner of living. Humility is the standard of Christ, pride is that of Antichrist, or rather pride is the standard of his leader the devil, who has command over all the children of pride; pride was his sin from the very beginning.

Let us therefore rejoice, brethren, that we are poor for Christ, but let us at the same time take care that we are also humble with Christ. No one is more worthy of our scorn than a poor man who is proud; but no one is more deserving of our pity than he, for his poverty afflicts him in this life and his pride damns him for all eternity. A poor man who is humble, however, though purged by fire in the furnace of poverty,[31] rejoices in the consolation of the treasure he holds within himself. He finds his comfort in the promise which holy hope holds out to him, knowing in his mind and feeling in his bones that his is the kingdom of heaven. That kingdom he is already carrying in seed or germ within himself,[32] the first-

---

30. Mt 19:27.   31. Is 48:10.   32. Lk 17:21.

fruits of the Spirit³³ and the guarantee of eternal inheritance.³⁴ So it has fallen to your lot, my brethren, as you must know for yourselves, to have the almost continual opportunity of plucking those delicious fruits of blessed joy, fruits which once tasted make all the sweetness of the world seem bitter by comparison. Unless I am mistaken you have all experienced this taste and so realize that the business you are engaged in is good.³⁵ In exchange for things which ought indeed to be despised and rejected, you have obtained the highest good. The kingdom of God does not mean food and drink but righteousness and peace and joy in the Holy Spirit.³⁶ If we feel these within us, why do we not proclaim confidently that the kingdom of God is within us?³⁷ What is within us truly belongs to us, for no one can take it away from us against our will.

6. Therefore when our Lord was proclaiming the blessedness of the poor he was correct in saying that the kingdom of heaven is theirs, not that it will be theirs. It is theirs by an unimpeachable right. But it is also theirs because of a most certain pledge and their happy enjoyment of it. It is theirs not only because it was prepared for them from the beginning of the world,³⁸ but also because they have already begun to enter into some sort of possession of it. They already have heavenly treasure in earthen vessels;³⁹ they already bear God in body and heart.⁴⁰ How blessed is the nation whose God is the Lord.⁴¹ How near must they be to the kingdom of God if they already possess and carry within their hearts their own King. To serve this King is to reign. In the words of the Psalmist: "The lot marked out for me is my delight, welcome indeed the heritage that falls to me."⁴² Worldly men may quarrel among themselves about the allotment of the inheritance that they expect in this life; "Lord, it is you who are my portion and my cup."⁴³ Let them fight among themselves and see which of them needs the most pity; for my part, I envy them none of those things for which they are struggling. My soul and I, we shall take our delight in the Lord.⁴⁴

33. Rom 8:23.
34. Eph 1:14.
35. Prov 31:18.
36. Rom 14:17.
37. Lk 17:21.
38. Mt 25:34.
39. 2 Cor 4:7.
40. 1 Cor 6:20.
41. Ps 32:12.
42. Ps 15:6.
43. Ps 15:5.
44. Ps 103:34.

O wonderful Inheritance of the poor, O blessed Possession of those who possess nothing. You provide us not only with all that we need; you overflow, giving all glory; you abound, giving to all happiness and joy, like the measure in a man's lap, overflowing on every side.[45] With you are riches and glory, the highest riches and justice.[46]

7. O you poor, O you humble, let your hearts be filled with pride. Let your souls glory in their humility and scorn all the lofty dignities of the world which lie so far beneath their feet. Let them judge it no longer worthy of their own glory to degrade their majesty by a desire for cheap pickings. It is amazing. You are on the point of being taken up into heaven and is this the moment you would choose to sink back at last into the mire? The world of eternity stands ready for you, and would you prefer the world of fleeting things, things with no more substance than dreams? The whole court of the saints is waiting to greet you, and would you now prefer the company of demons?

How wretched is the man who, "when he was in honor, did not appreciate it and so can be compared to a senseless beast and has become like one."[47] This verse clearly refers to those who, by the practice of blessed poverty, have become honorable in the sight of heaven, remarkable in the sight of the world, and to include all, terrible in the sight of hell, but who have subsequently become so blinded that they have come to look upon their poverty as misery and their humility as cowardice.[48] In their desire to become rich they have but fallen into the snares of temptation held out to them by the devil.[49] When they were lords of all creation they sold themselves without bothering to name a price[50] for the sake of what is nothing. Woe to those who have forsaken perseverance

---

45. Lk 6:38.   46. Prov 8:18.   47. Ps 48:21.

48. Bernard of Clairvaux foresaw this danger also and in the development of his commentary on the beatitudes noted how aptly the second beatitude followed the first. Since the afflictions of poverty can readily lead to murmuring and impatience one does need the meekness of the second beatitude. Cf. Bernard, *loc. cit.*, n. 9.

49. 1 Tim 6:9.   50. Ps 43:13.

and have turned aside into crooked ways. What will they do when the Lord begins to examine them?[51] They will see what will become of them.

But to you, brethren, who look upon your poverty as a friend, and find your pleasure in humility of spirit, to you Truth unchangeable gives the certainty of possessing the kingdom of heaven. He declares it belongs to you and he guards it safe, laid up in readiness for you. All you have to do is to guard the hope of it deep in your heart[52] to the very end, with the help of our Lord Jesus Christ, to whom belongs all honor and glory, through endless ages. Amen.

51. Sir 2:16f.   52. Job 19:27.

SERMON 54

A SERMON FOR AROUSING DEVOTION AT PSALMODY

WHOSE VOICE IS FITTINGLY HEARD in the assembly of brethren and friends, that is, in the Church of the saints, the Bridegroom himself indicates when he says: "You who dwell in the gardens, friends are listening; let me hear your voice."[1]

It is not I to whom this should be said; I am not one who dwells in gardens—I seem to myself rather to be of those who dwell in tombs.[2] For what are the bodies of sinners but tombs of the dead? Therefore they who are devoted to their bodies dwell not in gardens but in tombs and exasperate God until he who leads forth prisoners in strength[3] cries with a loud voice: "Lazarus, come forth"; and he gives his disciples the command: "Loose him and let him go free."[4]

To be sure there is a great difference between tombs and gardens. The former are full of every filth and of dead men's bones, the latter are full of flowers or fruits in all their sweetness and grace. What if tombs are sometimes seen in gardens? For the Lord was buried in a garden.[5]

If there are tombs in a garden surely there are not gardens in tombs? Yet perhaps there are, but in the tombs of the just. There indeed a certain most agreeable pleasantness which belongs to gardens will flourish as in spring, the springtime, that is, of their

1. Song 8:13.   2. Ps 67:7; Is 65:4.   3. Ps 67:7.
4. Jn 11:43f.   5. Jn 19:40f.

resurrection when their flesh will blossom again.[6] Not only the bones of the just man will sprout like grass[7] but also the whole of the just man will sprout like a lily and bloom forever before the Lord.[8] Not so the godless, not so.[9] They are buried with the burial of an ass.[10] Without any hope of a better resurrection, they are subject to corruption, as a foretaste of their future fate. Concerning their tombs I had begun to say that as great as is the difference between their filth and the beauty of gardens in flower incomparably greater is the difference between the delight of spiritual men and the pleasure of carnal joys.

2. It is you then, if I am not mistaken, who dwell in gardens, you who meditate on the law of the Lord day and night[11] and walk about in as many gardens as you read books, pick as many apples as you select fine thoughts. And blessed are you for whom all the apples, both old and new, are kept, that is, for whom the words of the prophets, evangelists and Apostles are laid up, so that to each of you those words of the Bride to the Bridegroom seem to be said: "All the apples, new and old, my Beloved, I have kept for you."[12]

Search the Scriptures then. For you are not mistaken in thinking that you find life in them, you who seek nothing else in them but Christ, to whom the Scriptures bear witness.[13] Blessed indeed are they who search his testimonies, seek them out with all their heart.[14] Your testimonies are wonderful, Lord, therefore my soul has searched them.[15] There is need for searching not only in order to draw out the mystical sense but also to taste the moral sense. Therefore you who walk about in the gardens of the Scriptures do not pass by heedlessly and idly but searching each and every word like busy bees gathering honey from flowers, reap the Spirit from the words. "For my Spirit," says Jesus, "is sweeter than honey and my inheritance surpasses the honeycomb."[16] So, proving by experi-

6. Ps 27:7.   7. Is 66:14.   8. Hos 14:6.   9. Ps 1:4.
10. Jer 22:19.   11. Ps 1:1.   12. Song 7:13.   13. Jn 5:39.
14. Ps 118:2.   15. Ps 118:129.

16. Sir 24:27. It is interesting to note here that Guerric attributes to Jesus the words of the Wise Man.

ence that hidden manna is savory, you will break forth into those words of David: "How sweet to my mouth are your words, sweeter than honey and the honeycomb to my palate."[17]

3. From these gardens the Bridegroom will lead you, if I be not mistaken, into others where rest is more hidden and enjoyment more blessed and beauty more wonderful. When you are absorbed in his praises with accents of exultation and thanksgiving, he will take you into his wonderful tenting place, into the very house of God,[18] into the unapproachable light in which he dwells,[19] where he feeds, where he lies down at midday.[20] For if the devotion of those who sing psalms or pray has something of that loving curiosity of the disciples who asked: "Rabbi, where do you dwell?" they deserve, I think, to hear: "Come and see." "They went," we read, "and saw and stayed with him that day."[21]

As long as we are with the Father of lights, with whom there can be no change, no swerving from his course,[22] we know nothing of night, we enjoy a blessed daylight. When we fall thence, we relapse into our own darkness. Woe is me: how quickly my days have passed away,[23] how quickly I have dried up like grass.[24] As long as I was in the garden with him, I was vigorous and flourishing like God's Paradise. With him I am a garden of delight;[25] without him, a place of horror and utter wilderness.[26]

For I think that the man who enters his garden becomes a garden himself, his soul is like a watered garden,[27] so that the Bridegroom says in praise of him: "A closed garden is my sister, my bride."[28] Are they not a garden in which there comes about what the Gardener himself says to the plantation which his Father planted?[29] "Give heed to me," he says, "scions of the divine stock. Burgeon like a rose-bush that is planted by running water. Yield the fragrance of incense. Blossom like the lily, and smell sweet, and put forth leaves for your adornment."[30]

17. Ps 118:103.
18. Ps 41:5.
19. 1 Tim 6:16.
20. Song 1:6.
21. Jn 1:38f.
22. Jas 1:17.
23. Ps 89:9.
24. Ps 101:12.
25. Ezek 26:35.
26. Deut 32:10.
27. Jer 31:12.
28. Song 4:12.
29. Mt 15:13.
30. Sir 39:13f.

4. O Lord Jesus, true Gardener, effect in us what you demand of us. For without you we cannot do anything.³¹ You are the true gardener, the same Creator who cultivates and protects your garden. You plant by your word, water with your Spirit, give growth by your power.³² You were mistaken, Mary, when you thought he was the gardener of that poor and tiny garden in which he was buried.³³ He is the gardener of the whole world, he is the gardener of heaven, he is the gardener of the Church, which he plants and waters here until its growth is completed and he transplants it into the land of the living by streams of living water,³⁴ where it will not be afraid when heat comes, but its foliage will be green and it will never cease to bear fruit.³⁵ Blessed are they who dwell in those gardens of yours, Lord, for ever and ever they will praise you.³⁶

Paul dwelt in them, he whose true home was in heaven.³⁷ In spirit he often soared aloft and walked about in the paradise of blessed enjoyment, the gardens of God's delights.³⁸ Passing by the roses of the martyrs and the lilies of the virgins³⁹ and ceasing even to wonder at the height of God's cedars, he would take pleasure rather in picking fruit from the tree of life which is in the middle of paradise,⁴⁰ in it tasting more fully and more happily how sweet is the Lord.⁴¹ When he came back from there he would pour forth at length to his listening friends what he remembered of its abounding sweetness. His mouth would overflow from the abundance of his heart.⁴² Because his soul was filled as with marrow and fat therefore his mouth gave praise with exulting lips.⁴³ For "the wise man's heart will instruct his mouth and lend grace to his lips."⁴⁴ So his heart would pour forth a goodly word⁴⁵ and from

---

31. Jn 15:5. 32. Cf. 1 Cor 3:7. 33. Jn 20:15.
34. Ps 1:3. 35. Jer 17:8. 36. Ps 83:5.
37. Phil 3:20. 38. 2 Cor 12:4.

39. "Among [the Church's] flowers are both roses and lilies." These words, taken from a sermon attributed to the Venerable Bede [PL 94, 450 c], were known to Guerric from a responsory sung on the feast of All Saints.

40. Gen 3:3. 41. Ps 33:9. 42. Cf. Mt 12:34.
43. Ps 62:6. 44. Prov 16:23. 45. Ps 44:2.

his good treasure the good man would bring forth good things[46] and delight as with an agreeable song the Bridegroom himself who would be listening among his friends.

It was indeed a joyful song and a delightful melody, when so harmonious an instrument of the Holy Spirit sang of Christ Jesus, his heart's jubilation, with behavior and speech so well in accord, with such sweetness of love, such graciousness of countenance. For if a sweet tongue were not itself a song it would not be written: "Flute and psaltery make a sweet melody but a sweet tongue surpasses them both."[47] If the Psalmist did not know that God is delighted with a song of this sort he would not say: "May my word be pleasing to him."[48] Neither would the Bridegroom himself say: "Make me hear your voice; let your voice sound in my ears. For your voice is sweet[49] because your mouth exults in God[50] as one dwelling in gardens, in the delights of Paradise."

On the contrary praise in the sinner's mouth is not seemly,[51] because he dwells in tombs.[52] For when a man's life exasperates God his tongue gives him no pleasure. Rather he is dreadfully rebuked by the divine voice: "Why do you recount my just decrees?[53] I will not listen to the music of your lyre."[54]

5. But since the Scriptural text which I had taken as an excuse for a sermon has furnished the occasion and the material for the sermon, if it please you let us finish what we had begun to say on it. The Bridegroom's words: "You who dwell in the gardens, friends are listening; let me hear your voice,"[55] can be understood in two ways: either he is inviting a devoted lover to sing psalms or pray, or he is stirring up a holy preacher to speak. To reinforce his plea he mentions that friends are listening, that is, the angels to him who prays or sings psalms, the faithful to the preacher.

In this let us consider first with what discipline of heart and body we ought to sing psalms or pray in the sight of the angels,[56] lest

46. Mt 12:35.
47. Sir 40:21.
48. Ps 103:34.
49. Song 8:13; 2:14.
50. Ps 149:6.
51. Sir 15:9.
52. Is 65:4.
53. Ps 49:16.
54. Amos 5:23.
55. See note 1 above.
56. Ps 137:1.

they be sent away empty and send us away empty, they who had come to carry our prayers up and bring back gifts; lest indeed they should withdraw as enemies who had come as friends. The Bridegroom himself who stands at the door and knocks,[57] if no worthy devotion answers him from within and opens the door, will go away complaining and saying: "I have given heed and listened: no one speaks what is good. There is no one who repents of his sin and says: 'What have I done?' They are all set on their course, like a horse plunging headlong into battle."[58]

If however he is exhorting a preacher, he gives him confidence to speak from the goodwill and the attention of his hearers. They do not refuse belief and interrupt or argue, they do not compete with him and take away his good name or mock him, they are not lukewarm and do not go to sleep or yawn. Rather they are friends, attentive and listening; their love and their merit can obtain the gift of the Word and of the Spirit for him who preaches the Gospel to them.

And it is well said: "friends are listening." For it is the mark of a friend to listen devotedly to the Bridegroom's voice, as John says: the Bridegroom's friend is he who stands by, not wandering in mind or prostrated by sleep, and listens, rejoices too, rejoices at hearing the Bridegroom's voice which he recognizes even in his servants.[59] Let us then also, whether the Bridegroom's voice sounds through the mouth of one speaking or reading or singing, prove ourselves to be friends by so standing and listening that it may give joy and gladness to our hearing[60] and we may not only receive the word with joy but also bear fruit in patience.[61]

---

57. Rev 3:20. 58. Jer 8:6. 59. Cf. Jn 3:29.
60. Ps 50:10. 61. Lk 8:13ff.

ANALYTIC INDEX

The first number refers to the Sermon; the number(s) after the colon refer to section(s) within the Sermon. Sermons 1-21 are in volume one (Cistercian Fathers Series 8); Sermons 22-54, in this volume.

Abandonment, 23: 1 ff; 39:5.
  of Christ, 31:2.
Abbatial office, ideals of, 36:1f.
  see also Spiritual paternity, Prelates.
Abishag, the Shünammite, figure of the warming fire of Wisdom, 15:2.
Abraham, 2:2; 17:1; 32:2; 35:2; 42:1; 43:3; 47:4.
Acedia, 11:4.
Achaz, 28:2.
Achsah, 23:6.
Active life
  Christ also reveals himself to those justly and devoutly engaged in activity, 35:4.
  preparation for contemplative life, 23:6; 33:2; 35:5; 45:3; 50:4; 53:2.
  striving after moral perfection, 23:6.
  see also Leah, Martha.
Adam, 12:6; 34:2; 47:2.
  sons of, 27:1.
Advent, Sermons for, 1-5.
All Saints, Sermon for the Feast of, 53.
Alms giving, 18:5f.
Angels, 2:1; 3:1; 4:3; 6:1ff; 12:4; 13:4; 19:5; 22:6; 23:1, 3, 6; 48:1ff; 49:4.
  Christ mounted above all, 37:4.
  Christ not born before, 8:1.
  cruel, 4:2.
  guardian, 23:3.
  Mary exalted above, 47:6.
  Species: Thrones, 47:6.
Anna, 16:4ff.
  gives us an example of prayer and fasting, 16:7.
  name signifies *grace,* 16:4.
Annunciation
  prophecies of, 28:1.
  Sermons on, 26-28.
Antichrist, 53:5.
Apostles, 14:4; 22:3; 24:6; 26:3; 37:4; 39:1; 54:2.
  Christ's love for, 37:1.
  the Twelve, 22:4.
  true Israelites, 33:2ff.
  see also John, Matthew, Paul, Peter.
Aridity, see Dryness.
Ascension, Sermon for the Feast of, 37.
Assumption of the Blessed Virgin Mary, Sermons for the Feast of, 47-50.

Balaam, 30:6.
Baptism, 12:1.
  Christ's, 14:4ff.
  not for himself but for us, 14:4.
  rebaptism through humility, 14:7.
  with faith and the Eucharist, it makes us Christians, 14:1.
Beatitude, 46:6.

219

P

Analytic Index

Beatitudes, 53:1ff.
  eight steps to evangelical perfection, 53:1.
Beginners in the spiritual life, state of conversion and penance, 11:5f.
Behemoth, 43:5.
Benedict of Nursia (St)
  a new Moses, 25:1f.
  filled with the spirit of all the saints, 25:1.
  Legislator of the Cistercian way of life, 5:3.
  lived as he taught, 25:1.
  Sermons for, 22–25.
  see also Meekness, Rule.
Bernard of Clairvaux (St)
  exegete of the Holy Spirit, 46:1.
  Master, 46:1.
Blessed Sacrament, *see* Eucharist.
Blessed Trinity, 36:3; 42:4.
  images of 36:4.
  see also Christ, Father, God, Holy Spirit.
Body (flesh)
  in relation to the spirit (soul), 1:3; 3:2; 5:3; 11:2.
  treasures of good works and riches of devotion are hidden in it, 11:2.
  of Christ, *see* Mystical Body.
Bread of Life, *see* Eucharist.

Cana, 12:1; 50:1.
Chanaanite woman, 3:3.
Charity, 23:5; 36:4; 52:4.
  faith working through love, 15:3.
  fraternal, 24:3ff.
  God's, 9:3.
  order of, 18:6; 50:2.
  spotless law of the Lord, 39:1.
  see also Fraternal correction, Friendship, Love.
Chastity, 4:3; 15:1; 26:4ff; 27:4; 51:5.
  St John's, 48:4; 50:3.
  see also Mary, Turtledove, Virginity.
Christ
  all is given with him, 2:4.
  attitude toward his Mother, 47:1ff; 48:3ff; 50:1ff.
  Bridegroom, 54:4f.
  of the Church, 26:7.

bud, fruit and flower, 27:3.
Champion, our, 47:5.
child, 6:3ff; 8:4; 10:7.
example for us, 28:6f; 29:2; 31:4.
flesh not conceived prior to the incarnation, 27:1.
forms of Christ: flesh, spiritual master, Word, 52:1ff.
forsaken on the cross, 23:2.
Gardener, true, 54:3f.
gives us the whole pattern of the religious life in the mode of his birth, 10:4.
glory of, 31:2ff.
God humbled in the flesh, 1:3; 6:2ff; 8:2ff; 10:6; 28:4, 6; 32:5.
work of mercy, 6:2.
high priest, 37:5.
Liberator, 26:2.
makes God present to all the senses, 10:1ff.
Mediator, 6:2; 30:6; 37:2, 5.
mother and nurse, 45:2.
Old Testament prophecy of, 8:4ff.
Partaker of our nature, 22:5.
Rock, 27:1f; 32:5.
  mighty but not hard, 22:3.
  that gives living water, 22:3.
Root of Jesse, 28:3.
Savior, 1:8; 2:1, 3, 10; 4:12; 6:2; 26:2.
Second Adam, 34:2.
Son of the Father, 28:2f; 30:6; 31:3; 32:1.
to be sought and known no longer according to the flesh but according to the spirit, 35:2; 39:5; 52:1.
Truth, 4:5, 9, 13; 5:3; 17:2.
Word heard in silence, 4:4.
see also Annunciation, Ascension, Coming of Christ, Death, Epiphany, Humility, Light, Meekness, Miracles, Mystical Body, Passion of Christ, Wisdom.
Christianity, three things make us Christians: faith, baptism, Eucharist, 14:1.
Christmas, Sermons for, 6–10.
Church, 13:1; 17:2, 6; 26:3; 45:1f; 47:3; 49:3; 53:3; 54:4.

Analytic Index

assembly of brethren and friends, 54:1.
Body of Christ, 26:7.
Bride of Christ, 52:5.
gazelle, type of the Church, 45:3.
includes good and evil, 28:6.
Jerusalem illumined by Christ, 13:1.
left to Peter's care, 50:3.
Mary, type of the Church, 47:2.
primitive, 32:4.
true Israel, 28:3.
universal joy at Christ's birth, 7:1.
virgin mother, 7:1f; 8:4.
see also Christ, Jerusalem, Magi, Mary.
Cistercian life, 5:4ff.
chapter meetings, carnal contend against the spiritual, 8:5.
deserts made fruitful, 4:3.
fulfilling Rule, comes before private prayer, 5:2.
holy way, 5:4.
narrow way, 5:4.
second baptism, 5:4.
solitude with companionship, 4:2.
see also Religious life.
Coming of Christ, 2:2ff; 7:3.
intermediate, 2:3ff.
spiritual, hidden, wonderful, 2:3.
see also Eucharist, Visits of God to the soul.
final, 1:4f.
confidently expected, 1:4.
corporal, public, glorious, 2:3ff.
time unknown, 3:1.
first, 2:3ff; 7:3.
corporal, hidden, lowly, 2:3.
Community
complementarity in, 45:4.
consolation of companionship, 4:4.
dissension in chapter, 8:4.
see also Monastic life.
Compassion
God's in Christ, 8:2.
purifies from sin, 18:5f.
Compunction, 11:3; 26:2.
gifts of the Holy Spirit, 39:5f.
tears of—refreshing waters, 23:7.
see also Mourning, Myrrh, Repentance.

Confession, in preparation for the coming of the Lord, 3:3f.
Confidence, 23:1ff.
Christ's words on, 23:2.
causes the healing of body and soul, 23:1.
effects of, 23:2.
faith in God, 23:2.
see also Hope.
Consolation, 22:4; 41:2.
from confidence in God, 23:5f.
often received in the fulfillment of the exercises of the monastic life, 22:5.
preceded by mourning, 39:6.
Spirit of, 39:6.
sweetness of the Lord, 22:4.
see also Community, Scriptures.
Contemplation, 25:3; 35:5; 37:5; 41:1, 5; 45:3; 53:2; 54:3.
should pray for it, 45:5.
sweet and happy state of absorbed admiration, 2:4.
Contemplative life, 23:6; 49:1ff.
of Mary, 48:1; 50:3.
relation to the active life, 23:6.
see also Active life, Mary Magdalen.
Continence, see Chastity.
Conversion, 4:2; 39:2.
Correction, fraternal, 24:6; 39:3.
Covetousness, 53:4.
Creation
bears witness to Christ through responding to commands, 12:2.
points to the Creator in the same way as Sacred Scriptures, 53:3.
Cross of Christ, 28:3.
glory in, 30:4.
sign of, 30:4ff.

Daily life at Igny
disputes in chapter, 8:5.
suffering from the cold, 11:6.
work, 49.
Damascus, etymologically "city of blood," 14:5.
Daniel, the Prophet, 12:5; 16:2.
Darkness, 13:2.
David (King), 3:2f; 5:4; 8:2; 9:2; 15:2, 4; 26:1f: 28:1; 30:5; 32:1; 41:4; 42:1; 43:4; 46:4; 53:6; 54:2.

Disciple of the anointing, 13:6.
Holy Man, 22:5.
house of, 14:5; 15:1.
Psalmist, 5:2; 35:2; 38:4; 39:5;. 44:4.
Death, 1:4; 3:1f.
   Christ's, 2:2.
   freely chosen, 1:4.
   comes unexpectedly, 1:2, 4; 3:1.
   overcome by Christ's, 34:2; 41:3.
Desert, *see* Solitude.
Detachment, 1:1.
   from earthly affairs, 1:3f.
   ready to do good and suffer evil, 3:2.
Detraction, 38:5; 42:5f.
Devils, 24:2; 42:5f; 53:5.
   ancient serpent, 23:3.
   believe and shudder, 25:5.
Devotion, 26:7.
   tears of, 23:7.
Discipline, 44:5.
   always to keep the Lord before our eyes, 44:5.
Discretion, 31:4.
Distractions, 22:6.
Divine Office, *see* Office.
Dryness, 23:5.

Easter, 33:1.
   Sermons for the Feast of, 33–35.
   see Resurrection.
Egypt, 25:1ff; 49:3.
Elijah, 42:4; 44:1, 5.
Elisha, 14:5ff; 35:5.
Elizabeth, mother of John the Baptist, 40:2.
Emmaus, 33:1f; 35:3.
Enlightenment, 13:1ff; 15:4f.
   measure of: knowledge of one's deficiencies, 13:1.
Enoch, 44:1.
Envy, leads to detraction, 42:6.
Epiphany of Christ,
   at Cana, 12:1.
   birthday of the Church, 14:1.
   in his Baptism, 12:1f.
   in the coming of the kings from the East, 12:2.
   Sermons for, 11–14.
   through his miracles, 12:2.

Esau, 23:1.
Eucharist, 9:4f; 10:9; 18:6; 19:4; 22:4; 27:1; 28:6; 29:1; 33:6; 34:4f; 38:5; 50:5; 51:4.
   given us as a means of holiness, 7:3.
   institution, 37:1.
   prefigured at Cana, 12:1; 14:1.
   principle by which we are grounded in Christ, 34:4.
   refreshing waters, 23:7.
   with faith and baptism, makes us Christians, 14:1.
Evangelists, 54:2.
   see also John, Luke, Mark, Matthew.
Eve
   contrasted with Mary, the Mother of Christ, 18:1; 47:2; 51:1.
   more stepmother than mother, 47:2.
   mother of all the living, 47:2.
   mother of prevarication, 18:1.
Evil thoughts, how to guard against them, 22:6.
Experience, 51:4.
   of God, 2:5ff.
   those who have it rejoice in it, those who do not should be eager for it, 35:4.
   see also Visits.
Ezekiel, 19:4; 23:5; 27:2; 53:1.

Faith, 1:4; 2:4; 10:3f; 12:1; 14:1ff; 23:5; 25:1ff; 36:4; 44:5; 51:4; 52:5.
   definition, 25:5.
   feigned, 25:5.
   lamp in the heart, 15:3f.
   light of, 13:3ff.
   of the Magi, *see* Magi.
   of Mary, Mother of Christ, 27:4.
   of St Paul, 27:4.
   of the Shepherds at Christ's birth, 10:8.
   overcomes the world, 23:1.
   purifies from sin, 18:5f.
   stages of, 12:5.
   taught to monks by the example of Moses and Benedict, 25:1.
   various meanings, 25 5.
   see also Confidence.

Analytic Index

Father (First Person of the Blessed Trinity), 12:4; 23:1, 4; 28:2f; 30:6; 31:3; 32:1; 50:2; 51:3; 54:3.
  bears witness to Christ, 12:1f.
  Christ's prayer to, 37:2f.
  of lights, 12:3.
Fathers, 15:1; 26:4.
  guiding light for us, 12:7.
  have given us sufficient and abundant doctrine, 14:2.
  peacemakers, 53:2.
Fear, 19:6; 20:6; 22:6.
  allows nothing to enter the mind without careful examination, 22:6.
  arises from judgment and yet judges, 17:4.
  of death, 3:1.
    blessed to be without, 3:2f.
    cleansed by it, 3:3.
  of judgment, 22:5.
  of the Lord, 5:3; 24:2; 25:4, 6; 30:5.
    does not take away but guards true joy, 38:2.
    effects, 17:5.
    source of confidence, 23:4.
    tester of thoughts, 22:6.
Flesh, see Body.
Fraternal correction, see Correction.
Friendship
  lies between silly amiability and proud aloofness, 24:4.
  must first be a friend to yourself, 24:3.
  variant natural predispositions, 24:5.
  with God, 24:2.
  see also Charity, God, Grace, Love.

Gabriel (Archangel), 48:3, 5f.
Gentleness, 4:4.
  Divine gentleness in Christ, 6:3.
Gifts of the Holy Spirit
  compunction, 39:5.
  praise of God, 39:1f.
  speaking in tongues, 39:1.
God
  all-seeing, 22:1ff.
  Creator, 53:3; 54:4.
  friendship with, 24:2.
  generous to all without respect of person, 38:3.
  presence of, 25:4ff.
  see also Christ, Father, Holy Spirit.
Gold
  offering of the perfect, 11:5.
  of the Magi
    symbolizes glory, 11:1.
    symbolizes wisdom, 11:7.
Good example, 15:3.
Good works, 23:5.
  lamps burning in the hands, 13:4; 15:3.
  see also Justice.
Gospel, 16:4f.
Grace, 2:3f; 7:3; 24:1.
  fullness of time as abundance of grace, 8:1ff.
  God's friendship the sum total and cause of all grace, 24:3.
  hidden and manifest, 23:6.
  illuminating, 15:4.
  man must cooperate with, 13:6.
  not lessened by use but increased, 28:6.
  see also Penance.
Guerric of Igny
  bewails his negligences, 19:3; 20:4ff; 24:2.
  desires to give Christ in his sermons, 10:3.
  did not wish to be elected, 38:1.
  does not consider himself to have attained the state of perfection and wisdom, 11:7.
  fears his piety is only apparent, 14:3f.
  limitations, 36:1; 39:4; 46:1.
  more concerned with moral instruction than dogmatic speculation, 27:4.
  profession of faith, 44:2.
  use of Sacred Scripture, 46:1.

Habakkuk, the Prophet, 20:5.
Happiness, arises from abiding in Wisdom, 22:1.
Hard heart, 22:3; 24:6.
Hate among the brethren, 24:6.
Herod, 43:2.
Herodias, 43:2.

Analytic Index

Holy Spirit, 6:1; 7:3; 8:5; 9:1; 10:3; 15:4; 21:4; 23:1; 25:3; 26:4; 27:1, 5; 28:5; 32:1f; 33:6; 34:5; 35:5; 37:1; 42:4; 44:2; 45:5; 49:4ff; 50:5; 51:2; 53:1; 54:4f.
   bears witness to Christ, 12:1f; 23:6.
   in our hearts, 50:3.
   came to the world for judgment, 39:6.
   Consoler, 38:4.
   distributes gifts according to his will, 13:6.
   gift of Christ, 33:4.
   grace of, 23:5f.
   mark of adoption and guarantee of inheritance, 38:2.
   Shining Oil, 44:1f.
   the Anointing which teaches, 13:5f; 44:4.
   see also Pentecost.
Hope, 1:1ff; 22:4; 23:1, 5; 25 3ff; 36:4.
   greater in times of trial, 22:4.
   of David, 26:1.
   overcomes fear, 23:1.
   overcomes the world, 23:1.
   see also Confidence.
Horace, 39:4.
Hosea, the Prophet, 13:5; 22:2; 23:1; 41:1; 50:4.
Humility, 2:4; 6:2f; 10:3; 14:5ff; 16:2; 21:4ff; 23:6; 24:2; 42:3ff; 47:4f; 53:5, 7.
   best way to win the favor of men, 42:6.
   gift, 35:3ff.
   of Christ, 1:1; 2:3; 4:4; 6:2ff; 10:3ff; 28:4; 29:1ff; 31:4; 32:4; 37:1; 49:4.
   seven qualities, 14:7.
   of God, 27:4; 28:4.
   of Mary, 15:1; 26:4; 49:4.
   pre-eminent value, 21:4ff.
   rebaptizes by the mortification and burial of sin, 14:7.
   resting place of Christ, 49:4.
   straightest and easiest way to glory, 42:6.
   see also Poverty.

Idolatry, the opposite of wisdom, 22:1.

Incense
   offering of those making progress, 11:5.
   signifies honor, praise, devotion, 11:1, 5.
Instability, 22:4.
Instruments of good works, 22:2.
Intention, 15:3f.
   pure intention does not preclude mistakes and ignorance, 13:1.
Isaac, 26:6; 51:3.
Isaiah, the Prophet, 1:2; 5:2; 10:2; 22:5; 23:1; 27:2; 28:1ff; 29:3; 31:1; 32:4; 46:6; 47:4; 48:3; 49:5f; 50:2; 52:4.
Israel, *see* Jacob.
Issachar, 49:1.

Jacob (Israel), 33:1; 35:1ff; 41:1; 50:4.
   type of the Apostles, 33:2.
   type of Christ, 26:6.
James (Apostle), 31:2; 46:5.
Jealousy, 24:6.
Jeremiah, the Prophet, 19:4; 22:5; 23:5; 25:5; 28:1; 41:2; 44:3f; 49:4.
   figure of the Baptist, 40:1, 6.
Jerome (St), 48:1f.
Jerusalem, 23:6.
   figure of the Church, 12:1, 3; 13:1.
   heaven, 14:4.
   Lamb is its light, 15:5.
Jesus, *see* Christ.
Jews, 16:2, 28:1ff; 30:3; 31:5; 32:3; 43:2; 49:3.
   rejection of Christ, 7:1· 8:2f.
   replaced by the Church, 7:2; 8:3.
Job, 2:4; 31:2, 5; 42:1; 43:5f; 46:6.
Joel, 20:4.
John the Baptist (St), 4:1ff; 5:2, 4.
   bears witness to Christ, 12:1f.
   Forerunner, 42:2ff.
   Friend of the Bridegroom, 42:4.
   humility of, 42:4.
   prophet, 40:2.
   Sermons for the Feast of, 40-43.
   see Jeremiah.
John the Evangelist (St), 37:5; 42:3; 49:4; 52:4; 54:5.
   Apostle, 37:1.
   Christ's beloved heir, 50:3.

Analytic Index

Mary's companion, 48:4; 49:4; 50:3.
  most loved by Christ, 48:5; 50:3.
  see Chastity.
Jonah, 28:3.
Jordan, 12:1; 14:4ff.
  etymologically: "their descent," 14:4.
  true Jordan, descent of the humble, 14:7.
Joseph (Patriarch), 33:1.
  type of Christ, 33:2ff.
Joshua, 30:6.
Joy, 2:2; 23:5f.
  at the coming of Christ, 2:2.
  Christ comes joyfully to us, 3:4; 4:2.
  in the Holy Spirit, 53:5.
  true and false, 38:2f.
Judgment, 17:4; 25:4.
  final, 25:6.
Justice, 17:4; 53:2.
  abounding justice of a few makes up for the infidelity of many, 16:5.
  light of, 13:3ff.
  Simeon, an example for us, 17:4.

Kings
  all Christians are kings, 15:5.
  see also Magi.
Knowledge, 44:5.
  experiential, 51:4.
  light of, 13:3, 5f.
  Spirit distributes various kinds, 13:6.

Labor, *see* Manual labor.
Law, 25:1.
  end of law: charity, 36:4.
  New Law of charity written in the heart, 39:1.
  Old Law, 16:4, 7.
    of Moses, 36:4.
    time of Old Law comes to an end with John the Batpist, 40:3.
  see also Rule.
Leah, type of the active life, 50:4.
Lectio Divina, 22:5; 54:2.
  exercise of wisdom, 22:5.
  tepidity at, 38:4.

Lent, 26:1; 33:1.
  Sermon for, 20.
  Sermon for the Saturday of the Second Week of, 21.
Leviathan, 46 6.
Light
  Christ, 12:1ff; 13:1; 15:2; 23:1.
  source of all light, 15:5.
  theme of, 12:1ff; 13:1f.
Liturgy
  means of ascent to the experience of God, 2:3.
  psalmody, 3:4; 5:2.
  see also Office.
Love, 2:4; 39:1.
  false love, 24:3.
  God, 2:4; 52:5.
  importance of seeking it from our brethren, 24:3ff.
  merits visit from God, 2:4.
  primacy of love of God in intensity, not in time, 24:4.
  stronger than death, 41:3.
  source of confidence, 23:4f.
  true love commends itself, 24:5.
  types of love: sinful or unclean, natural, worldly, fair, 52:5.
  see also Charity, Friendship.
Luke the Evangelist (St), 33:2; 42:3.
Lust, 43:4.
Luxury (*luxuria*), *see* Wantonness.

Magi, 12:2ff.
  first-fruits of the nations, beginnings of the Church, 12:5.
  their faith rewarded, 12:4.
  see also Epiphany.
Malachi, the Prophet, 16:2.
Manual labor, 35:4; 39:4; 49:1ff.
  Christ sometimes comes unexpectedly at work, 35:4.
  exercise of wisdom, 22:5.
Mark the Evangelist (St), 13:2, 42:3.
Martha (St), 50:1.
  type of active life, 49:2; 50:3f.
Martin (St), 3:1.
Mary of Bethany (St), 50:1.
  compared with the Blessed Virgin Mary, 50:1.
  type of the contemplative life, 49:2, 50:3f.
  see also Mary Magdalen (Note:

Guerric would have identified the two).
Mary Magdalen (St), 33:2, 35:2; 48:5; 54:4.
  repentant sinner, 48:5.
  see also Mary of Bethany and note there.
Mary, Mother of Christ, 7:1; 8:3; 9:1; 10:2, 4; 12:4.
  chosen of God, 47:1, 5; 48:6.
  election, 47:1.
  exalted above all angels and men, 26:4; 47:6, 50:3, 5.
  free from all sin, 48:5.
  fullness of grace, 40:2; 47:5.
  glorification, 47:1, 6.
  immaculate, 6:1.
  instructed Christ, 10:1.
  maternity
    divine, 47:1f.
    spiritual, 27:4f; 47:2ff; 50:3; 52:4.
  Mother of purity, 15:1.
  Mother of the Most High, 47:4.
  perfect chastity, 4:1; 26:4; 47:6.
  poverty, 10:4; 47:6.
  Queen, 47:6; 48:6; 49:3.
  source of grace, 40:2.
  spiritual martyrdom, 26:4; 48:4; 50:1.
  type of the Church, 10:4; 47:2.
  virginity, before, after and in childbirth, 15:1; 18:1; 26:4; 27:1ff; 28:4; 47:2; 50:3; 51:1, 5.
  virtues, 47:6.
  way of life after ascension of Christ, 48:2.
  see also Annunciation, Assumption, Christ, Eve, John, Humility, Nativity, Purification, Visitation.
Maternity, see Mary, Spiritual Maternity.
Matthew the Evangelist (St), 11:5; 31:1; 42:2.
Mediator, 53:2.
  see also Christ, Mary.
Meditation, 22:1ff; 23:7.
Meekness, 25:1ff; 53:2.
  necessary to complement with zeal, 26:2.
  of Christ, 25:2; 31:4; 49:4; 52:2.

taught by the example of Moses and Benedict, 26:1ff.
Mercy, 53:2.
  motive of the incarnation, 6:1.
Micah, the Prophet, 20:6; 25:4.
Miracles
  changing water into wine at Cana, 12:1.
  of Christ, clear witness to him, 12:2.
Moderation in carrying out monastic observances, 5:3.
Modesty, 51:5.
Monastic life, 23:7; 25:1ff; 40:5.
  apostolic life, 44:3.
  compared with the Exodus, 25:1.
  conversion of, 38:2.
  exercises of, 22:5.
  holy way, 5:4.
  John the Baptist's example of, 43:1.
  monastic community comes together to win heaven by force, 41:2.
  partly carnal, partly spiritual, 20:1.
  second baptism, 5:4.
  see also Benedict, Observance, Rule.
Monasticism, School of Christian Philosophy, 22:4.
Mortification, 30:5f; 40:5; 41:1f; 43:3f.
  see also Penance.
Moses, 41:2; 42:1; 44:1, 5; 46:4.
  type of St Benedict, 25:1f.
  see also Law, Meekness.
Mother
  Eve, mother of all the living, see Eve.
  Mary, Mother of God, Spiritual Mother of Men, see Mary.
  see also Church, Spiritual maternity.
Mourning, 53:2, 5.
  see also Compunction.
Myrrh
  offering of beginners, 11:5.
  signifies repentance: sorrow of heart and corporal labor, 11:3.
  why Christ refused to drink it, 11:3.
Mystical Body, 21:2; 26:3.
  Christ the Head, 4:2; 23:7; 32:5; 34:1; 47:2.

Analytic Index

members of Christ, 47:2.
mortified bodies are members of Jesus, 11:4.
see also Church.

Naaman, 14:5ff.
Name of Christ, 14:2.
Nativity
  of the Blessed Virgin Mary, Sermons for the Feast of, 51–52.
  of Christ, *see* Christmas.
Nature
  law of, 18:6.
  man's natural endowments, seedbed of all virtue, 11:2.
Nazareth, 27:3, 42:3.
Negligence
  offset by fear and hope, 25:4.
  purging away one's, 19:2ff.
  undermines faith, 25:4.
Noah, 42:1.

Obedience, 53:2.
  until death, 22:4.
Observances (monastic), 11:3f; 19:6; 22:5.
  bitter for beginner 11:3
  exercises of wisdom, 22:5.
  give the appearance of piety, 14:3.
  importance of, 5:2.
Office (*Opus Dei*), 11:7; 22:5.
  exercise of wisdom, 22:5.
  tepidity at, 38:4.
Old Testament, speaks clearly of New, 33:2.
see also Sacred Scripture.
Openness, 27:3.
Opus Dei, see Office.
Original sin, *see* Sin.

Palm Sunday, Sermons for, 29–32.
Pardon, 21:1ff.
Passion of Christ, 11:3; 29:2; 30:1ff; 31:1; 41:3; 48:3; 49:3; 50:1; 51:4.
  comparison with John the Baptist, 31:2.
  form freely chosen, 1:7.
  forsaken on the cross, 23:2.
  wounds are places of refuge and pardon, 32:5ff.

Patience, 22:3.
  Christ's example, 31:4.
Paul the Apostle (St), 2:4; 12:5; 24:1f; 25:2ff; 27:2; 29:3; 30:1ff; 34:1ff; 35:5; 36:4; 37:3; 39:1; 41:1; 46:4; 49:2, 5; 54:4.
  the Apostle, 2:3; 6:1; 7:1; 8:1; 9:2; 11:1; 13:5; 14:2ff; 18:51; 20:6; 38:5; 39:3; 49:2.
  contemplation, 54:4.
  conversion, 45:2.
  instrument of the Holy Spirit, 54:4.
  ministry compared with Mary's, 47:3.
  rapt to the third heaven, 37:5.
  Sermons for the Feast of Sts Peter and Paul, 44–46.
  Servant of Christ, 47:3.
  stigmata, 30:5.
  Teacher of the Nations, 25:5; 49:5.
Peace, 4:2; 5:2; 17:3; 23:3, 5; 53:5.
Peacemakers, 53:2.
Penance, 4:1; 5:2; 11:3ff.
  baptism of, 4:3.
  Cistercian life, 5:4.
  comes before grace, 5:2.
  example of John the Baptist, 42:4.
  pertains even to the perfect, 11:7.
see also Mortification.
Pentecost, 45:2.
  Sermons for the Feast of, 38–39.
see also Holy Spirit.
Perfect, offering of the perfect, the gold of wisdom, 11:7.
see also Stages of spiritual growth.
Perseverance, 4:1; 22:4; 23:5; 30:6; 41:2ff; 43:3.
  in Cistercian way of life, 5:5.
  in spite of falls, 4:13.
Peter the Apostle (St), 10:5; 11:1; 14:4; 22:4; 31:5; 39:1f; 51:2.
  Christ's heir, 50:3.
  confession of faith in Christ, 22:4.
  loved most by Christ, 50:3.
  power to open and close heaven, 45:5.
  Prince of the Apostles, 39:2.
  Sermons for the Feast of Sts Peter and Paul, 44–46.
  sons of, 20:2.

Pharaoh, 25:2.
Philosophy, empty philosophies, 22:5.
see also Monasticism.
Piety, is unfeigned charity, true humility, long-suffering patience and prompt obedience 14:3.
Pigeon, signifies simplicity, 15:1.
Plato, soul learns before being united to the body, 11:2.
Poor in spirit, 53:1ff.
Poverty, 14:5f; 18:6; 34:4; 49:4.
   blessedness of the poor, 38:3.
   Christ dwells by preference with the poor, 49:4.
   example of Christ, 10:4; 14:7; 32:3; 47:5.
   example of Mary, 18:6.
   of spirit, more humility of heart than privation of possessions, 53:5.
   rich if Christian and voluntary, 11:1.
   see also Humility.
Praise
   not seemly in sinners, 54:4.
   of Christ, 32:2ff.
   of God, gift of Holy Spirit, 39:1f.
Prayer, 3:4; 13:7; 15:3ff.
   importunate, 3:3.
   of Christ to the Father, 37:1f.
   perseverance in, 22:5.
   private, 22:5.
      exercise of wisdom, 22:5.
   see also Contemplation, Liturgy, Meditation, Office.
Preaching, 54:5.
Predestination, 12:1.
Prelates, 36:2.
   receive the grace of preaching, 37:2.
Presence of God, 22:1ff.
Presentation of Christ in the Temple, see Purification.
Pride, 14:5f; 24:3; 53:5.
   isolating, 5:2.
   leads to envy and detraction, 42:6.
Prodigal Son, 21:1ff.
Progressors in the spiritual life, see Stages of spiritual growth.
Prophets, 2:1ff; 8:2f; 40:2; 41:1.

see also Daniel, Elizabeth, Habakkuk, Isaiah, Jeremiah, Joel, John the Baptist, Micha, Zachary.
Providence of God, 24:2.
Prudence, 11:7; 22:1.
Psalmist, see David.
Psalmody, Sermon for arousing devotion at, 54.
Purgatory, 3:1; 19:2.
Purification, 20:5f.
   of the Blessed Virgin Mary.
   example of humility and obedience, 16:7.
   Sermons for, 15-19.
   true purification at the incarnation, 18:3ff.
   seven kinds, 18:3ff.
Purity of heart, 53:2.

Rachel, type of the contemplative life, 50:4.
Recollection, 22:6.
   see also Meditation, Silence.
Religious life, pattern in Christ's birth, 10:4.
Renunciation, 53:5.
Repentance, 11:3; 21:1ff; 40:5f; 54:5.
   violence done to the kingdom of heaven, 41:1.
   see also Compunction, Myrrh.
Resurrection, 6:1; 51:5.
   final, 37:4.
   of Christ, 34:1.
      first resurrection bringing about the resurrection of our souls and also bringing about the second resurrection, that of our bodies, 34:1f; 35:1.
   for our justification, 34:3.
   joy in, 35:2f.
   see also Easter.
Rogation Days, Sermon for, 36.
Romans, 16:2.
Rule
   guidelines for us, 5:3.
   of St Benedict, 23:1.
      compared with the Law of Moses, 25:1.
   Gospel teaching, 25:1.
   see also Cistercian life.

Analytic Index

Sacrament, 23:7.
supporting arms, 7:3.
see also Eucharist, Washing of the Feet.
Sadness
offset by fear and hope, 25:4.
undermines faith, 25:4.
Saints, exemplars, 12:6f.
see also All Saints.
Salvation, uncertain, 24:2.
Satan, see Devil.
Scandal, 24:5.
Scripture, 22:5; 26:3; 39:1ff; 44:1.
basic rations during our warfare, 7:3.
bears witness to Christ, 54:2.
consolation through, 4:1.
opened to us by Christ, 35:4.
purpose, that we might believe, hope and love, 36:4.
refreshing waters, 23:7.
relates the mysteries of redemption in such a way as to indicate our response, 18:1.
senses
allegorical, 36:4; 51:2.
historical, 36:4.
moral, 36:4, 54:2.
mystical, 54:2.
sometimes heard without interest, 10:1.
see also Lectio divina, Old Testament.
Service, those attaining to the state of the perfect and wisdom are to use it for the brethren, 11:7.
see also Abbatial office.
Shadows, spiritual
darkness of error, 46:2.
evil spirits of men and devils, 46:2.
from things of creation, 46:3, 6.
from things of God, 46:3ff; 49:1.
something of unspeakable splendor, 46:4.
transitory experience, 46:6.
Silence, 4:4; 10:2; 22:5; 50:2.
example of the Word, 28:5.
exercise of wisdom, 22:5.
interior silence must correspond to exterior silence, 4:2.
nourishes, forms and strengthens the spirit, 28:5.
reasons for silence, 10:2.
Simeon, 15:1ff; 16:1ff; 17:1ff.
gives us an example of piety and devotion, 16:7.
his justice, 17:4.
Simplicity, 2:4; 17:2.
of faith, 10:4.
of God, 22:6.
see also Pigeon.
Sin
mortal, 13:3.
original, 6:2.
Sion
daughters of, 18:2f.
signifies the soul contemplating heavenly things, 17:2f.
Slander, 38:5.
Sloth, 46:6.
Solitude, 4:1ff.
desert, 4:1f.
Christ consecrated, 4:1.
in community, 4:2.
of pride, 5:1.
Solomon, 4:2, 4; 5:2; 9:4; 12:4; 17:1; 18:5f; 22:1f; 26:4, 7; 28:5; 42:1.
God, our Solomon, 8:4f.
presides in chapter meetings giving award to the spiritual, 8:5.
ivory throne, type of Mary, 26:3ff.
not equal to Simeon, 17:6.
type of Christ, 26:4.
wisdom of, 15:4.
Wise Man, 5:2; 15:4; 20:6; 21:4.
without prejudice, 22:1f.
Son of God, see Christ.
Sorrow, see Compunction.
Spirit
that gives life, 28:6.
of understanding, 35:5.
of wisdom, 35:5.
see also Holy Spirit.
Spiritual dryness, see Dryness.
Spiritual maternity, 8:5.
see also Mary.
Spiritual paternity, 53:2.
Spiritual reading, see Lectio divina.
Spiritual shadows, see Shadows.
Spiritual sloth, see Sloth.
Stability of place, 22:2ff.
see also Transfer (transitus)

Stages of spiritual growth, 12:4f; 19:6; 27:3; 35:5.
 compared with the offerings of the Magi, 11:5ff.
 eight steps of the Beatitudes, 53:1.
 four:
  knowledge, fear, hope, love, 53:4.
  light of faith, of justice, of knowledge, of wisdom, 13:3ff.
  predestined, called, justified, glorified, 51:4.
 three:
  attracted, sanctified, glorified, 51:4.
  beginners, progressors, perfect, 11:5.
  fear of judgment, love of holiness, rest of wisdom, 22:6.
  good works, prayer, contemplation, 35:5.
 see also Faith.
Stephen, Protomartyr (St), 38:3.
Study, 10:5.
Superfluities, 18:6.
Suspense, a good, 1:3f.

Tears, see Compunction.
Temptation, 22:6.
Terence (*Comicus*), 24:6.
Timothy (St), 11:4.
Transfer (*transitus*), 22:2.
 instability, 38:4.
 see also Stability of place.
Trinity, see Blessed Trinity.
Turtledove, signifies chastity, 15:1.

Understanding, spirit of, 35:5.

Vainglory, 42:5.
Vanity, 24:3.
Virgil, 46:2.
Virginity, 51:1ff.
 see also Chastity, John the Evangelist, Mary.
Virtue, the bones of Christ, 27:4.
Visits
 of God to the soul, 2:3ff; 3:3; 7:3.
 of the Word, 26:7.
Visitation of the Blessed Virgin Mary to Elizabeth, 40:2.

Wantonness, 11:3f.
Washing of the Feet, example of humility and a sacrament of forgiveness, 37:1.
Way
 end of
  Christ, 3:2.
  to be kept in mind, 5:5.
 of Christian life
  preparing the way by penance, 5:1ff.
  no limit, 5:1.
 of Cistercian life, 5:4.
Will, goodwill the straight way, 4:4.
Wisdom, 5:2; 22:1ff; 23:4, 7; 24:6; 25:2; 31:5; 49:3; 51:2.
 casts out fear, 22:6.
 exercises of, 22:5.
 false, 5:3.
 God's foolishness, 5:3, 6:2.
 must be accompanied by prudence, 22:1ff.
 of God: Christ, 6:2; 10:3f; 15:2; 17:1; 22:6; 35:2f.
 of the perfect, 11:7.
 of Solomon, 15:4.
 rejected because of pride, lust, inconstancy, frivolity, 22:2f.
 sought only through love, 16:2.
 source of happiness, 22:1.
 spirit of, 35:5.
 stability necessary to the growth of wisdom, 22:2f.
Wise Man, 42:4; 43:5; 50:4; 52:4.
 see also Solomon.
Witness, see Good example, Holy Spirit, John the Baptist, Miracles.
Work, 22:5, 25:4, 49:1, 5.
 part of monastic asceticism, 11:3f.
 Work of God, see Office.
 see also Good works, Manual labor, Miracles.
World, will pass into a new state of incorruptibility, 18:4.

Zechariah, 44:1.

CISTERCIAN PUBLICATIONS

TITLES LISTING

CISTERCIAN TEXTS

Bernard of Clairvaux

- Apologia to Abbot William
- Five Books on Consideration: Advice to a Pope
- Homilies in Praise of the Blessed Virgin Mary
- Letters of Bernard of Clairvaux / by B.S. James
- Life and Death of Saint Malachy the Irishman
- Love without Measure: Extracts from the Writings of St Bernard / by Paul Dimier
- On Grace and Free Choice
- On Loving God / Analysis by Emero Stiegman
- Parables and Sentences
- Sermons for the Summer Season
- Sermons on Conversion
- Sermons on the Song of Songs I–IV
- The Steps of Humility and Pride

William of Saint Thierry

- The Enigma of Faith
- Exposition on the Epistle to the Romans
- Exposition on the Song of Songs
- The Golden Epistle
- The Mirror of Faith
- The Nature and Dignity of Love
- On Contemplating God: Prayer & Meditations

Aelred of Rievaulx

- Dialogue on the Soul
- Liturgical Sermons, I
- The Mirror of Charity
- Spiritual Friendship
- Treatises I: On Jesus at the Age of Twelve, Rule for a Recluse, The Pastoral Prayer
- Walter Daniel: The Life of Aelred of Rievaulx

John of Ford

- Sermons on the Final Verses of the Songs of Songs I–VII

Gilbert of Hoyland

- Sermons on the Songs of Songs I–III
- Treatises, Sermons and Epistles

Other Early Cistercian Writers

- Adam of Perseigne, Letters of
- Alan of Lille: The Art of Preaching
- Amadeus of Lausanne: Homilies in Praise of Blessed Mary
- Baldwin of Ford: Spiritual Tractates I–II
- Geoffrey of Auxerre: On the Apocalypse
- Gertrud the Great: Spiritual Exercises
- Gertrud the Great: The Herald of God's Loving-Kindness (Books 1, 2)
- Gertrud the Great: The Herald of God's Loving-Kindness (Book 3)
- Guerric of Igny: Liturgical Sermons Vol. I & 2
- Helinand of Froidmont: Verses on Death
- Idung of Prüfening: Cistercians and Cluniacs: The Case for Cîteaux
- Isaac of Stella: Sermons on the Christian Year, I–[II]
- The Life of Beatrice of Nazareth
- Serlo of Wilton & Serlo of Savigny: Seven Unpublished Works
- Stephen of Lexington: Letters from Ireland
- Stephen of Sawley: Treatises

MONASTIC TEXTS

Eastern Monastic Tradition

- Besa: The Life of Shenoute
- Cyril of Scythopolis: Lives of the Monks of Palestine
- Dorotheos of Gaza: Discourses and Sayings
- Evagrius Ponticus: Praktikos and Chapters on Prayer
- Handmaids of the Lord: Lives of Holy Women in Late Antiquity & the Early Middle Ages / by Joan Petersen
- Harlots of the Desert / by Benedicta Ward
- John Moschos: The Spiritual Meadow
- Lives of the Desert Fathers
- Lives of Simeon Stylites / by Robert Doran
- The Luminous Eye / by Sebastian Brock
- Mena of Nikiou: Isaac of Alexandra & St Macrobius
- Pachomian Koinonia I–III (Armand Veilleux)
- Paphnutius: Histories/Monks of Upper Egypt
- The Sayings of the Desert Fathers / by Benedicta Ward
- Spiritual Direction in the Early Christian East / by Irénée Hausherr
- The Spiritually Beneficial Tales of Paul, Bishop of Monembasia / by John Wortley
- Symeon the New Theologian: The Theological and Practical Treatises & The Three Theological Discourses / by Paul McGuckin
- Theodoret of Cyrrhus: A History of the Monks of Syria
- The Syriac Fathers on Prayer and the Spiritual Life / by Sebastian Brock

CISTERCIAN PUBLICATIONS
TITLES LISTING

Western Monastic Tradition
- Anselm of Canterbury: Letters I–III / by Walter Fröhlich
- Bede: Commentary...Acts of the Apostles
- Bede: Commentary...Seven Catholic Epistles
- Bede: Homilies on the Gospels I–II
- Bede: Excerpts from the Works of St Augustine on the Letters of the Blessed Apostle Paul
- The Celtic Monk / by U. Ó Maidín
- Life of the Jura Fathers
- Maxims of Stephen of Muret
- Peter of Celle: Selected Works
- Letters of Rancé I–II
- Rule of the Master
- Rule of Saint Augustine

Christian Spirituality
- The Cloud of Witnesses: The Development of Christian Doctrine / by David N. Bell
- The Call of Wild Geese / by Matthew Kelty
- The Cistercian Way / by André Louf
- The Contemplative Path
- Drinking From the Hidden Fountain / by Thomas Spidlík
- Eros and Allegory: Medieval Exegesis of the Song of Songs / by Denys Turner
- Fathers Talking / by Aelred Squire
- Friendship and Community / by Brian McGuire
- Gregory the Great: Forty Gospel Homilies
- High King of Heaven / by Benedicta Word
- The Hermitage Within / by a Monk
- Life of St Mary Magdalene and of Her Sister St Martha / by David Mycoff
- Many Mansions / by David N. Bell
- Mercy in Weakness / by André Louf
- The Name of Jesus / by Irénée Hausherr
- No Moment Too Small / by Norvene Vest
- Penthos: The Doctrine of Compunction in the Christian East / by Irénée Hausherr
- Praying the Word / by Enzo Bianchi
- Rancé and the Trappist Legacy / by A. J. Krailsheimer
- Russian Mystics / by Sergius Bolshakoff
- Sermons in a Monastery / by Matthew Kelty
- Silent Herald of Unity: The Life of Maria Gabriella Sagheddu / by Martha Driscoll
- The Spirituality of the Christian East / by Thomas Spidlík
- The Spirituality of the Medieval West / by André Vauchez
- Tuning In To Grace / by André Louf
- Wholly Animals: A Book of Beastly Tales / by David N. Bell

MONASTIC STUDIES
- Community and Abbot in the Rule of St Benedict I–II / by Adalbert de Vogüé
- The Finances of the Cistercian Order in the Fourteenth Century / by Peter King
- Fountains Abbey and Its Benefactors / by Joan Wardrop
- The Hermit Monks of Grandmont / by Carole A. Hutchison
- In the Unity of the Holy Spirit / by Sighard Kleiner
- The Joy of Learning & the Love of God: Essays in Honor of Jean Leclercq
- Monastic Odyssey / by Marie Kervingant
- Monastic Practices / by Charles Cummings
- The Occupation of Celtic Sites in Ireland / by Geraldine Carville
- Reading St Benedict / by Adalbert de Vogüé
- Rule of St Benedict: A Doctrinal and Spiritual Commentary / by Adalbert de Vogüé
- The Rule of St Benedict / by Br. Pinocchio
- St Hugh of Lincoln / by David H. Farmer
- The Venerable Bede / by Benedicta Ward
- Western Monasticism / by Peter King
- What Nuns Read / by David N. Bell
- With Greater Liberty: A Short History of Christian Monasticism & Religious Orders / by Karl Frank

CISTERCIAN STUDIES
- Aelred of Rievaulx: A Study / by Aelred Squire
- Athirst for God: Spiritual Desire in Bernard of Clairvaux's Sermons on the Song of Songs / by Michael Casey
- Beatrice of Nazareth in Her Context / by Roger De Ganck
- Bernard of Clairvaux: Man, Monk, Mystic / by Michael Casey [tapes and readings]
- Bernardus Magister...Nonacentenary
- Catalogue of Manuscripts in the Obrecht Collection of the Institute of Cistercian Studies / by Anna Kirkwood
- Christ the Way: The Christology of Guerric of Igny / by John Morson
- The Cistercians in Denmark / by Brian McGuire
- The Cistercians in Scandinavia / by James France
- A Difficult Saint / by Brian McGuire
- A Gathering of Friends: Learning & Spirituality in John of Ford / by Costello and Holdsworth
- Image and Likeness: Augustinian Spirituality of William of St Thierry / by David Bell

CISTERCIAN PUBLICATIONS

TITLES LISTING

- Index of Authors & Works in Cistercian Libraries in Great Britain I / by David Bell
- Index of Cistercian Authors and Works in Medieval Library Catalogues in Great Britian / by David Bell
- The Mystical Theology of St Bernard / by Étienne Gilson
- The New Monastery: Texts & Studies on the Earliest Cistercians
- Nicolas Cotheret's Annals of Cîteaux / by Louis J. Lekai
- Pater Bernhardus: Martin Luther and Saint Bernard / by Franz Posset
- Pathway of Peace / by Charles Dumont
- A Second Look at Saint Bernard / by Jean Leclercq
- The Spiritual Teachings of St Bernard of Clairvaux / by John R. Sommerfeldt
- Studies in Medieval Cistercian History
- Studiosorum Speculum / by Louis J. Lekai
- Three Founders of Cîteaux / by Jean-Baptiste Van Damme
- Towards Unification with God (Beatrice of Nazareth in Her Context, 2)
- William, Abbot of St Thierry
- Women and St Bernard of Clairvaux / by Jean Leclercq

MEDIEVAL RELIGIOUS WOMEN

edited by Lillian Thomas Shank and John A. Nichols:
- Distant Echoes
- Hidden Springs: Cistercian Monastic Women (2 volumes)
- Peace Weavers

CARTHUSIAN TRADITION

- The Call of Silent Love / by A Carthusian
- The Freedom of Obedience / by A Carthusian
- From Advent to Pentecost
- Guigo II: The Ladder of Monks & Twelve Meditations / by Colledge & Walsh
- Halfway to Heaven / by R.B. Lockhart
- Interior Prayer / by A Carthusian
- Meditations of Guigo II / by A. Gordon Mursall
- The Prayer of Love and Silence / by A Carthusian
- Poor, Therefore Rich / by A Carthusian
- They Speak by Silences / by A Carthusian
- The Way of Silent Love (A Carthusian Miscellany)
- Where Silence is Praise / by A Carthusian
- The Wound of Love (A Carthusian Miscellany)

CISTERCIAN ART, ARCHITECTURE & MUSIC

- Cistercian Abbeys of Britain
- Cistercians in Medieval Art / by James France
- Studies in Medieval Art and Architecture / edited by Meredith Parsons Lillich
  (Volumes II–V are now available)
- Stones Laid Before the Lord / by Anselme Dimier
- Treasures Old and New: Nine Centuries of Cistercian Music (compact disc and cassette)

THOMAS MERTON

- The Climate of Monastic Prayer / by T. Merton
- Legacy of Thomas Merton / by P. Hart
- Message of Thomas Merton / by P. Hart
- Monastic Journey of Thomas Merton / by P. Hart
- Thomas Merton/Monk / by P. Hart
- Thomas Merton on St Bernard
- Toward an Integrated Humanity / edited by M. Basil Pennington

CISTERCIAN LITURGICAL DOCUMENTS SERIES

- Cistercian Liturgical Documents Series / edited by Chrysogonus Waddell, ocso
- Hymn Collection of the…Paraclete
- *Institutiones nostrae:* The Paraclete Statutes
- Molesme Summer-Season Breviary (4 volumes)
- Old French Ordinary & Breviary of the Abbey of the Paraclete (2 volumes)
- Twelfth-century Cistercian Hymnal (2 volumes)
- The Twelfth-century Cistercian Psalter
- Two Early Cistercian *Libelli Missarum*

STUDIA PATRISTICA

- Studia Patristica XVIII, Volumes 1, 2 and 3

CISTERCIAN PUBLICATIONS
HOW TO CONTACT US

Editorial Queries

Editorial queries & advance book information should be directed to the Editorial Offices:

- Cistercian Publications
  WMU Station
  1201 Oliver Street
  Kalamazoo, Michigan 49008

- Telephone   616 387 8920
- Fax   616 387 8390
- e-mai   mcdougall@wmich.edu

How to Order in the United States

Customers may order these books through booksellers, from the editorial office, or directly from the warehouse:

- Cistercian Publications
  Saint Joseph's Abbey
  167 North Spencer Road
  Spencer, Massachusetts   01562-1233

- Telephone   508 885 8730
- Fax   508 885 4687
- e-mail   cistpub@spencerabbey.org
- Web Site   www.spencerabbey.org/cistpub

How to Order from Canada

- Novalis
  49 Front Street East, Second Floor
  Toronto, Ontario M5E 1B3

- Telephone   416 363 3303
                         1 800 387 7164
- Fax   416 363 9409

How to Order from Europe

- Cistercian Publications
  97 Loughborough Road
  Thringstone, Coalville, Leicester LE67 8LQ

- Fax   44 1530 45 02 10
- e-mail   MsbcistP@aol.com

Cistercian Publications is a non-profit corporation. Its publishing program is restricted to monastic texts in translation and books on the monastic tradition.

A complete catalogue of texts in translation and studies on early, medieval, and modern monasticism is available, free of charge, from any of the addresses above.